UNDER NEW OWNERSHIP

Privatizing China's State-Owned Enterprises

SHAHID YUSUF
KAORU NABESHIMA

AND

DWIGHT H. PERKINS

D1563273

A COPUBLICATION OF STANFORD ECONOMICS AND FINANCE,
AN IMPRINT OF STANFORD UNIVERSITY PRESS, AND THE WORLD BANK

A copublication of Stanford Economics and Finance, an imprint of Stanford University Press, and the World Bank.

Stanford University Press	The World Bank
1450 Page Mill Road	1818 H Street, NW
Palo Alto, CA 94304	Washington, DC 20433

World Rights except North America	*North America*
ISBN-10: 0-8213-5624-0	ISBN-10 (soft cover): 0-8047-5390-3
ISBN-13: 978-0-8213-5624-1	ISBN-10 (hard cover): 0-8047-5389-X
eISBN: 0-8213-5625-9	
DOI: 10.1596/978-0-8213-5624-1	

Library of Congress Cataloging-in-Publication Data has been applied for.

CONTENTS

Figures

Tables

PREFACE

This is the fifth volume in a series of publications emerging from a study cosponsored by the government of Japan and the World Bank to examine the future sources of economic growth in East Asia. The study was initiated in 1999 with the objective of identifying the most promising path to development in light of emerging global and regional changes.

The first volume, *Can East Asia Compete?*, published in 2002, provided a compact overview of the relevant strategic issues and future policy directions. *Innovative East Asia*, the second volume and published in 2003, analyzed each of the main issues and consequent policy choices, drawing comprehensively from recent empirical research and the findings of surveys of various firms conducted for the study. Its principal message was that sustained economic growth in East Asia will rest on the ability to retain the strengths of the past (stability, openness, investment, and human capital development), to overcome the sources of current weaknesses (in the financial, corporate, judicial, and social sectors), and to implement the changes required by the evolving economic environment, particularly with regard to technology development. The third volume, *Global Production Networking and Technological Change in East Asia*, published in 2004, was the first of two volumes of papers commissioned for the East Asia study. It presented detailed information, analysis, and case studies showing that the economies in East Asia must adapt to the changing character of global production networks and nurture and develop their technological capabilities in order to sustain their growth prospects. The fourth volume, *Global Change and East Asian Policy Initiatives*, also published in 2004, included a separate set of papers that examined some of the key institutional weaknesses identified in *Innovative East Asia*. Contributors to this volume explored in-depth topics ranging from regional issues arising from monetary and financial cooperation, trade, and harmonization to the national issues of public expenditure, corporate and public governance, the legal system, tertiary education, and finance. They also presented an array of policy options of value to East Asian economies. Some, if not all, of these issues are relevant to every country in East Asia. Both of the edited volumes complement *Innovative East Asia* and are addressed to researchers, students, and policymakers.

While the first four volumes in this series presented a macroeconomic perspective, *Under New Ownership* focuses on the microeconomics of business organization and reform—issues that are of considerable importance for China. To compete in a globalizing market, Chinese firms need to pursue strategies that will promote efficiency and innovation. Much of the cross-country evidence to date suggests that state-owned firms are slow to adopt such strategies; and because these firms are generally subject to a different set of incentives than are their private counterparts, their managers are less zealous in implementing those strategies. Chinese state-owned firms are not exceptions. If they are to compete in the global market with other firms, especially the established, large, multinational firms, privatization is a necessary step to attaining international competitiveness.

This volume first reviews the experience with state-enterprise reform in China since the early 1980s, and surveys the outcomes from privatization in other transitional and industrializing countries. Then, with the help of newly collected survey data, it analyzes the recent results of corporatization in China and compares corporatized state firms with privately owned firms and joint ventures. The findings reinforce the lessons from cross-country experience. Full privatization is not a panacea for underperforming firms, but it definitely dominates all other options for manufacturing enterprises.

The financial backing of the government of Japan, through its Policy and Human Resources Development Fund, has provided vital support for this project, as have senior public officials who gave generously of their time. We are deeply grateful to Haruhiko Kuroda, Takashi Kihara, Naoko Ishii, Masahiro Kawai, Kiyoshi Kodera, Rintaro Tamaki, Junichi Maruyama, and Takatoshi Ito. The staff of the World Bank's Beijing office facilitated our field work in China, and we greatly appreciate the assistance provided by Jianqing Chen and Hong Mei. The study also benefited from an Asia Europe Meeting (ASEM) grant, which was instrumental in providing financial support for training enumerators from the National Bureau of Statistics of China and conducting the enterprise survey.

We owe special thanks to Messrs. Wang and Lei and to the staff of the Enterprise Survey Organization of the National Bureau of Statistics of China for managing the survey of firms in China for our study.

The draft manuscript of this book was presented at the Seminar on State-Owned Enterprise Reform in China and Eastern Europe in Prague, cohosted by the Center for Economic Research and Graduate Education of the Charles University and the Economic Institute of the Academy of Science of the Czech Republic (CERGI-EI) on September 22, 2003. We thank Jan Hanousek, Daniel Munich, and Lubomir Lizal for organizing and cohosting this workshop. The comments received there helped the authors revise the draft. We would like to thank Harry Broadman, Stijn Claessens, Jacek Cukrowski, Laszlo Halpern, Yasheng Huang, Mark Schaffer, Edward Steinfeld, Ksenia Yudaeva, and other participants at the workshop. Prior to being accepted for publication, the manuscript was subjected to a careful review by Luis Guasch and two anonymous academic referees. We are grateful for their many insightful suggestions.

At the World Bank, the Development Research Group provided a home for the study, and the East Asia and Pacific Region contributed consistent and unflagging support. We are especially indebted to Alan Winters, Paul Collier, Jemal-ud-din Kassum, and Homi Kharas for their encouragement and their faith in the value of the study. We also thank Anjum Altaf, Deepak Bhattasali, Sudarshan Gooptu, Bert Hofman, William Mako, and Chunlin Zhang for their comments and guidance.

The study team was ably supported by the research and organizational skills of Yifan Hu and Shiqing Xie. We are grateful to them, and also to Simon J. Evenett and Marc Shotten, who contributed to the initial phase of this study. The manuscript was edited by Kim E. Kelley; and Paulina M. Flewitt and Rebecca Sugui assisted with the revisions and production. Patricia Katayama and Janet H. Sasser of the World Bank's Office of the Publisher delivered yet again. We thank them all for adding value in many ways.

ABBREVIATIONS AND ACRONYMS

$	All dollar amounts are current U.S. dollars unless otherwise specified
ASEAN	Association of Southeast Asian Nations
CEO	Chief executive officer
CIS	Commonwealth of Independent States
COE	Collectively owned enterprise
CSRC	China Securities Regulatory Commission
DEA	Data envelopment analysis
FDI	Foreign direct investment
FIE	Foreign-invested enterprise
GLC	Government-linked corporation
GDP	Gross domestic product
GVIO	Gross value of industrial output
ICOR	Incremental capital-output ratio
ICT	Information and communication technology
IMF	International Monetary Fund
IPO	Initial public offering
IT	Information technology
LLC	Limited liability company
LLSC	Limited liability shareholding company
LMEs	Large and medium-size enterprises
NAFTA	North American Free Trade Agreement
NBS-ESO	China National Bureau of Statistics Enterprise Survey Organization
NPL	Nonperforming loan
OECD	Organisation for Economic Co-operation and Development

OEM	Original equipment manufacturer
OLS	Ordinary least squares
PAYG	Pay-as-you-go
PBC	People's Bank of China
PCs	Personal computers
PIPO	Privatization initial public offering
PPP	Purchasing power parity
ROA	Return on assets
SASAC	State-Owned Assets Supervision and Administration Commission
SEZs	Special economic zones
SMEs	Small and medium-size enterprises
SMSOEs	Small and medium-size state-owned enterprises
SOE	State-owned enterprise
TFP	Total factor productivity
TVE	Township and village enterprise
VAT	Value-added tax
WTO	World Trade Organization

CHAPTER 1

CHINA'S INDUSTRIAL SYSTEM: WHERE IT IS NOW, WHERE IT SHOULD BE HEADED, AND WHY

I n December 1978, the Third Plenum of the Eleventh Central Committee issued a low-key communiqué whose directives have since reverberated throughout the Chinese economy. The communiqué called for a solution to economic imbalances and for an end to the "disorder in production, construction, circulation, and distribution." It then crucially defined the medium-run objectives for the government, which were to seek "comprehensive balance [and] lay a solid foundation for rapid development." The communiqué's cautiously voiced ambitions to reduce the centralization of economic management, reform the commune system, and raise living standards opened the door to economic change of extraordinary scope, which shows no signs of abating even after more than two decades (Riskin 1987, p. 284).

The first round of reforms initiated the dismantling of the team-based, communal agricultural system and granted increasing production autonomy to individual farming households (Perkins and Yusuf 1984; Riskin 1987). The reforms also established four special economic zones (SEZs) along the coast of Guangdong and Fujian provinces to increase China's export earnings, attract foreign investment, and enlarge trade flows.[1] These limited and exploratory actions swiftly produced results. Growth of

---

1. Reardon (1998) discusses the evolution of development thinking away from import substituting industrialization in China during the 1960s and 1970s. He describes the formation of a post-Great Leap Forward Coalition that by the time of the Third Plenum had convinced the ruling elites to support a strategy embracing a very different vision. This strategy called for a new approach that would promote exports, encourage foreign direct investment (especially from the

agricultural output rose to almost 8 percent per year between 1979 and 1984. Foreign direct investment (FDI) in Shenzhen alone climbed to $580 million, and trade increased from $21 billion to $54 billion during 1978–86 (Carter, Zhong, and Cai 1996; Kleinberg 1990; Lardy 1992). By the mid-1980s reformers were emboldened to shift more of their attention to the enterprise sector, which was then and remains the principal driver of the Chinese economy. Starting with six enterprises in Sichuan, a modest initiative was launched to increase the share of profits retained by industrial enterprises and to permit them to sell output in excess of plan targets (Naughton 1995). This led during the 1980s to initial tinkering with the management of enterprises and the authority wielded by enterprise-level Communist Party committees. It was followed in 1986–9 by contracting arrangements that rewarded the manager with a share of the enterprise profits for meeting performance targets such as sales or profitability. When this yielded indifferent results, the government sought to lease out enterprises in return for a share of the profits.

Nearly two decades later, China's industrial system is greatly changed, but the reform agenda is far from complete. In fact, it is only now entering the most critical phase as the state gingerly, and with many reservations, transfers the ownership of state-owned enterprises (SOEs) partially or wholly into private hands, starting with the smaller SOEs.

The purpose of this chapter is to establish the importance of this phase of the reform for the future competitiveness of Chinese firms and the growth of the economy. It does so by providing a historical perspective on China's reforms and on the efforts to privatize and corporatize state enterprises; by comparing the outcomes of reform in China with those of other economies in transition; by analyzing empirically the effects, thus far, of reform on the performance of former SOEs relative to other types of firms with the help of survey data gathered for this study; and by drawing lessons from privatization in other countries.[2] Finally, based on Chinese and worldwide experience to date, the chapter suggests how changes in the direction of ownership reform, combined with other institutional reforms, could lead to better results.

---

overseas Chinese community), and use SEZs to earn foreign exchange, promote technology transfer, and provide an impetus for the reform of economic management. A series of post-Third Plenum initiatives in 1979 formally defined the new, more outward-looking strategy. The first SEZ was set up in January 1979, in Shekou, within what is now Shenzhen. This was followed by SEZs in Shantou, Xiamen, and Zhuhai. In June 1979, China introduced its first law sanctioning Sino-foreign joint ventures (Howell 1993; Kleinberg 1990).

2. Research on enterprise reform reported in Garnaut and others (2005) complements and enriches the authors' findings.

THE CHANGING ECONOMIC LANDSCAPE SINCE 1979

China's efforts to develop a modern economy began from a modest economic base. In 1979, its GDP was $177 billion (at 2002 prices), and with a per capita income of $183, more than half generated by agriculture, China was among the world's poorest countries.[3] Thereafter, a combination of mainly fiscal incentives to subnational governments that provoked local entrepreneurial initiatives coupled with the pruning of controls on trade, foreign direct investment, and prices together with the gradual creation of markets for goods, labor, capital, foreign exchange, and housing were responsible for growth rates averaging nearly 9 percent per year during 1979–2004.[4]

By the end of 2004, China's GDP had risen to almost $1.65 trillion, and per capita GDP, at over $1,268, had moved squarely into the lower-middle-income range. After Japan, China is by far the largest economy in the East Asian region, accounting for a quarter of the output from developing Asia. In fact, the GDP of the Yangtze Valley region ranks just below that of Taiwan (China), and the economy of the Pearl River Delta is larger than the economies of Malaysia, the Philippines, and Singapore (Ohmae 2002). China's progressive adoption of market institutions and its integration into the global system have not only provided the underpinnings for growth but have, in addition, pushed the country to the front rank of trading nations and made it one of the foremost recipients of FDI. In 2004, with exports and imports of over $1.1 trillion, China was the world's third-largest trading nation, having edged out Japan.[5] During that year it utilized close to $61 billion in FDI, second only to the United States, and equivalent to a tenth of China's gross investment. Cumulative FDI exceeded $500 billion (as against $25 billion in 1990), much of it in export-oriented activities responsible for one-half of China's outward trade flows.[6] If this amount is added to the $433 billion of FDI in Hong Kong, China is second only to the United States, where the stock of FDI had reached $1.35 trillion by 2002 ("China Closes Foreign Investment Gap" 2003). Because of the steady inflow of FDI into high-technology industries, by 2003 China had

---

3. See http://www.stanford.edu/~ljlau/Presentations/Presentations/030502.pdf.

4. Although administrative decentralization commenced in the 1970s, fiscal decentralization was mainly the result of actions taken in 1981 and 1985. See Lin and Liu (2000).

5. See "China Overtakes" (2005).

6. This FDI helped create 44,000 foreign-invested enterprises in 2004 as against 41,000 in 2003 ("The Flows Reformulate" 2005). On the pattern of China's FDI, see Prasad and Wei (2005).

emerged as the second-largest producer of information technology hardware after the United States. In 1990 China accounted for 0.69 percent of global high-technology exports. Ten years later this had risen to 4.7 percent, with China producing nearly 37 percent of all personal computers manufactured in the world ("Technically Speaking" 2003).

Early in the 19th century, about 36 percent of global GDP originated in China, then the leading world economy. After 1820 China rapidly lost ground because of domestic strife, challenges from abroad, huge advances in industrial technology made by the West, and constraints imposed by domestic institutions and the resource base (Maddison 1998; Pomeranz 2000). But by dint of reform and deregulation, China in the early 21st century, was the sixth-largest economy in 2003 (on the basis of nominal exchange rate calculations). When measured using purchasing power parities (PPPs), China in 2001 was ranked second in the world behind the United States and ahead of Japan.[7]

Government policies, together with the regulatory framework and market institutions, undoubtedly define the incentives and shape the behavior of economic agents, but the nature of outcomes depends on the actions of myriad market participants. Much of China's growth since 1979 has been propelled by the response to reforms first directed toward agricultural production and marketing and subsequently toward collectively owned enterprises (COEs), township and village enterprises (TVEs), and to a lesser extent state-owned enterprises (SOEs).[8] With many of the initial and easier stages of reform completed and the economy significantly deregulated, growth now depends more on institutions governing market competition, how industrial organization evolves, and what firms do. The transfer of ownership of state- and collectively owned enterprises into private hands, perhaps more than any other policy, will affect the efficiency of industrial resource utilization and technological gains.

Why is ownership reform so crucial? How has it evolved? What are some of the consequences of the ownership reforms implemented thus far? And how can the future course of enterprise privatization and the

---

7. According to the data on PPP-based per capita incomes, China's per capita income was $3,950 in 2001 (East Asia Unit 2003).

8. Since the mid-1980s and through much of the 1990s, the growth of industrial production, employment, and exports was strongly supported by the multiplication of TVEs, beginning in some of the coastal provinces and later extending into the interior regions. The phenomenon resulted from the policy of decentralization, which uncapped latent local entrepreneurial energies. Although the TVE sector had begun to stabilize by 2000, in that year it accounted for 30 percent of GDP and employed 128 million people in 21 million TVEs (Ding, Ge, and Warner 2002).

competitiveness of firms in China be informed by the experience of other developed and transition economies? These are the questions briefly addressed in this chapter and explored more fully in later chapters. As Qian (2002) has observed, the enterprise sector is an area in which China's reforms have yielded relatively meager returns. This sector has acted as a brake on the efficiency of resource use and has constrained reform efforts in other areas as well. With a fourth generation of leaders now at the helm in China, a completion of enterprise ownership reforms could serve as the hinge for the finalizing of associated financial and social security reforms (Ewing 2003; Fewsmith 2002). It would not be an exaggeration to say that the future level of growth in China will depend on completing the prolonged transition of the enterprise sector from a planned system to a market-based economy. The next two sections explain how growth is inextricably linked with what happens to Chinese firms and why privatization deserves continuing priority.

THE IMPACT OF REFORMS ON PRODUCTIVITY AND GROWTH

Close to 80 percent of China's industrial GDP originated in the state sector at the time that the Eleventh Central Committee issued its landmark edict. This was comparable to other socialist economies around that time. The rest was produced by collective enterprises. There were no private enterprises and the 150,000 individual proprietorships generated only 1 percent of GDP.[9] Enterprise reforms initiated during the mid-1980s and the explosive growth of nonstate entities have substantially altered the composition of the industrial sector. By 2004 the share of industrial value added by SOEs had shrunk to 40 percent ("China: SOE Reforms" 2005). Collectively owned enterprises and individual, private, wholly foreign-owned firms and joint ventures accounted for the remaining 60 percent. About one-third of this (20 percent of industrial GDP) was attributable to individual proprietors and private enterprises. In other former socialist economies, the share of the private sector in GDP ranged from 20 percent in Belarus to 70 percent in Russia and 80 percent in Hungary (Gang 2002). China's reforms led to rapid and far-reaching sectoral shifts in the distribution of GDP and a dramatic acceleration in growth. Agriculture's share of GDP fell from 43 percent in 1979 to 14.6 percent in 2003, and agricultural employment declined from 70 percent of the labor force to 50 percent.

---

9. See http://www.stanford.edu/~ljlau/Presentations/Presentations/030502.pdf.

Table 1.1 Percentage Contribution of Total Factor Productivity to Growth

France	65
Germany, Fed. Rep. of	66
Japan	39
United States	49
United Kingdom	57

Source: Kim and Lau (1994, table 7.2, p. 259).

Meanwhile, the share of exports in GDP climbed to 23 percent (in terms of value added) from negligible levels in the pre-reform era.[10]

Sources of Growth

During 1979–95, China's GDP grew at an annual average rate of 10 percent, as a result of intersectoral transfers of resources combined with heavy investment in industry and infrastructure. Since 1997, however, growth has slowed to about 8 percent per year, and the economy appears to be moving to a new equilibrium at which the pace of growth is likely to be subject to other forces as well. From the recent history of successful middle- and high-income economies, it appears that the rate at which total factor productivity (TFP) increases will more strongly influence overall performance once the returns from increasing factor inputs start to diminish (see table 1.1). Changes in TFP are derived mainly from "super normal profits, externalities and some of the other free lunches" arising from intersectoral shifts in resources and technological advances over and above the resources consumed directly and indirectly in making product and process innovations (Carlaw and Lipsey 2003). Although the growth of TFP is the end result of many actions, it is the way firms behave, how they organize production, and how they innovate that arguably exert the greatest leverage.

An analysis of the sources of growth in China, by Heytens and Zebregs (2003), underscores the importance of reforms that could enlarge the share of TFP in the future. Table 1.2 shows that between 1979 and 1998, capital accumulation contributed the bulk of the growth. In fact, the share of capital rose from 63 percent in 1979–89 to 67 percent in 1990–8. But

---

10. The ratio of the nominal value of exports to GDP was approximately 31 percent in 2003. About 45 percent of China's exports are processed goods, with value added at about 55 percent. Value added in the rest is in the range of 80–90 percent. A 75 percent average value added is assumed for total exports.

Table 1.2 Contributions to Output Growth
(percentage of GDP)

Model	1971–8	1979–89	1990–8
Potential output growth	4.9	9.3	9.5
Capital accumulation	4.8	5.7	6.4
Labor force growth	0.7	1.0	0.5
TFP growth	−0.5	2.5	2.6

Note: Percentage of GDP refers to period averages; TFP, total factor productivity.
Source: Heytens and Zebregs (2003).

these figures are somewhat deceptive because capital investment is the vehicle for embodied technological advance, which is responsible for a significant part of the growth. The contribution of TFP rose from 2.78 percent in 1979–84, after agricultural reforms were initiated, to 2.81 percent in 1990–4, when the third round of reforms focused on decontrol and "marketization" accelerated, before declining to 2.30 percent during 1995–8 (see table 1.3).

A decomposition of the productivity numbers shows that between 70 percent (1979–84) and 90 percent (1995–8) of the gains were derived from the transfer of labor out of the primary sector to higher-value-adding activities in secondary and tertiary industries, some of which benefit from rapid technological change (see table 1.3). Structural reforms contributed one-third of TFP growth in the earlier period and 17 percent in 1995–8 (Heytens and Zebregs 2003). This suggests that China thus far is obtaining relatively little benefit from technological progress by urban industrial enterprises.

The estimate of TFP reinforces the message conveyed by the trend in incremental capital-output ratios (ICORs). Since the mid-1990s, China's gross domestic investment has remained at close to 40 percent of GDP,

Table 1.3 Contributions to TFP Growth

Contributor	1971–8	1979–84	1985–9	1990–4	1995–8
TFP growth	−0.53	2.78	2.11	2.81	2.30
Structural reform	0.38	0.94	0.76	0.83	0.39
Labor migration out of primary sector	2.34	2.01	1.52	2.15	2.08
Exogenous trend	−3.25	−0.17	−0.17	−0.17	−0.17

Note: Period averages, based on estimation results in table 1.2; TFP, total factor productivity.
Source: Heytens and Zebregs (2003).

Table 1.4 Incremental Capital-Output Ratio, Selected Countries

Country	1975–9	1980–4	1985–9	1990–4	1995–9	2000	2001	2002
China	−0.44	3.96	4.45	4.39	4.49	4.51	5.19	5.40
Korea, Rep. of	3.70	−0.06	3.72	5.26	3.18	3.02	8.81	4.12
Thailand	3.70	5.22	3.80	4.60	−2.04	4.90	13.37	6.86
Brazil	4.56	6.35	−40.54	−3.87	51.22	4.94	13.98	14.99
India	3.08	4.05	4.05	8.06	3.77	5.79	4.17	4.64

Note: Simple average of ICOR for a five-year period; ICOR, incremental capital-output ratio.
Source: World Bank Unified Survey (2002).

among the highest in the world (World Bank 2003). However, the average growth rate has diminished, with ICORs rising from 3.96 in 1980–4 to 5.40 in 2000–2 (see table 1.4). Clearly, China is pouring an enormous volume of capital into developing its economy (approximately $600 billion per year if the ratio of gross investment to GDP is converted into dollars)—more than any large developing country has done in such a sustained fashion. But the growth outcome, while high in comparison with other countries, is not commensurate with the input of resources. It is likely that a sizable portion of the investment is being inefficiently allocated and that market incentives inducing firms to pursue technological advances and introduce organizational changes are insufficiently forceful, as shown by the analysis in chapter 5 of this volume.

Rapid growth must remain a key objective for China over the foreseeable future, so as to raise living standards throughout the country;[11] reduce the numbers of those living in poverty (still in the range of 595 million under the $2 per day poverty line in 2001, World Bank 2004a); and provide employment each year to from 8 million to 9 million new entrants (the labor force is growing by about 1 percent per year) and workers being laid off by the state sector (almost 50 million by early 2003), not to mention the army of underemployed in the rural sector who are seeking jobs in industry.[12] Adding to the pressure for jobs is the rising number of university graduates. Between 2002 and 2003, the size of the graduating class

---

11. This objective is in addition to increasing emphasis on the sustainability of rapid growth and the containment of income inequality between the rural and urban populations and among regions, signaled by the Eleventh Five-Year Plan.

12. Up to 200 million people are likely to migrate from the rural to the urban sector within the next two decades, and close to 100 million are seeking work or are underemployed in the urban sector ("A Dragon Out" 2002; "China Banks Extend" 2002; "China's Unwelcome Growth" 2003).

Table 1.5 Productivity Dynamics

Economy	Initial productivity ranking relative to U.S. (1970s)	Subsequent productivity ranking (late 1980s)
Hong Kong (China)	24	2
Japan	19	17
Korea, Rep. of	51	31
Malaysia	82	82
Philippines	61	65
Singapore	29	22
India	77	74
Israel	21	21
Brazil	37	34

Source: Islam (2003).

expanded by 46 percent, to over 2 million; and with enrollments continuing to expand, more rather than fewer graduates will be entering the job market.[13] This pressure is likely to increase if the employment elasticities in the manufacturing sector continue their downward trend and if productivity gains in services reduce elasticities in that sector as well.

Resource inputs will continue for some time to be the principal determinants of growth. By increasing the contribution of TFP, China could appreciably diminish the cost of development. Stated differently, the experience of the leading Organisation for Economic Co-operation and Development (OECD) economies, and of Hong Kong (China), Singapore, and Taiwan (China) suggests that measures that enhance allocative efficiency and technological advance, broadly understood, can significantly cut waste. Furthermore, Islam's (2003) study of productivity dynamics indicates that gains were greatest in open economies that made the most determined efforts to restructure or raise technological capability in industry and services. The business sector in Hong Kong (China), for instance, virtually reinvented itself in the 1985–90 period. Manufacturing of low- and medium-tech products was moved to the Pearl River Delta area, with firms in Hong Kong (China) mainly concentrating on upstream manufacturing; financial, marketing, advertising, and finishing services; supply chain management; and logistics (Berger and Lester 1997). During this period, when firms redefined and focused on their areas of core competence, Hong Kong's productivity ranking rose from 24th relative to the United States in the 1970s, to 2nd in the late 1980s (table 1.5). Hong Kong (China) established itself as one of the world's most competitive economies

---

13. See "Prospects 2003" (2002); "The Human Tide" (2003); and "Young, Bright" (2003).

in the eyes of the international business community.[14] Singapore also moved decisively into higher tech manufacturing and producer services in the second half of the 1980s, and its ranking improved from 29th to 22nd according to Islam's index.

Reform of Business Organization

For a brief period in the late 1990s, the industrialized world seemed to be on the threshold of a new technological epoch. Some of the initial exuberance proved to be irrational, but there is little doubt that the pulse of technological change has quickened.[15] Feldstein (2003) ascribes this, in part, to advances in and assimilation of information and communication technology (ICT) (see also OECD 2004). He also links the robustness of productivity to changes in business organization and management practices, new approaches to networking and interfirm collaboration, and the building of technological capability and supply chain management. In a globalizing market environment, these practices affect survival and profitability and are actively pursued by leading Western and East Asian firms. These practices are no less important for firms in China that are or increasingly will be competing on the same level playing field in markets for more sophisticated products against new competitors.

As argued in this and later chapters, efforts to complete the process of enterprise reform are a matter of urgency. And after a transition that has already extended over a quarter-century, further delay in modernizing enterprises and associated market institutions in China will not only constrain competitiveness but have a dampening effect on the growth of the economy. Moreover, because the scale and performance of the state sector have a direct bearing on the condition of the banking sector, delaying enterprise reform will make it harder to strengthen the health of banks in keeping with the financial liberalization agreed to as part of China's accession to the World Trade Organization (WTO). Steinfeld observes that "as long as the commercial banking sector serves as the chosen vehicle for pumping SOE policy loans, the central state cannot credibly threaten to stop bailing out insolvent banks. The government, in effect, loses the

---

14. See Thompson (2002), who also notes that in 2000–1, Hong Kong's ratings began to plummet because of concerns with respect to governance and adherence to the rule of law.

15. Although the surge in U.S. productivity growth associated with the "new economy" slowed somewhat after 2000 (see Baily 2002), the United States continued to register respectable gains in TFP during 2001–4 (Gordon 2003).

few levers it has to force ostensibly commercial banks actually to operate on a commercial basis" (1998, p. 71). Enterprise reform also impinges on the integration of the domestic economy. Although the domestic market is more unified now than it was in the late 1970s, market integration has been hampered not only by transport constraints (especially the underdeveloped state of China's physical infrastructure and multimodal transport), but also by local regulations that introduce barriers to entry, a weak legal system that makes it difficult for firms to enforce contracts, preferential treatment of local producers, and taxes that restrict interprovincial—and sometimes intercounty—trade, permitting inefficient producers supported by local governments to survive and to continue receiving loans from banks.[16] According to research by Alwyn Young (2000), partial integration is costly for China and detracts from full exploitation of regional comparative advantages.[17]

Much has been written about the nonstate sector, whose share of industrial output now overshadows the state sector. Nevertheless, over one-half of industrial value added is in the state sector, and its absolute size remains large, as does its claim on resources. SOEs in China held close to two-thirds of all net fixed assets in 2000, and the percentage of fixed assets in total assets of SOEs had risen to 44, up from 36 in 1994 (Heytens and Karacadag 2003, p. 177). At the start of the Ninth Five-Year Plan in 1996,

---

16. The situation is even more serious in Russia, where provincial governments have been slow to harden budget constraints on the large SOEs and have used trade barriers to sustain their industrial policies (Sonin 2003).

17. Naughton's (1999) estimates of interprovincial trade among 23 provinces for the period 1987–92 (derived from input-output statistics) pointed to a rising trend. Exports to other provinces and to the rest of the world increased from 52 to 69 percent of provincial GDP, while imports climbed from 53 to 68 percent. This compared favorably with intercountry trade in the economies of the European Union, the North American Free Trade Agreement (NAFTA), and the Association of Southeast Asian Nation (ASEAN). Between 1992 and 1997, however, interprovincial trade fell steeply. Poncet (2003) has estimated that in 1992, the composition of provincial absorption was as follows: 27 percent were goods produced in other provinces, 68 percent were locally made goods, and 5 percent were imports from other countries. By 1997, the percentages were, respectively, 20 percent, 72 percent, and 8 percent, reflecting gains in intraprovincial and international trade at the expense of interprovincial trade. Poncet (2003, p. 17) observes that "barriers to trade between Chinese provinces to be closer in magnitude to that on international trade than that on trade flow within a single country. Chinese domestic market integration is low. . . . This evolution underlines the failure of reforms to promote domestic market integration and the growing division of the Chinese domestic market into cellular submarkets." Such a tendency is unlikely to be reversed so long as the state sector continues to loom large and provincial authorities feel compelled to shelter relatively inefficient SOEs from competition from private enterprises, joint ventures, and TVEs. More recent research suggests that product market integration has picked up in the past few years, although the failure of institutions to enforce contracts continues to hamper cross-provincial trade (Tan 2004).

the government announced plans to modernize the enterprise sector by creating a number of enterprise groups at the national and subnational levels. The central government identified 512 enterprises to be formed into 57 groups, each with a main bank relationship similar to some of the Japanese *keiretsu* (an alliance among suppliers, intermediaries, and other firms that operate vertically and horizontally, are centered around a financial entity, and often have interlocking business relationships and shareholdings). Other groups were forged by provincial governments (Smyth 2000). In 2000 there were 2,655 such groups, accounting for over a fifth of China's total exports and 57 percent of its industrial assets. The state had a majority ownership in the largest 1,605 of these—which together held 92 percent of assets and were responsible for 87 percent of sales. By virtue of their size and importance for the economy, and their association with most of China's leading firms, these groups exert an effect far out of proportion to their actual contribution to GDP. Some of these enterprises and groups have a vital role to play in China's future development; however, for reasons explained in the following section and further developed in chapter 6, they are more likely to do so if they can fully and flexibly respond to the rapidly evolving global business environment. This volume argues that the full privatization of most industrial SOEs and a strengthening of enabling market institutions are the best ways to provide the incentives, induce the dynamism, and build the industrial organization needed to enhance competitiveness.

Performance of China's SOEs

The new generation of Chinese leaders faces the politically delicate and complex task of preparing the Chinese economy for the conditions that must be fulfilled following China's accession to the WTO in 2002. They must decide on the degree to which the state will continue to direct the enterprise and financial sectors, and on whether retaining majority public ownership of the larger enterprises and the banks—directly or through holding companies—is necessary for the role envisaged by the state. These decisions will inevitably call for the balancing of an array of political and economic concerns, including the likelihood that privatization could lead to the layoffs of many of the nearly 50 million urban workers currently employed by SOEs.[18] A substantial downsizing of the state bureaucracy that supervises the state sector and a diminution of the controls exercised by different levels of government over industrial entities are likely as well.

---

18. See Tenev, Zhang, and Brefort (2002, p. 19).

During the socialist era, China devised an elaborate bureaucratic apparatus to direct industry activity. Although detailed physical planning has been circumscribed and many supervisory agencies have merged or been eliminated, a planning apparatus remains intact and continues to exert substantial oversight over broad sectoral development—at times extending to micro-level decisions. The newly streamlined supervisory agencies, according to Steinfeld, "still intervene in basic managerial decisions, still maintain an iron grip over personnel decisions . . . and still retain the power to pull money out of a state firm" (1998, p. 61).

So the reform of state enterprises deserves priority for four main reasons: first, to stem the direct costs to the economy from the inefficient use of resources and reduce the pressures that the production of loss-making enterprises imposes on healthier firms that must register normal profits to survive and grow; second, to protect the health of the banking system, which has invested heavily and often unwisely in SOEs—and whose fortunes are likely to remain linked for some time with those of current and former SOEs so long as the flow of nonperforming loans (NPLs) continues as a result of related lending; third, to facilitate and promote the reform of market and legal institutions that support transition, social security, and intraprovincial trade; and fourth, to heighten the responsiveness of the SOEs to market forces, thereby stimulating changes needed to enhance factor productivity and the innovativeness of firms. This chapter will comment on the significance of the first two priorities but focus mainly on the third, and explain why privatization might be the first best option for the manufacturing sector in China.

Although reforms of SOEs strengthened performance in the latter half of the 1980s, and formally sanctioned exit via bankruptcy in 1988, the sector has remained a drag on the economy.[19] Ten years after enterprise reforms were launched in earnest, nearly 40 percent of China's small and medium-size state-owned enterprises (SMSOEs) were insolvent—almost 120,000 enterprises in all ("Corporatizing China" 2002); and in the late 1990s, almost half of all SOEs were running losses, up from a quarter in

---

19. From a very small start of 32 in 1989, the number of bankruptcies rose to between 7,000 and 8,000 per year in 1998–2002, half of them being SOEs. This is still a fairly small number but is related to the inadequacies of the bankruptcy law, which assigns much of the decisionmaking power to government agencies, and is vague with regard to the treatment of different types of firms and the valuation of assets. Moreover, some bankrupt enterprises are resurrected by local governments as new firms, and many others are bought up by healthy firms, often at the suggestion of subnational governments, at prices that significantly overstate the value of their assets. A new bankruptcy law that has been 11 years in the making (since 1994) could eliminate some of the problems, but it has still to be approved by the National People's Congress (NPC) ("Busted" 2003).

1997 (see also Tenev, Zhang, and Brefort 2002).[20] By 2002, the situation was less serious following the divestment or closure of thousands of SMSOEs;[21] nevertheless, 30 percent of the remaining SOEs were still "in the red," with the median return for better-performing listed companies at only 7 percent.[22] During 2003–4, the performance of SOEs reportedly improved further. Nevertheless, many SOEs that do break even are in a precarious liquidity position, because of an anemic cash flow that makes it difficult to cover interest costs and renders them highly susceptible to movements in interest rate. According to one recent survey, "a moderate rise in the interest rates or drop in sales could cause 40–60 percent of the debts of all firms to become unserviceable" (Heytens and Karacadag 2003, p. 180). Furthermore, the high ratio of receivables and inventories to total assets suggests that, as in the past, SOEs persist in producing goods for which demand is weak or nonexistent. Those that do diversify too often target commodity products for which entry barriers are low, competition is fierce, and profits are correspondingly small. Steinfeld (2004a; 2004b) reports that firms such as Konka have responded to the pressures in the market for televisions by entering into the production of mobile phones. Similarly, Galanz, which specializes in the manufacture of microwave ovens, has jumped into the already saturated market of air-conditioning units.

Moreover, the assets of SOEs might be valued more generously than is warranted. This also has implications for leverage—which averaged 144 percent in 2000 and would be significantly more if assets and inventories were properly valued (Heytens and Karacadag 2003, p. 178).

Other measures corroborate the evidence from financial indicators. Studies extending back into the latter half of the 1980s (discussed more fully in chapter 3) have repeatedly shown that the efficiency and productivity of SOEs lag behind COEs, TVEs, and joint ventures. Using data for 1995 from China's third industrial census, Wen, Li, and Lloyd (2002) established that the technical efficiency of SOEs was lower than that of COEs and joint ventures for each of the industrial subsectors in their

---

20. About 12 percent of SOEs were making losses in 1980, and these amounted to 2.43 percent of net industrial output (Cheng and Lo 2002).
21. Although very few SOEs were declared bankrupt during 1988–96, the numbers swelled to 17,000 between 1998 and 2002 ("Busted" 2003).
22. There were 9,300 large and 181,000 small and medium-size SOEs in 2002 ("Privatization Revived" 2003). A figure of 174,000 is quoted in "China Lays Out" (2003). More recently, the number of SMSOEs in 2002 is stated to have been 149,000; and there were 8,752 medium-size and large ones ("China: SOE Reforms" 2005).

Table 1.6 Cyclical Behavior of Total Factor Productivity
(percentage annual growth)

Time period	SOE	COE	ODE	FIE
1985(P)–1998/89 (P)	2.29	3.38	n.a.	n.a.
1988/89(P)–1993(P)	2.45	5.40	3.63	3.31
1981(T)–(1983) (T)	3.40	4.79	n.a.	n.a.
1986(T)–(1990) (T)	1.58	2.95	n.a.	n.a.
1990(T)–(1996) (T)	0.65	4.40	3.41	1.14

Notes: (P) and (T) denote the cyclical peaks and troughs based on price movements; COE, collectively owned enterprise; FIE, foreign-invested enterprise; ODE, other domestic enterprise, including domestic private enterprises, domestic joint ventures, and small residual category; SOE, state-owned enterprise.
Source: Jefferson and others (2000).

sample. This is in line with results published by Otsuka, Liu, and Murakami (1998), which indicate that of the enterprises they studied (using data for 1985 and 1990), SOEs were the least efficient. It is also comparable to the findings of Jefferson and others (2000) based on production data for 1985–8, 1990, 1993, and 1996. They determined that SOEs occupied the lowest rung on the total factor productivity ladder, with other types of enterprises ranked in between.

Research on the total factor productivity of Chinese enterprises comes to broadly similar conclusions, and some recent work also suggests that reforms might not be producing the desired results. Table 1.6 shows that TFP increased substantially for all classes of enterprises in the second half of the 1980s, and that TFP growth of COEs and of privately owned enterprises remained robust in the period 1990–6. However, TFP growth of SOEs was noticeably weaker in the 1980s and slowed to a crawl during the first half of the 1990s.[23] But Jefferson and others also find that the TFP performance of reformed SOEs was equally meager. This latter result is not supported by the survey findings presented in chapter 5 of this volume.

Since 1996, the efforts to reform SOEs through corporatization, employee ownership, and other schemes (table 1.7) have been greatly

---

23. To Jefferson and others, "these consistently weak results represent a serious threat to the Chinese reform agenda because it depends heavily on the expectation that shareholding arrangements, which are key elements in the restructuring of both state enterprises and rural collectives can provide effective mechanisms for monitoring enterprise managers and operations. . . . Weak performance of foreign-invested firms and shareholding enterprises may signal that recent ownership reforms including new public-private partnerships as well as restructuring within the public sector have failed to deliver significant improvements in performance. These findings lend credence to critics who claim that neither joint ventures nor the new network of asset management companies established to exercise public ownership rights can eliminate the agency problems embedded in public ownership" (2000, pp. 805–6).

Table 1.7 Modes of Restructuring for Small and Medium-Size SOEs

Region	Number of SOEs	Trans-formed (%)	Restructuring method (percent)							
			Restruc-turing	Merger	Leasing	Contract-ing	Joint-stock company	Sale	Bank-ruptcy	Other
Coastal	17,629	83	17	13	11	9	22	8	8	12
Central	20,713	83	14	11	14	9	22	9	11	10
Western	21,068	80	20	12	9	8	19	9	11	12

Note: SOEs, state-owned enterprises.
Source: World Bank, based on a 2000 State Economic and Trade Commission survey.

intensified, with mixed results.[24] Between 1996 and 2001, close to 50,000 of the smaller and medium-size SOEs had been restructured (*gaizhi*) through a public offering, employee buyout, open sales, leasing, joint ventures, bankruptcy, or other means (Garnaut and others 2005). Many of the larger SOEs were restructured into shareholding companies—some of which have been listed on stock exchanges—but with state entities remaining the largest shareholders, with an average stake of 65 percent in 2005 in the form of nontradeable shares ("Big Names" 2005; Green 2003). According to a national survey reported by Garnaut and others (2005), 86 percent of all SOEs had been through *gaizhi* by the end of 2001, and 70 percent had been fully or partially privatized.

For the smaller SOEs, employee buyouts have often led to disappointing outcomes for reasons echoing the experience of other countries: Ownership is too diluted to give any single person much of a stake in the company's future, incompetent managers who own shares in the company cannot easily be discharged, dividends are typically generous, and governance exercised by boards of directors or others tends to be weak.[25, 26] As a result, by 2001, over half of all SMSOEs were unable to service their bank loans ("Corporatizing China" 2002). On balance, the bigger SOEs did better (as described in chapters 3 and 4), but even some of these firms were only marginally profitable.

---

24. In the mid-1990s, the government determined that nearly 40 percent of the nonfinancial SOEs were insolvent, mostly the smaller ones. See Zhang (2002) and Broadman (2001). Ownership reform is also ongoing in the TVE sector, as local governments and enterprises—many heavily indebted, running losses, and the source of serious environmental pollution—struggle to resolve a range of problems. See Smyth, Wang, and Kiang (2001).

25. A study of rural firms in China that were privatized points to a strong preference for insider privatization in spite of mixed results, because insiders enjoy the advantages of incumbency. Outsiders lack sufficient information, and with insiders, officials can continue to play a monitoring role and derive some financial gain (Li and Rozelle 2004).

26. See Tenev, Zhang, and Brefort (2002) for a comprehensive account of governance issues faced by enterprises in China.

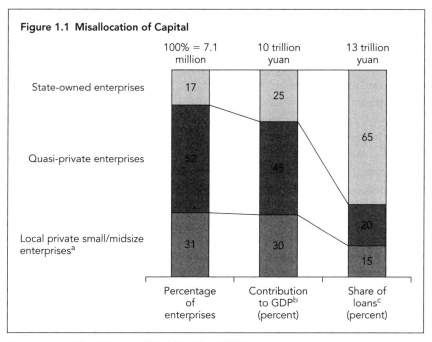

Figure 1.1 Misallocation of Capital

Source: Adapted from "Checking China's Vital Signs" (2004).

a. Includes companies with foreign investment and large local private enterprises.

b. Industrial output used as a proxy for state-owned enterprises, and industry value added used as proxy for local private small/midsize enterprises.

c. Financial liabilities used as proxy for bank loans in order to determine state-owned enterprises' share.

These findings reinforce earlier observations in this chapter on the economic costs of China's SOE sector. By virtue of their size, the industrial assets at their command, the inefficient use of resources, and outright waste on redundant or suboptimal production capacity and on inventories for which there is no market, the dismal economic and financial performance of SOEs is a serious drain on the economy—with ramifications extending well beyond the enterprise sector. With the help of subnational governments and their own personal connections (*guanxi*), the managers of SOEs have borrowed huge sums from banks (about 65 percent of the total loans in 2002), a sizable fraction of which the SOEs will not be able to repay (see figure 1.1).[27] As much as 42 percent of all lending by the banking system is in the form of policy loans directed by the government (Broadman 2001; Gordon 2003; Steinfeld 1998). This relationship

27. *Guanxi* refers to personal connections that lubricate business and political dealings. See Gold, Guthrie, and Wank (2002) on the many faces and changing character of *guanxi*.

between SOEs and state-owned banks is responsible for the accumulation of NPLs in the portfolios of commercial banks, credit cooperatives, and other lending institutions. Although at the end of 2004, the NPLs of the 16 largest commercial banks were reported to be 13.2 percent as against 26 percent at the end of 2002, the improvement largely reflected the transfer of bad debts to asset management companies and the infusion of $45 billion by the People's Bank of China.[28] However, China's main banks remain in a relatively fragile state. It is a fragility that China needs to rectify before the country can liberalize its capital account and before it is ready to face the competition from foreign banks under the agreed terms of its WTO accession.[29]

The slow nature of SOE reforms has permitted another problem to fester. China needs to craft a social security system that will, at a minimum, achieve two objectives. The first is to provide an acceptable degree of social assurance for urban workers affected by frictional unemployment and the millions of others who have been rendered jobless (some permanently) by the restructuring or closure of SOEs. SOEs have already laid off millions of workers, and many more would join this pool if SOE reforms were to accelerate.[30] Larger SOEs have created a diversified network of subsidiaries to employ redundant workers, often at considerable cost. The Shougang Group, for example, has set up businesses in the real estate and services sectors in order to minimize layoffs (Nolan and Yeung 2001). The employment insurance system created in 1986 and modified in 1999, in principle, covers a high percentage of the urban working population and offers a relatively high replacement rate. But the scheme is not yet viable and is already incurring annual losses.

To unemployment assurance must be added a second objective: the provision of a safety net for retirees and the elderly, whose numbers will

---

28. Several questions remain about the classification of bank loans by the Bank of China, such as the "number of days past due." Standard & Poor's, for example, estimates the bad debts of the banking system at about 50 percent (Bottelier 2002; "China: Burdened Banks" 2003). Whether the weight of NPLs seriously endangers the banking system so long as it is underwritten by the government is questioned by Gordon (2003).

29. Lo (2004) maintains that the adopted approach of repackaging bad loans is not likely to affect the flow of such loans. To do that, the government must address the problems of poor governance, accounting, and biased lending policies. Measures introduced in mid-2004, by fixing quotas on offshore borrowing by foreign banks to lend to local customers, will circumscribe their ability to compete with Chinese banks and expand their loan portfolios ("Beijing Tightens" 2004).

30. One estimate puts the number of layoffs from restructuring between 1998 and 2002 at 24 million workers. In the next four years, the government plans to close down 2,500 large mines and SOEs, which could lead to the displacement of an additional 5 million workers ("No Right to Work" 2004).

swell rapidly. Between 1990 and 2030, the percentage of the population
that is over 60 years of age will rise from 9 percent to 22 percent (Wang
and others 2004). For decades, SOEs provided the safety net for urban
workers through the so-called "iron rice bowl"—income and benefits for
the entirety of an individual's working life and the duration of retirement.
This arrangement saddles enterprises with enormous (and usually)
unfunded obligations. And now that life expectancy is rising and the SOEs
are no longer assured high profits by a system of state-determined prices
and market controls, the burden on the enterprises is increasingly unsus-
tainable. However, in the absence of an adequate safety net, SOE reform
through privatization (by multiplying the number of redundant workers)
would further strain the implicit social contract between the government
and the core urban workforce.

Although the Chinese state began tackling the pension issue in 1986
through a pooling of pension obligations across enterprises, this and subsequent arrangements, and further efforts aimed at creating a three-tier
system, have not yet advanced beyond the pilot stage.[31] Thus, retirees
depend on inadequately funded, municipal pay-as-you-go (PAYG)
schemes and often survive on government subsidies. Meanwhile, the
pension funding gap has widened to 40 billion yuan by 2000 (Wang and
others 2004). Quite apart from the costs of supporting workers laid off by
privatized SOEs and those that exit voluntarily, there is the risk of political turbulence dangerously in excess of the level already aroused by
reforms introduced since the mid-1990s.[32] This strengthens the hands of
government and party officials opposed to SOE reform of a radical sort,
who in turn are supported by many managers and workers in the SOEs.
Policymakers thus face the unenviable task of weighing the political costs
of layoffs and increased social security payments by the state against the
costs of implicit subsidies and protection to unreformed SOEs—plus
the nonperforming loans accumulated by banks as a result of their loans to
the state sector.

Can China continue to incur the direct and indirect costs of the gradu-
alist approach to SOE reform? The answer is, most certainly, yes. The
current growth momentum, the small size of the official public sector

31. The three pillars are the following: a state pension that would provide an amount equal to
one-fifth of the provincial average wage, an individual pension account administered by the state
that accumulates 11 percent of an individual's salary, and voluntary pension arrangements
("China: State Pension" 2002).

32. Resistance from workers has been especially marked in the industrial cities in northeast
China, but it has erupted in Sichuan and the central provinces as well ("A Dragon Out" 2002;
Cai 2002; "China Local-Level Protests" 2003; "Out of Business" 1999; Tanner 2004).

debt—local and foreign (18 percent in 2002)—the size of foreign exchange reserves (over \$660 billion in March 2005), and the sheer volume of domestic savings (47 percent of GDP in 2003) provide a cushion sufficient to offset for several years the excess resources consumed by inefficient SOEs and the symbiotically associated bureaucracy that controls them. China thus has the means to accommodate an inefficient public sector; but sustaining waste on such a scale, perhaps politically expedient in the medium term, reduces the gains from growth and saps the vitality of the economy. As China proceeds down the path toward greater integration with the global economy, the need for quickly restructuring enterprises becomes more acute, and the advantages of decisive action over gradualism are clearly evident.[33]

Urgent calls for reform have been voiced before—of the banking sector, of social security, of enterprises—but with little impact on the actual pace of implementation. Much of the time those suggesting haste have worried that delay would lead to a faltering of the reform drive, a severe domestic crisis, political unrest, or a sharp (possibly irrevocable) slowing of the growth rate. But China has coped with crises as they have arisen, without the economy losing its stride. As a consequence, further pleas for action are unlikely to motivate the kind of urgent action required unless it can be shown that the situation has become appreciably more acute. The message here is that the added risk China now faces stems from the apparently inexorable process of globalization. This risk derives both from the nature of competition in the global economy and from the response this demands from business participants.

HOW FIRMS CAN SUCCEED UNDER THE NEW COMPETITION

Successful industrial firms worldwide share a number of features. First, the overwhelming majority are privately owned.[34] Dynamic industrial firms in which the public sector has a controlling share are a rarity, which

---

33. Research using data from 140,000 manufacturing firms in the United Kingdom during 1980–92 shows that restructuring involving the exit and entry of firms was responsible for most of the growth in TFP and about one-half of the increase in labor productivity (Disney, Haskel, and Heden 2003).

34. There are exceptions, of course. In Korea, prior to its privatization, POSCO was one of the most efficient and profitable steel companies in the world. It has since emerged as the leader in terms of cost competitiveness and efficiency. Several of Singapore's government-linked companies, which operate as profit-maximizing commercial entities, have also done well financially (Ramirez and Tan 2003).

is why privatization of China's SOEs is a necessary step to expedite the exit of failing entities and unlock the full potential of the ones that can survive.[35] Successful firms tend to focus on a dominant line of business where they excel and are able to acquire a sizable share of the market for their principal product. They are companies in which the management provides strong leadership and a strategic vision but remains accountable to shareholders, with their actions continually scrutinized through effective governance institutions. The significance of good corporate governance is reflected in the stock market premium enjoyed by firms that are viewed as being more accountable to shareholders. Firms such as General Electric (GE) and Microsoft have benefited from investor perceptions of their accountability and transparency. In addition, competitive firms devote much effort to continuously enhancing efficiency in small and large ways—and motivate and reward employee initiative. Such firms plough a sizable share of their cash flow into the search for product and process innovation, to hone their competitive edge. Leading firms in the tradable subsectors increasingly adopt a global perspective. They actively pursue opportunities in international markets, and as they build market share and design and technological capability, seek to acquire the brand recognition needed to secure a profitable niche that will generate rents to fuel future growth. Last, but not least, these firms recognize that growth via the ladder of technology and global marketing can require that they enter markets adjacent to their own and leverage expertise in their core area, their marketing network, and brand name; embark upon advantageous collaborative arrangements with other firms; harness pools of knowledge in other countries by way of intercompany technology transfers, create research centers, or acquire promising companies.[36] Growth may require foreign direct investment in greenfield ventures as well.

By building companies with these characteristics and capabilities, China can sustain rapid growth. And the research on leading firms indicates that the way forward calls for a move away from past patterns of ownership and industrial management. Among China's bigger firms are several that have acquired a large share of the domestic market for their products and potentially could grow and compete on equal terms with the multinational

---

35. This step is also required in order to realize a competitive market environment, which in transition economies (and others) leads to more rapid productivity growth and to innovation (see Carlin, Shaffer, and Seabright [2004]).

36. An example of this approach is provided by ST Microelectronics, which developed its system on chip solutions by tapping expertise in France, Ireland, Singapore, the United Kingdom, and the United States (Santos, Doz, and Williamson 2004).

corporations—firms such as Haier, Huawei, TCL, Lenovo (formerly Legend), Konka, Galanz, and Sichuan Changhong Electric.[37] But the majority of SOEs bear no resemblance to Lenovo. To nurture more of these enterprises that are equal to the challenge of global markets, most SOEs will need to be extensively reshaped, because the top-down, hierarchical Chinese manufacturing enterprise, with its limited managerial, marketing, and technological capabilities, is far removed from the streamlined, flexible, and adaptive firms now competing in the corporate sea ("China Struggles" 2002). The purpose of this volume is not to prescribe norms. Instead, by highlighting aspects of the transformation that is now under way in the international corporate world, this study shows why it will take the privatization of industrial enterprises to attain China's development objectives. Corporatization will not succeed if it allows the state to retain dominant shares of firms and leaves existing controls and organizational structures largely in place.

Management and Strategy

One of the major consequences of privatization is an upheaval in management, although managerial capability is likely to be influenced by parallel changes in the institutions that affect corporate governance, the legal system, property rights of minority shareholders, and the entry and exit of firms. These are discussed in later chapters. A wealth of research shows that the architecture of a business organization, how it develops and utilizes innovation to acquire competitive advantage (by way of enhanced operational effectiveness and new products), and the path it takes to growth are all related to management, strategy, and execution. Whether a firm succeeds on a global scale, merely survives in the national market, or faces outright failure, the quality of its management is likely to be at the root. A company's management defines strategy anchored to a business model describing the company's objectives within a dynamic system. Articulating such a strategy, along with the underlying business model and mode of execution, is the management's defining purpose—and is fundamental to the effective functioning of a firm. For example, an emphasis on technological innovation as a means of obtaining a competitive edge, a reliance on open innovation systems, and the creative use of information technology are strands of company strategy that are not yet common among either China's SOEs or its reformed SOEs according to the

---

37. See Sull and Wang (2005).

findings presented in chapter 5.[38] Closely related to the execution of a company's strategy is the culture that the management instills. This culture influences the form of governance (that is, the role and efficacy of a board of directors, internal auditors, and other bodies within the firm that are responsible for oversight), employee initiative and loyalty, risk-taking, grassroots feedback, and rules governing both mobility within the company and the selection of management, which in turn determine the quality of those who run a company.[39]

Strategy needs to be designed with the wants of customers and partners at the forefront. A strategic frame provides answers to questions managers must confront every day and guide them in their search for and screening of information. This includes questions such as, What business are we in? How do we create value? Who are our competitors? Which customers are crucial, and which can we safely ignore? (Sull 1999, p. 4). Such a strategic frame is likely to be lacking, and customer orientation is generally weaker in state enterprises because the budget constraints tend to be softer. But nonfinancial and noncommercial concerns can loom large in state enterprises, and a bureaucratic culture that seeks safety in inaction can discourage boldness in decisionmaking and the readiness to innovate.

Dynamic private firms regularly fine-tune their strategies as circumstances change and a fresh approach is needed. Hayes and Pisano (1994, p. 78) correctly point out, "In a turbulent environment . . . the goal of strategy becomes strategic flexibility. Being world class is not enough, a company also has to have the capability to switch gears—from, for example, rapid product development to low cost production—relatively quickly and with minimal resources. The job of manufacturing—is to provide that capability." Again, SOEs that are subject to softer budget constraints and buffered to varying degrees from competition are less likely to have a coherent strategy and are much less inclined to unstitch and restitch the strategy to keep in step with market contingencies. This approach extends to execution and organizational structure. The leading firms are conspicuous in their efforts to serve the customer, tap latent wants or create entirely new ones, and run a tight ship, financial and otherwise. Moreover, these firms ensure that employees are committed to the strategy adopted, that decisionmaking authority is optimally decentralized, and that it is

---

38. See Chesbrough (2003a; 2003b) on the advantages of capitalizing on research done by others. This openness encourages firms to seek innovations more widely, restrains in-house research costs, and is a necessity where products call for integrating research from several disciplines.

39. On the role of management and some leading causes of its failure, see Nohria, Joyce, and Roberson (2003) and Charan and Useem (2002).

coordinated with the right mix of incentives. Organizations can complement strategy when employees are encouraged to work cooperatively to find innovative solutions to the wants of consumers and to search for the procedural simplifications that augment productivity.

In some cases, Chinese firms have been able to fashion strategies and successfully execute them by responding to changing domestic market conditions and their deep knowledge of the Chinese market institutions and the consumer. For example, Lenovo, the maker of China's best-selling line of personal computers (PCs), has captured 30 percent of the market share; the nature of its management and ownership structure contributes to its performance. And Lenovo's acquisition of IBM's PC division in April 2005 will raise its annual sales to $12 billion, positioning the firm to challenge Dell and Hewlett-Packard in global markets.[40] Haier and Changhong Electric have also shown managerial adeptness and marketing savvy in devising strategies that first captured a large share of the domestic market for home appliances (such as washing machines) and then established a foothold in the U.S. market for wine coolers and small refrigerators.[41] Similarly, Huawei has with remarkable speed entered the technologically demanding international market for lower end routers. It should be noted, however, that neither Lenovo nor Huawei is an SOE. Instead, they are quasi-private firms (or *minying qiye*); and Huawei is a private firm registered in Shenzhen, with past links to the People's Liberation Army (PLA).

Most SOEs, even reformed ones, remain subject to many handicaps. In some instances, too much authority is concentrated in the hands of the chief executive officer (CEO) or a few members of the senior management—who are subject to few checks from a board of directors or a supervising ministry and shielded from unwelcome information about the functioning of the enterprise or group.[42] Other managerial problems include a continuing predilection to vertical integration of the production process (as is the case with Lenovo) or diversification into unrelated fields for the sake of growth, which dilutes core competence and leads to ever greater unwieldiness. Worst of all are the inefficiencies that arise when a hierarchical organization, with a weak incentive system and tenured

---

40. "Lenovo Buys" (2004) and "Deal On" (2005).

41. Haier's "Little Prince" washing machine quickly exploited a large market in China for small-load washers. See Williamson and Zeng (2004). In the United States, Haier has captured 35 percent of the small refrigerator market (Gilmore and Dumont 2003).

42. On how boards of directors can contribute to the success of firms, see the overview of recent research by Daily, Dalton, and Cannella Jr. (2003). See also Smyth and Qingguo (2003).

employees, has lived far too long subject to soft budget constraints in the quasi-protected world of the public sector.[43] Under these circumstances, it is difficult to escape the grip of inertia; and even when the enterprise acts, the actions taken are often inappropriate (Sull 1999). Arguably most serious is the continuing interference by government agencies that retain control rights even after the SOE has been partially corporatized or wholly transferred into private hands.[44] The meaningfulness of shareholder rights is often questionable in a system where the rule of law and courts are generally unable to pass or to fully enforce rulings against the state, as described in chapter 2. Steinfeld (1998, p. 62) observed that "the currency of the bureaucracy is authority, not rights. The bureaucratic agencies of the old system continue interfering in the firm, and they do it not as owners of the firm but as agents of the state. They could care less what rights the firm has."

Innovation Capability and Firm Size

The quality of management and the effectiveness of strategy will determine the capacity of the leading Chinese firms to routinize product innovation and sustain competitive advantage (Steinfeld 2004b). Innovation of many kinds—process, product, financial, organizational, logistical, and technological—has long been associated with competition and growth. What has changed since the mid-1980s—a period that witnessed the spread of development based on free markets, intensifying global integration, and a revolution in information and communication technologies that have provided some of the impetus—is its degree of centrality. Innovation has become the key to competitiveness and a major contributor to growth. One reason for the weaker performance of the former socialist economies was that a system based on public ownership placed little premium on continuous technological advance and undermined the efficiency of research and development. Baumol has correctly drawn attention to the role of innovation in the context of market competition. He writes, "No earlier or alternative recent form of economy seems to have had as its main driving mechanism free competitive markets, using innovation as the prime weapon—[its] absence need not prevent the exercise

---

43. For a review of the large literature on soft budget constraints and their consequences, see Kornai, Maskin, and Roland (2003).

44. While governments are reluctant to relinquish their hold on companies, both reformed SOEs and private firms actively pursue relationships with government departments to seek favors and, in particular, gain access to financing.

of ingenuity . . . but [it] does seem to weaken or even undermine the subsequent innovation steps—the steps that lead to widespread use of inventions, to fuel rapid economic growth" (Baumol 2002, p. 261). He goes on to note the emergence of an "arms race" among firms competing on the basis of innovative capability. This is a contest, "in which all players are forced to keep running as fast as they can in order to stand still. This is an engine of growth of great power, and it is a game that participants cannot easily quit. It is also the prime support for the optimism about the prospects for the continuation of the market economy's historically unprecedented innovation explosion and its acceleration during the twentieth century" (Baumol 2002, p. 287).

Global markets, by raising both the stakes and the level of competition, are forcing firms to move simultaneously on two fronts: first, to extend their reach beyond local and national markets to international markets; and second, to harness innovation as a means of achieving a global presence and combine this with a marketing strategy to launch and sustain a brand name.[45] Multinational firms such as Logitech, Samsung, Sony, and Canon are conspicuous in this regard. Among Chinese firms, Haier was one of the first to seek an international role, invest in overseas production facilities, and attempt to carve out a brand image in white goods such as refrigerators and coolers. And Pearl River Piano is competing against Korean firms and Yamaha in Japan to capture a share of the lower price range of the international market for pianos.

In a world where the rules of competition have been redrawn, firms must change course as well. Under the terms of the "old" competition, firms struggled to drive down prices and costs. The "new" form of competition requires a "marriage of productivity and innovation . . . whereas productivity and innovation were a trade-off in the old competition, they have become a dynamic in the new" (Best 1997, p. 9).

Production efficiency will certainly remain a major attribute of firms that successfully participate in the market beyond their national borders. They will need to focus on design and product innovation not just in a few high-tech areas, but also across the spectrum of traditional manufacturing industries—from garments to toys. And to back this up with innovations in process and supply-chain management, firm finances must be handled efficiently, with close attention to the scale of risks (Nichols 1994). In other words, to penetrate world markets and enlarge market share, Chinese firms will need to match their competitors, compress the

---

45. Garrett (2001) and Zweig (2002) discuss the effects on China of increasing openness and globalization.

design-production innovation cycle that is now measured in months, not years—and offer consumers a steady supply of affordable new products, produced at the least possible cost with attention to customer convenience.[46] International experience suggests that firms with these characteristics tend to concentrate on a few core areas, invest heavily in research and development, and seek to grow mainly on the basis of market-aware technological prowess—often through the takeover of small, new firms with promising technologies. This is not a route that most Chinese SOEs are likely to embark upon unless ownership and incentives are altered.

Because technology and productivity are so central to global competition, investment in research and development has arguably become a driving force behind the internal growth of a firm. In the East Asian context, a recent study of 136 major Taiwanese manufacturing firms by Wang and Tsai (2003) shows that expenditure on research and development had a direct bearing on the productivity of firms during the latter part of the 1990s. A World Bank–sponsored survey of Chinese and other East Asian firms conducted in 2000–1 arrived at similar findings (Yusuf and others 2003; Yusuf and Evenett 2002). However, the survey indicated that Chinese SOEs reaped fewer benefits from research and development than foreign joint ventures and wholly foreign-owned firms (Jefferson and Zhong 2004). Furthermore, while nearly half of all firms reported introducing some innovations in shop-floor production and management, very few referred to product innovations that earned large profits (Steinfeld 2004b). These results reinforce the findings from research on Chinese enterprises by Hu (2001) and Zhang, Zhang, and Zhao (2003). Hu (2001) shows that research and development expenditure is closely linked to rising productivity in private firms and to SOEs. He also finds little correlation between public research and development activity and the productivity of private businesses. Zhang, Zhang, and Zhao's (2003) empirical analysis of data from the 1995 General National Survey establish that the intensity and efficiency of research and development are related to productivity and profitability. They further show that the efficiency of such activities is much greater in private firms, joint ventures, and foreign firms. While SOEs have fairly high research and development intensity, the efficiency of this expenditure is limited and the productivity gains are

---

46. Agarwal and Gort (2001) estimate that the life cycle of a consumer product was compressed from an average of 33 years at the beginning of the 20th century to less than 3½ years from 1967 to 1996. Today it is measured in months. As Williamson and Zeng (2004) observe, a few Chinese firms have been able to fight back against the multinational corporations in their home market by mastering just this skill.

relatively meager. Nurturing the expansion of a firm through innovation is an art form in itself and not merely a function of the resources spent, although these certainly matter. This is an art that some Chinese firms are beginning to master and that many more need to learn.

Since the mid-1990s patenting activity and scientific publications have risen sharply in China, although from a very slender base; patent applications alone rose by close to 15 percent per year from 1994 to 1999. The enterprise sector responsible for 60 percent of spending on research and development has taken the lead, but overall total spending by businesses is only 0.6 percent of GDP compared to 1.37 percent in France, 2.04 percent in the United States, and an OECD average of 1.56 percent.[47] This expenditure is low in light of the findings of Hu and Jefferson (2004), who show that the return from research and development is close to 16 percent in the electronics industry and up to 54 percent in chemicals. Furthermore, Chinese domestic patenting still comprises mainly utility and design patents with limited innovative content, while applications for foreign patents numbered only 200 in 1995 and rose to only 299 in 1997 (Cheung and Lin 2004; OECD 2002, pp. 259, 261). This may be the result of a continuing concentration of research in government laboratories (which still absorbed two-thirds of all science and technology personnel in 1999) and the limited amount of research conducted in universities (Sun 2002). However, there is encouraging news on a number of fronts. First, the number of scientists and engineers engaged in research reached 802,000 in 2002. Second, China's ranking in the science citation index rose to 8th place in 2003, up from 26th in 1985. Third, a study of 20,000 medium- and large-size enterprises over the period 1995–9 points to intensifying research and development activity among such firms and suggests that a few are developing strong innovation capability. In 1995, no company in China applied for 100 or more patents; however, three did in 1996, and eight in 1999 (Jefferson and others 2003). Still, it is not evident that even the leading SOEs have moved with much alacrity. The changes in structure, management, strategy, culture, and technological capability warranted by the imperatives of China's growth objectives and the global market environment are not yet apparent.

Innovation capability that enhances commercial performance is made up of many parts. One part is the building of research capacity within the firm, by finding able knowledge workers, giving them adequate facilities,

---

47. In the aggregate, China's research and development spending as a percentage of GDP rose to 1.3 percent in 2003; and adjusted for PPP, it ranked third in the world after the United States and Japan.

and creating an environment of incentives that encourages not just the researchers but the entire organization to make innovation the principal competitive goal.

A second attribute of competitive firms is size. They exploit early successes in achieving production efficiency and in innovating to expand by investing in additional capacity and merging with other firms that produce similar or related products.[48] That is, successful firms try and leverage their advantages to initiate a virtuous cycle of growth which, in turn, provides them with the resources needed to conduct research and fuel innovation, sell under their brand name, and support the marketing infrastructure needed to enhance their international image.

There is plenty of evidence from the higher-income economies suggesting that small firms are more innovative and inventive on a per worker basis, and also that new starts can be a fruitful conduit for innovations. However, the findings from Japan, Korea, and even Taiwan (China) suggest that large firms are in a position to be much more innovative (though not inventive) on a sustained basis (Amsden and Chu 2003; Urata and Kawai 2002).[49] Even among the leading OECD countries, the serial innovators with the global brand names are large firms that command the cash flow to pour vast sums into research and development and identify the market opportunities that can justify a massive, multifaceted outlay on innovation. Innovation capability on the scale and excellence required to participate in the "new competition" on global markets calls for large firms with an international reach and the potential for achieving brand recognition. Size can matter more in globalized markets in which competition is keyed to innovation. Size can make it easier for a firm to take steps to expand its portfolio of technological options and establish its presence in foreign markets. However, size is an asset for the focused and efficiently managed company with a strategy based on technological capability. For many large conglomerates with a diffuse range of activities, size is of no

---

48. A study of Chinese iron and steelmaking enterprises by Kalirajan and Yong (1993) found that the larger firms were, on balance, more efficient technically. Using a database for European countries, Pagano and Schivardi (2003) found that size of firms and their research and development intensity were correlated with productivity growth. Cross-country research by Kumar, Rajan, and Zingales (1999) has established that the efficacy of the judicial system is positively correlated with the growth of firms. Because legal institutions exert more influence on the information-intensive rather than capital-intensive subsectors, firms that are dependent on research and development and knowledge are most likely to grow with sound judicial institutions.

49. Or, large firms are at least much more effective in capitalizing on an innovation by adapting it for the market and investing in the required production facilities. Microsoft has not been a great innovator, but it has shown remarkable skill in building on innovation by others.

help and can adversely affect the willingness to recognize internal problems or external threats and to take, if needed, radical steps. These issues are discussed with respect to China in chapters 2, 3, and 6 of this volume.

Innovation at the frontiers of fields such as electronics, biotechnology, or biopharmaceuticals has become increasingly costly. For the majority of firms, even the largest such as IBM and Intel, technological advances that translate into commercial success depend upon alliances, joint projects, and collaborative arrangements with other compatible firms—or with firms nurturing new products.[50] The incessant demand for fresh products, the attempt to telescope product cycles, and the extraordinary costs of pushing the technological frontiers are enormous challenges. And a task that involves large outlay on facilities, a critical mass of workers with highly specialized skills, and taking an idea from design to commercial fruition tests the management capacity of even the biggest multinationals and can be well beyond the reach of most midsize firms or the vast majority of Chinese SOEs. But a trickle of reformed SOEs is now entering into alliances and merging with foreign firms. TCL—a manufacturer of television sets, mobile telephones, and personal computers—has merged its television facilities with those of Thomson of France (which earlier acquired the RCA brand), creating the largest global producer of television sets. SVA Electronics has partnered with NEC of Japan to produce liquid crystal display (LCD) panels; and Pearl River Piano has entered into a joint venture with Yamaha of Japan. This initial trickle needs to swell.

Collaboration at many levels and in different areas also means going beyond the company to universities and research institutes that can be a fertile source of advances in basic science as well as commercially viable technologies. Contracting with universities is one avenue more frequently taken by the large, more entrepreneurial firms (see, for example, Veugelers and Cassiman 2003). The bridges established between the business sector on the one side and universities and research institutes on the other

---

50. Interfirm collaboration on technological matters and strategic technical alliances is the most rapidly expanding form of business cooperation. From a modest 30–40 partnerships per year in the 1970s, the number has risen to 600 and more annually in the decades since (Caloghirou, Ioannides, and Vonortas 2003). Companies have found that a closed, self-sufficient innovation system is costlier and less productive than an open system that allows for an active and potentially fruitful interaction with others. As Chesbrough (2003a, p. 37) remarks, in an open system "the boundary between a firm and its surrounding environment is more porous enabling innovation to move easily between the two." But for collaboration to generate value and produce the desired spillovers, management must design and implement an appropriate strategy and to devise incentives that maximize the returns from joint research projects, licensing, investment in start-ups, and other approaches.

have tended to galvanize research and innovation, to the benefit of all parties. The interchange is promoted by demand from the most dynamic private companies, aided both by institutions that protect intellectual property rights and provide incentives to researchers and by government policies that allow public research entities to contract with the private sector and derive commercial advantage from research and from a host of other measures—including those that enable access to venture capital (Yusuf and others 2003). But everywhere, the initiative of private businesses remains critical. Where firms have firmly embraced a strategy of growth through innovation, they are likely to take the lead that can stimulate research capacity in universities and make them a fruitful source of innovation.[51]

Establishing overseas research labs is another way that firms draw upon specialized local expertise to build innovation capability (Boutellier, Gassmann, and Zedtwitz 2000; Kim 2003; Mathews and Cho 2000). This means hiring researchers in other countries, and can involve taking over foreign firms with significant technological potential—a strategy pursued by Samsung with considerable success (see Kim 1997)—to supplement or extend the research being done at the home base. This approach can be motivated by other objectives as well, such as that of adapting a product to suit the idiosyncrasies of foreign markets. To establish, coordinate, and derive value from an international research effort requires management skill and an organization with the structure, incentives, and ability both to motivate and fully harness such decentralized research. Leading American, European, Japanese, and Korean companies have set up laboratories on each other's home turf, in China, Israel, and in Taiwan (China), economies with the abundance of moderately priced skills needed to exploit the full diversity of global knowledge (Santos, Doz, and Williamson 2004). As evidenced by Lenovo, Haier, and Huawei, this will be the most likely future direction for some of China's emerging transnational companies as well.

Innovation capability can also be augmented through a carefully designed strategy of mergers with or the takeover of other firms that have technological or other potential. Mergers and acquisitions activity fuels the growth of leading Western firms that dominate some industry sectors, including chemicals, electronics, pharmaceuticals, and transport. These

---

51. Linder, Jarvenpaa, and Davenport (2003) find that almost half of all the innovation by the companies they studied was externally sourced. Though less for pharmaceutical companies (30 percent), external capacity was as high as 90 percent for retail companies.

industries have adopted well-crafted takeover strategies. An iconic example is Cisco Systems, which over the years has risen to dominance in the production of routers and telecommunication switches, not so much through home grown innovation as through investment in and targeted acquisition of firms—mainly smaller ones—with new technologies that could extend or complement Cisco Systems' own (Chesbrough 2003a). There are thousands of other examples, though none quite so spectacular as that of Cisco Systems.

This is not a pattern one observes in East Asia, excluding Japan. There are many large (frequently family controlled) conglomerates operating in Indonesia, Korea, and Thailand, and in China, but these comprise numerous firms that are far smaller than their Western counterparts.[52] Except in a few instances, such as when Hyundai and Kia were merged as a result of government pressure, market-based (hostile) mergers and acquisitions action is infrequent—primarily because the business culture, institutions, and financial practices discourage not only acquisitions but also the financing of this type of activity.[53] In China, however, mergers induced by the government—which have brought heterogeneous enterprises together into groups or have led to the assimilation of an ailing enterprise by a healthy one—have not generally led to the emergence of large, competitive firms. More often they have resulted in unwieldy conglomerates or compromised the vigor of strong enterprises by forcing them to absorb weaker ones.[54] This is a pattern that needs to change, as discussed in chapter 6 of this volume.

A small number of East Asian companies will be able to replicate the approach of Samsung and Hyundai by joining the ranks of the world's

52. The control and ownership of firms typically rest with families, in both high-income and lower-income countries. However, a corporate system with dispersed ownership is more prevalent in countries with strong legal institutions that can protect the rights of minority shareholders. Until a legal system capable of enforcing these rights is in place, the control of companies in East Asia is likely to remain concentrated in the hands of a few (Burkart, Panunzi, and Shleifer 2002; Claessens, Djankov, and Lang 2000).

53. Only one-third of equities are tradable shares, making takeover bids through the stock market difficult (Zhang 2004b).

54. This poorly conceived merger activity is comparable to the experience of the United States from the 1960s through the 1980s (Ravenscraft and Scherer 1989) and again from 1995–2000. During the latter period, deals totaling $12 trillion cost shareholders $1 trillion in wealth (Selden and Colvin 2003). These findings are echoed by research on postmerger performance in Japan, much of which has been disappointing. See Yeh and Hoshino (2002) and the research cited by them. However, takeovers that were carefully targeted, effectively implemented, and tied to the company's core competence yielded solid outcomes. Positive results from the U.S. experience have been reported by Smith (1990) and Healy, Palepu, and Ruback (1992).

leading companies.[55] They may be able to do so through their own management skill, access to long-term capital from banks, investment in research and development, and the acquisition of technology from others (Khanna and Palepu 2002; Mathews and Cho 2000). Changhong Electronics and Konka, both state-controlled companies, have been able to replicate the Korean model and successfully assimilate foreign technology (Xie and Wu 2003). But the number of large, dynamic firms is likely to be limited in the absence of mergers and acquisitions. As Peter Nolan (2002) has observed, in spite of the consolidation of SOEs in China, groups in some industries such as aerospace, automobiles, electrical equipment, petrochemicals, and steel are a fraction of the size of their Western competitors; and even the larger ones such as steel giants Baoshan Steel and Shougang lack the focus on core competence and the managerial expertise of their Western counterparts (Movshuk 2004; Nolan and Yeung 2001). This puts these firms at a disadvantage in the national market as it becomes more exposed to competition; and the disadvantage is even greater in the global market. Moreover, the persistence of a regulatory regime reluctant to sanction market-based mergers and acquisitions activity constrains both the effective commercial exploitation of innovation and the diffusion of innovation among firms (Jovanovic and Rousseau 2002; Norton and Chao 2001). New entrants with a good product, or small firms that have perfected a potentially highly profitable technology, frequently need the backing of a powerful sponsor with deep pockets to refine and market a product. When acquisition is impeded, good ideas can go to waste. Thus, for firms that aspire to a significant role in the global market, developing innovation capability and actively using mergers and acquisitions to advance this must be a part of their strategy. Before this is feasible, the hurdles placed by the unavailability of public records pertaining to the assets of SOEs, the lack of financing for takeovers through the issuance of debt, and the difficulty of obtaining approval from relevant supervisory bodies will need to be addressed (Norton and Chao 2001).

Deverticalization, Outsourcing, and Collaboration

When market competition demands that firms survive and grow through innovations that open "new ways to create value [for customers] and

---

55. Khanna and Palepu (2002) ascribe some success of the Korean *chaebol* (such as Samsung and Hyundai) to their diversified structure, which lowers the transaction costs of raising capital and recruiting talent. With respect to the Japanese *keiretsu*, Dewenter (2003) maintains that the primary motive during the 1990s was risk-sharing.

[define] new value to create" (Magretta 2002, p. 150), the organization and management of firms as well as incentives must be suitably aligned. The efficiency of markets and declining transaction costs make it much easier for firms to buy services and to outsource rather than produce in-house. This, together with the need to move quickly in identifying and seizing opportunities, profoundly influences organizational structure and—in the majority of industrial circumstances—undermines the advantages of vertical integration.

Today organizations can be much "flatter" and focus on a more narrow range of activities in which they can add the greatest value.[56] From their study of 300 large firms in the United States, Rajan and Wulf (2003) find that companies have stripped away layers of middle managers, enlarging the CEO's span of control and transferring more decisionmaking authority to managers on the frontlines. This, in turn, is buttressed by much steeper salary and bonus structures that reward achievement. The heightened concern for focus stems from evidence showing that conglomerates are less successful than smaller firms in generating shareholder value, and that the acquisition of new plants can lead to a deterioration in the productivity of existing ones (Schoar 2002).[57]

Among the larger companies, Boeing, for example, has determined that its expertise lies in design, systems integration, assembly, and after-sales service rather than in the manufacturing of parts; and this is reflected in its willingness to outsource 70 percent of all parts, including the wings of its new 787 airliner, to non-U.S. suppliers ("Nose to Nose" 2005). Similarly, Sun Microsystems is oriented toward research and design, while Nike is primarily geared toward marketing. Both of these companies have farmed out manufacturing to other suppliers. To capitalize on this tendency, Taiwanese firms such as TSMC have set up silicon chip foundries in China (as have domestic firms such as SMIC) to take full advantage of China's lower wage and infrastructure costs (Geppert 2005). By combining Taiwanese design expertise with lower production costs, they hope to fully exploit the outsourcing wave. By the end of 2005, one-fifth of all wafer fabrication will be located in China. By 2010, it is projected that half of all chip production will be outsourced and that the Taiwan-China

---

56. Large and focused corporations are also more likely to generate the entrepreneurial energies that spawn new firms (Gompers, Lerner, and Scharfstein 2003).

57. Bieshaar, Knight, and Van Wassenaer (2001) note that while many mergers do not create additional shareholder value, those that do are ones where a company is engaged in horizontal expansion, entering new markets for its existing range of products or strengthening its marketing capacity.

ventures could gain 40 percent of the world market ("China Foreign Entrants" 2003). This is a model now being widely adopted, with companies outsourcing not only manufacturing but also a host of back-office services, design, and research. It is a model that calls for a high degree of organizational flexibility and a fundamental rethinking of management practices to match the "clockspeed" of business processes in a "nonlinear world" (Hout 1999, p. 163, Fine 1998). One response on the part of firms, referred to earlier, is to diverticalize so as to maximize the gains from specialization and the ease of outsourcing. The centrality of the former has been obvious for generations; but the new information and communications technologies and advances in logistics are now dramatically facilitating the use of the latter. Instead of attempting (often inefficiently) to meet most of their needs in-house, as was the widespread practice throughout the world of large-scale manufacturing in the past—and still is in China—firms in the new market economies are learning to be selective in what they do and to leverage the strengths of other businesses. As businesses have gained in expertise and become more skilled at managing information, the trend is toward outsourcing and dealing directly with a few major suppliers, each of whom may have a number of subcontractors (see Yusuf and others 2003; and Yusuf, Altaf, and Nabeshima 2004).[58] A firm may have an arm's-length relationship with its suppliers if the technology demands, or it can work closely with them to develop and debug products and introduce improvements in processes.

This shift in the organization of production requires firms to be far more adept at capturing and utilizing information internal to the firm and from the outside. Constant screening of information updates a firm's options, including the option to vertically extend its production if that is considered cost-effective or the best way to achieve competitive advantage. This has been demonstrated by the Hong Kong–based Esquel Group that produces nearly 60 million garments annually and whose production is integrated all the way back to (long staple) cotton growing in Xinjiang Province.

Deverticalization and outsourcing are driving firms to build flexibility into their organizations and systems of production, and are inducing all types of companies to acknowledge the important role of information technology. In addition, the dependence on other suppliers has rendered supply chain management one of the central elements of competitive strategy. Magretta (2002, p. 35) observes that "supply chain management

---

58. For a discussion of the changing nature of global supply chains and of the behavior of firms, also see Steinfeld (2004a).

reflects a far more systematic way of thinking about how a company creates value for its customers: through what it buys, and not just the price it pays, through gains in speed and flexibility as well as cost, through access to suppliers know how and innovative capability as well as its goods."[59]

Paradoxically, the sharpening of competition across the global marketplace has led not just to specialization on the part of firms; it has also resulted in parallel surge in modes of cooperation that help companies gain competitive advantage while ameliorating the harshness of competition. Modes of cooperation are evolving, with no single one clearly the most effective; however, diverticalization and outsourcing appear to be striking deeper roots. For example, the linkages among members of the Japanese *keiretsu* are loosening, and the Korean *chaebol* (a conglomerate of many companies, which usually hold shares in one another and are often run by one family, clustered around one parent company; Korean translation of the Japanese word *zaibatsu*, or business conglomerate, and related to the *keiretsu* in Japan) are being pushed to reverse a long-running process of conglomerate diversification. As some relationships dissolve, others arise to take their place—many of a horizontal nature and less centered on banks or large holding companies (DiMaggio 2001).

What has become all too apparent is that governments are far less effective than markets in determining the shape of industrial organization. Rather than attempting to mold SOEs in a particular manner through reform, privatization and a reliance on orderly market-based processes that compel extensive restructuring are better calculated to yield more-enduring results over the longer term. Governments can add more value by building strong market institutions rather than through industrial policy.

It seems appropriate for the discussion in this section to end on a cautionary note. The corporate sectors in even the most advanced free market economies such as Germany, Japan, and the United States have proven all too susceptible to the failings of management, organization, and corporate governance. New management recipes are constantly being recommended, and too many of these have been found lacking. Frenzied bouts of restructuring during the 1980s and 1990s have been followed by hand-wringing regret. There is an excess of fads that are not quickly weeded out by a rigorously critical invisible hand.[60] A glance at the leading

---

59. In this connection it is worth drawing attention to process innovations such as cross-docking. This particular process, introduced by Wal-Mart, greatly reduced warehousing expenses (Hammer 2004).

60. Interestingly, the book that launched the fad phobia—*In Search of Excellence* by Tom Peters and Bob Waterman—was published in 1982 ("Why Are the Fads" 2003).

business journals warns against swallowing the free market and private enterprise myths without a bit of caution. Yet even allowing for the hype, private companies relative to their public sector cousins are generally conspicuous for their customer orientation, innovativeness, flexibility, and productivity. It is certainly desirable to weigh the merits of a corporatist halfway house between a socialistic enterprise system and a purely privatized one. China's own experience offers a good check. But it is also increasingly necessary to assess the relative advantages of full privatization of SOEs and of completing SOE reform.

PRIVATIZATION: WISDOM FROM EXPERIENCE

From a slow start in the 1980s, the pace of privatization quickly escalated during the 1990s, especially in the transition economies and in Argentina, Brazil, and Mexico. In 1980, state-owned enterprises accounted for about 11 percent of the GDP in the middle-income countries, but by 1997 the share had fallen to 5 percent (Kikeri and Nellis 2002) and from 15 percent to 3 percent in the low-income countries (Chong and López-de-Silanes 2005). Between 1989 and the mid-1990s, over 60,000 enterprises were privatized in the transition economies alone. Governments turned to privatization in an effort to improve the efficiency of firms and staunch annual losses that could reach 5 to 6 percent of GDP; obtain large, one-time additions to the budget; or (as in the former Soviet Union) to gain political support for further reforms[61] (Shleifer and Treisman 2000). Kikeri and Nellis (2002) estimate that in 1990–9, governments raised $850 billion from the sale of state firms. From this total, divestiture in developing countries netted $250 billion, with the largest share in Latin America, followed by Eastern Europe and Central Asia, and then by East Asia. By the end of 2002, a total of 3,535 privatizations worldwide had generated $1.127 trillion, 33 percent of this amount in the developing or transition economies (Bortolotti and Pinotti 2003).

The past two decades have yielded a wealth of knowledge on the sectoral mix of privatization, the methods used, and the speed with which firms are privatized. The role of the enabling market environment, the principal bottlenecks, and the gains in efficiency and profitability are well documented in the findings reviewed by Havrylyshyn and McGettigan

---

61. The budgetary costs imposed by the losses of smaller SOEs are among the principal reasons that subnational governments in China have pushed forward with privatization (see Tenev, Zhang, and Brefort 2002, p. 30; and Li and others 2001).

(2000), Megginson and Netter (2001), Djankov and Murrell (2002), and Kikeri and Nellis (2002), among others. Inevitably, the story is not simple, and the evidence does not speak with one voice; this evidence is reviewed in chapter 4 of this volume. But then, one must expect some degree of discord and contradiction to emerge from such varied and complex cross-country situations. That said, seven messages are reasonably clear.

First, the initial outcomes of privatization and longer-term trends in performance are clearer for manufacturing as compared to network industries (such as utilities, and the transport and communications industries). The former do better in a sustained fashion, whereas the performance of the latter, post-privatization, while broadly positive, is mixed (Kay 2003; Green and Haskel 2004).[62] In addition, networked industries and natural monopolies are more directly influenced by political pressures and the quality of regulation. Even the most advanced countries have struggled to consistently maintain a regulatory infrastructure that resists capture by industry and provides guidance that induces industries to remain focused, innovative, and efficient while meeting a few key social goals. With manufacturing, the advantages are more clear-cut and the issue of regulation rarely arises.

Second, at least in the industrialized countries, privatization is a policy more closely associated with right-wing governments in majoritarian electoral regimes that concentrate power. Such governments were more likely to use privatization to widen shareholdership among the average middle-class voters. The evidence also suggests that privatization has appeared most attractive to countries struggling with large public debts and that privatization has been facilitated by deep and developed capital markets (Bortolotti, Fantini, and Siniscalco 2003; Bortolotti and Siniscalco 2004). Moreover, privatization has also been viewed as a means of widening stock markets.

Third, a variety of methods have been attempted, ranging from management and employee buyouts to mass privatization. Again, there are no clear winners, but the evidence does tend to argue against insider buyouts that would favor a small group or entrench existing stakeholders to the detriment of future performance. Outsiders are more likely to restructure, infuse dynamism and introduce changes in governance, and bring in new technology.

---

62. Bortolotti and Faccio (2004) indicate that there are many instances where European companies with dominant state ownership have been able to equal or surpass the performance of private companies. Similarly, in Singapore, financial markets favor government-linked corporations with a higher market-to-book value relative to comparable private firms (Ramirez and Tan 2003).

Any method of privatization is more likely to deliver the desired outcomes when at least the basic institutions of the market are in place, which is the fourth point. Institutions—including those that determine corporate governance, the rights of minority shareholders, bankruptcy laws, the efficacy and independence of regulatory agencies, exit of firms, independence of the business media that influence corporate governance (Chong and López-de-Silanes 2005; Dyck and Zingales 2002), and the monitoring of performance—can modulate the behavior of insiders and subject outsiders to more-rigorous scrutiny. The absence of adequate institutional scaffolding was largely responsible for some of the privatization debacles in the earlier stages of transition in Eastern Europe and Russia.[63]

This, of course, raises the question of speed and a fifth message. Once a hotly contested issue, the pace of reform is now seen as linked to the degree of institutional preparedness and the ability, with external assistance, to achieve a threshold of adequacy. As Havrylyshyn and McGettigan (2000) point out, two fast movers, the Czech Republic and Russia, did poorly at the outset. Two others, Estonia and Latvia, which also plunged rapidly into privatization, did much better. So did Poland, which took its time; but those imitating Poland's pace have struggled to keep their bearings and their resolve. Many believe that success does not depend upon how privatization is paced but by the appearance and effectiveness of market and government institutions. However, a decade after privatizations were launched in Eastern Europe and the Commonwealth of Independent States (CIS), the fast movers appear to have grown faster and achieved better distributional outcomes than the ones that proceeded more gradually (Balcerowicz 2003; Havrylyshyn 2004).

The significance of a robust market system leads to a sixth message, which emphasizes the role of a thriving private sector that is open to the entry of new firms and the exit of failing ones.[64] The growth of a private sector stimulates the development of market institutions. It also prepares SOEs for entry into the market environment via privatization, forces them to adapt, presents them with models of what to do, enlarges the supply of managerial skills, and provides firms with a competitive milieu in which to find their feet if they can.

---

63. Some argue that effective corporate governance that exerts a positive influence on the performance of firms requires the presence of large and active institutional shareholders, such as pension funds and insurance companies (Mohan 2004).

64. A robust, highly contestable private manufacturing system with few barriers to entry and exit already flourishes in coastal provinces such as Fujian, Guangdong, and Zhejiang. This free market environment is very much in evidence in cities like Wenzhou, which is the center of a number of China's industries: shoes, eyeglasses, electrical transformers, and locks ("A Cauldron" 2003).

The final message is on performance. Here again, the findings inevitably do not speak with one voice—and for some types of industries, outcomes change over time. The overall impression, nevertheless, is broadly favorable across a number of indicators. Whether one uses profitability as the yardstick (net income divided by sales) or sales per employee, labor productivity, or growth in sales, privatized firms that survive, on balance, register measurable improvements; and analysis of privatizations in Latin America also shows that gains are distributed across society (Chong and López-de-Silanes 2005). There are instances where firms take time to shed workers and adjust to new modes of behavior. As a result, they may go through a spell of losses or low profits. In the networked industries, however, there are examples of performance diminishing after an initial spurt (Kay, 2003). Still, even allowing for the variation, false starts, and failures—privatization leads to better outcomes than under state ownership. By and large, the gains in performance can be directly ascribed to changes in the structure of the organization, often involving a reduction in the size of the workforce and decentralization of decision-making authority. Much of this is the necessary result of a change in management or outlook. It is management, after all, that must define strategy, restructure, and streamline the organization; put in place a new incentive regime; and transform the culture so that traditionally insular SOEs can be made to create value for customers and compete on the basis not only of production efficiency and quality but also (and importantly) of innovation.

As stated earlier, the literature on privatization is extraordinarily rich in details. These studies can add content, nuance, and qualifications to the essential story. They also provide a sense of the options available for partial privatization and for introducing full privatization. A too-careful screening of the options by China should not become an excuse for delaying the privatization of at least its manufacturing enterprises once reasonably functioning markets are in place—because how it is done may make a relatively modest difference at this stage.

A BRIEF OVERVIEW OF THE STUDY

Starting with the dismantling of rural collectives and the creation of four special economic zones in Guangdong Province, China has by slow degrees created a relatively open market economy. It is a market economy because the nonstate sector accounts for almost four-fifths of industrial production, most prices have been decontrolled, the nominal value of exports equaled 36 percent of GDP in 2004, and by 2002, cumulative foreign direct investment amounted to nearly 16 percent of total domestic investment. Moreover, China's financial, accounting, legal, and corporate institutions are slowly converging toward those of other market economies as its integration with the international economy progressively deepens. When one compares China in 2005 with the closed and tightly controlled economy that tentatively opened a small window onto the world in 1978, the changes have been truly immense. The centrally planned economy of yesteryear is little more than a shadow of its former self. Furthermore, the commitments made to win accession to the World Trade Organization have accelerated the pruning of many remaining regulations and a harmonizing of others with those of China's trading partners.

But in certain respects—and this is not a trifling qualification—China's reform process is radically incomplete. Xiaobo Hu (2000, p. 643) observes that,

> over the past two decades, Chinese reformers on a number of occasions have called for the separation of the state and enterprises and the delegation of economic decisionmaking power in SOEs to the director and managerial level. As of the late 1990s, however, bureaucrats and Party committees were still making decisions for many large- and medium-sized SOEs, and doing so on the basis of political concerns rather than economic logic. Furthermore, implementation of Premier Zhu Rongji's three-year revitalization plan not only had failed to reduce or eliminate government control of business enterprise, but ironically had created new connections between them.

Indeed, Chang and Wong's (2004) study of a group of firms listed on the Shanghai stock market in 1999 indicates that Communist Party control over enterprise and bank management impaired performance. One notable instance is the pressure exerted by Mianyong municipality on Sichuan Changhong Electric to sell TV sets to Apex Digital Inc., a distributor in California, in spite of doubts regarding Apex's creditworthiness. The unfortunate outcome of this transaction cost Changhong $500 million (Perry 2005). The control exercised by the Party Committee rather than the board of directors over the China Construction Bank was also highlighted when scandals forced a change of management in early 2005 ("China's Banks" 2005). These views and findings are echoed by Minxin Pei. "In spite of adopting policy changes that have propelled market reforms, Chinese leaders have not made state institutions market friendly. As a result, the state has maintained its command and control orientation and interferes excessively in the market place" ("The Real Test" 2003, p. 15). Although the relative size of the SOE sector has been much reduced, its contribution to industrial value added, its claims on financial resources, and the potential contribution of the larger SOEs to future industrial competitiveness and growth all point to the crucial significance of bringing the reform process to a speedy and successful close. The linkage between SOE reforms and those of the banking industry and of social security adds to the urgency, as does the necessity for preparing Chinese firms to compete on more equal terms with multinational corporations in domestic and global markets.

Since 1997, China has embraced the policy of *zhua da fangxiao* (grasp the large and free the small). This has entailed the divestiture and privatization (mainly through employee and managerial buyouts) of thousands of small and medium-size SOEs and the corporatization of a minority of the large SOEs. At the 15th Plenary Session of the Party's Meeting in September 2002, Premier Zhu Rongji called for a redoubling of efforts to diversify ownership of SOEs, including the larger ones. These are certainly positive steps and should improve performance. However, they need to evolve rapidly in three directions. First, privatization of the SMSOEs should be allowed to take a multiplicity of forms, with employee buyout as only one of the possible modes. In fact, private firms, joint ventures, and foreign companies should be encouraged to bid for SOEs through measures that free up the market for mergers and acquisitions. The findings reported in chapter 5 assign special importance to the contribution of foreign ownership.

Second, the current state policy of grasping the large and permitting only a cautious corporatization of the bigger SOEs, with the majority of the assets being held by the state's asset holding company and senior management screened and selected by the Communist Party, should be substantially loosened. A start was made in June 2005 with the floating on the stock market of nontradeable state-held shares of 42 of the SOEs, including those of Baoshan Steel, Yangtze Power, and Shanghai Port and Container ("Big Names" 2005). The Security Regulatory Commission has in parallel raised the limit on foreign investment in the stock market from $4 billion to $10 billion, which will serve to channel more foreign capital into the corporatized SOEs ("China: Stock Market" 2005). The desirable next steps for China's long-running SOE reform, described in chapters 2 and 3, would be the full privatization of industrial enterprises. Chapter 4 summarizes insights from research on privatization in other transition economies. Chapter 5 draws on information derived from a survey of 736 Chinese SOEs and other firms to show how reform affects performance. And chapter 6 examines future policy directions. It is only by emerging as full-fledged and autonomous firms that China's potentially most-dynamic SOEs can effectively compete in a globalizing world economy.

Through private ownership, firms can acquire a customer orientation and build management teams that will practice financial prudence, restructure the organization in the interests of flexibility and focus, enhance the technological capability needed to compete through innovation, continuously upgrade in-house and outsourced processes (such as inventory management, billing, and logistics), and actively pursue a strategy aimed at succeeding in global markets.

The third direction is not only to push for the privatization of the large SOEs, but also to create the conditions that will lead to the consolidation of firms into entities with a core strength that can match that of the multinational corporations that now dominate most industrial subsectors. Private ownership, size, a strong emphasis on innovation, and the readiness to compete internationally should be the central objectives of the new generation of Chinese reformers. As discussed in the following chapters, these objectives can provide the means for continuing rapid growth, driven by mutually reinforcing advances in technology and productivity.

CHAPTER 2

REFORM IN CHINA, 1978–97

China's efforts to reform state enterprises can be broken down into four distinct periods. The first period, from 1978 through early 1984, was characterized by reforms that emphasized agriculture and foreign trade but left central planning in industry largely (although not wholly) intact. The second period began with the October 1984 directive that launched a major industrial reform effort but assumed that the primary task was to reform the state enterprises through incentive contracts that rewarded managers for specified gains in enterprise performance. These contracts were later supplemented by enterprise leasing arrangements. In 1988, the passage of the state-owned enterprise (SOE) law took the major step of granting legal status to the SOEs, thereby replacing direct control by the state with a relationship that defined the state as an owner. The word "privatization" was never voiced by Chinese leaders in a favorable context during this period; but this period witnessed the rapid rise of the township and village enterprises (TVEs), out of seeds planted by the home-based rural industries—from an earlier era that during 1960–80 grew into collectivized industries (Friedman 2005).[1] This reform effort was interrupted, however, by the political turmoil of 1989 and the associated shift in government leadership.

With Deng Xiaoping's tour of China's southern provinces in 1992, the reform drive that commenced in 1984 was reinvigorated and an effort made to revive the flagging growth rate largely within the existing institutional parameters. It was not until after the launch of the Ninth

---

1. The flowering of township and village enterprises was not anticipated by the Chinese leadership but was a welcome development (Becker 2000, p. 68). A similar autonomous growth of small and medium-size enterprises occurred in Taiwan (China) during the 1960s and 1970s (Wu 2005).

Five-Year Plan in 1996 that China's economic policymakers appear to have made major changes in reform objectives in response to the persistent weakness of the state sector and the shock administered by the East Asian economic crisis of 1997–8. The term privatization was still not used at the policymaking level, but some of the large SOEs began to be called by new names. Most of these enterprises had by then been registered on the Shenzhen and Shanghai stock exchanges (created in 1990 and 1991, respectively), and a few were even registered on the Hong Kong and New York exchanges. Shares were being sold to the general public and to other institutions, although the state retained majority control over most of the larger state enterprises. Foreign direct investment (FDI) began to climb as early as 1992 and 1993, and rapidly became a major force influencing Chinese industry. Foreign-funded enterprises accounted for just under 30 percent of Chinese industrial output in 2001—an extraordinarily high figure for such a large country—and produced almost half of total exports in 2004.[2] Even if a third of this "foreign" investment was in reality Chinese money that had been filtered through Hong Kong and elsewhere in order to avoid Chinese taxes, real FDI would still have approached 20 percent of all Chinese industrial assets.[3] The influence of these foreign firms, however, was even greater than this figure of 20 percent indicates, since these firms brought with them not only money but technology and intangible assets as well. This is borne out by the findings of the survey on the performance of joint ventures discussed in chapter 5.

This chapter and chapter 3 both elaborate on the story sketched out in chapter 1, about the reform of industry in general and of the state-owned enterprises in particular. Because of the complexity and constantly evolving nature of these reforms, the subject will be presented in a historical context.

THE PRE-REFORM INDUSTRIAL SYSTEM

To understand what China has sought to accomplish through reform, it is important to take as a point of departure the system that the reformers inherited when they gained power over the economy in late 1978. What

---

2. The fact that nearly 30 percent of Chinese industry had foreign funding does not mean that foreigners controlled that large a share of Chinese industry.

3. This is a crude estimate since there is no reliable figure on the amount of foreign investment that actually originated from Chinese domestic sources. The $400 billion figure would convert to 3,300 billion yuan, but not all of this went to industry since there were also large investments in real estate and hotels. The total assets of all Chinese industry in 2001 were 13,540 billion yuan.

follows is a simplified overview of a state-owned and state-directed industrial system that evolved under the nationalist government in 1937–45, was further shaped by the Soviet model during the 1950s, and was tinkered with by the Chinese government over the following two decades.[4]

Chinese industrial firms of any size lost their legal person status and had come under state control by 1956, although a handful formally retained their status as joint state-private firms for a few years thereafter.[5] Control of these entities, which were treated as branches of the government and labeled as *gongchang* (or factories), was first and foremost the responsibility of the State Planning Commission, which operated through more than a dozen ministries dedicated to particular industrial sectors. These ministries dealt directly with the individual enterprises or through corporations that oversaw the work of several enterprises. As was true in the former Soviet Union, the Chinese enterprise was an independent accounting unit—but otherwise had very little decisionmaking autonomy. Basically, the enterprise received and implemented orders that were sent down through the hierarchy described earlier.

The orders were in the form of plan targets. A firm received input and output targets, plus a variety of financial targets (including profits). The individual enterprises, in turn, funneled information up the hierarchy that was used to determine these targets. For the most part, it was the State Planning Commission, industrial ministries, and provincial bureaus that had the main say in deciding how much to produce and with what inputs, although the larger enterprises did have some bargaining power. Because of the wide variety of technologies in use within a given industry in China, and the weak accounting systems within most firms, the planners worked with very poor information. As a result, the output targets were at times easy to realize and at other times impossible to achieve. In 1957, for example, the plan output targets for steel and coal were surpassed by 69.5 and 184.2 percent, respectively, while those for petroleum and cotton yarn were underfulfilled by 12.5 and 2.4 percent (Perkins 1968, p. 611). Enterprises focused primarily on fulfilling these output targets. By contrast, financial and input targets were frequently ignored because, as often as not, they were not consistent with meeting

---

4. For the wartime origins of the state enterprise system, in particular the ordnance factories established by the Nationalist government, see Bian (2005). For a more detailed analysis of this system as it operated in the 1950s and early 1960s under the Community government, see Donnithorne (1967, chapters 4 and 6) and Perkins (1966, chapters 5 and 6).

5. Foreign equity participation in Chinese firms more or less ended in 1955 (Prybyla 1978), when the actions of the government nullified the corporation law passed in 1904.

the firms' output targets. Although failure to meet the output targets could disrupt the plan and deprive other firms of needed production materials, missing input and financial targets had fewer implications for other firms.

Plan targets had the force of law, but the law in China was not a powerful force—for historical and contemporary reasons. At the time these reforms were instituted, actual enforcement of the law was largely achieved through the allocation of key inputs by ministries and bureaus, and these administrative allocations were supposed to follow and enforce the plan. But there was often more flexibility than this rigid system implied, as was true in the former Soviet Union. Enterprises with surplus allocation of some items could trade their surplus items with other firms in exchange for products for which their own allocation was insufficient. At times, the government even encouraged large meetings of enterprises to facilitate input swaps and thereby offset the allocation mistakes made by its planners.

Complementing this physical allocation of goods was a financial plan monitored by the People's Bank of China (PBC) as well as the State Planning Commission. The People's Bank was a mono-bank: the central bank and the sole commercial bank all rolled into one. Each enterprise was allowed to keep only a small amount of cash on hand and was required to deposit the rest of its money in the bank. When funds were needed, an enterprise could withdraw from its bank deposits, but the bank was supposed to confirm that the withdrawal was for purposes stated in the central plan. In practice, the PBC was often under great pressure from well-placed politicians and provincial governments not to interfere with efforts to achieve major increases in enterprise output. What on paper appeared to be a powerful institution was, in fact, very weak. For the most part, the People's Bank accommodated most of what the enterprises and the politicians asked for. This contributed to the "soft budget constraint" that has continued to plague Chinese industry to this day.

Prices in this industrial system were set by the state and rarely changed prior to 1978, although there were major adjustments in periods such as in the aftermath of the Great Leap Forward in the early 1960s. At these state prices, most enterprises made large profits. The exceptions were the producers of energy and raw materials whose prices were deliberately kept low so that these enterprises often ran losses. Demand for industrial inputs usually exceeded supply because firms, caring mainly about output targets, aggressively sought inputs through plan allocations and bartered deals with other enterprises, even if that frequently led to a large buildup of inventories for which there was little demand (a chronic feature of the

Chinese and other socialist economies). Prices were not brought down by competition, because competition was not allowed. For the most part, each enterprise had a monopoly of a particular local or provincial market. And even when the government began to push rural small-scale industries in the early 1970s, those industries typically were given a monopoly over their local township or county market.

Monopoly prices produce monopoly profits; but these profits, for the most part, had to be surrendered to the state and provided the bulk of government revenue. The exception was a small portion of the earnings from sales above plan targets that were retained by the enterprise. This was designed to enhance the attractiveness of profit targets, a process of experimentation that began in the late 1950s, almost as soon as the system of central planning was established.

An enterprise did not have many resources of its own to plough back into the business. The profits that were transferred to the government treasury were allocated to various investment projects, but the enterprise did not control the growth of its own plant and equipment. The expansion of enterprise fixed assets was turned over to enterprises created to implement the investment plan. When the investment was completed, the assets were then transferred to the operating enterprise.

Chinese leaders, and Mao Zedong in particular, were dissatisfied with the rigidity of this system and attempted to modify it right from the start. During the Great Leap Forward in 1958–9, an attempt was made to decentralize decisionmaking to the enterprise level in industry and to the newly formed communes in agriculture. But decentralization was conducted without any method for coordinating inputs and outputs. Although the central plan was effectively ignored, no market mechanism was allowed to take its place. The result was chaos—and a sharp decline in industrial output. Moreover, the effort of local groups to develop small-scale industries (notably the backyard iron and steel factories) discredited small-scale industries in general for a decade, until a more sensible approach to the promotion of these industries was devised.

Decentralization in an economy as large and diverse as China's, however, made obvious sense. Beijing did not have the information needed to centrally control an industrial sector that included 30,000 large and medium-size firms (by Chinese definitions of size) and nearly 150,000 small firms. Because a great many of these firms produced for their local market and obtained most of their inputs from that same market, it was feasible to decentralize decisionmaking to the individual provinces and even to individual counties and below. This type of decentralized administrative planning began around 1957. In the early 1960s, after the failure of the Great Leap Forward, there was an effort to recentralize some controls; but much planning and control activity remained at the provincial level. In fact, the Cultural Revolution, by almost paralyzing the central government, again strengthened decentralizing tendencies—as did the rural small-scale industry program in the 1970s that devolved a great deal of industrial planning and control to the county and commune levels.

With the exception of the rural small-scale industry program, the years of the Cultural Revolution (1966–76) did not lead to much further experimentation with the planning and management of state enterprises or of industry in general. Because so many government officials (including many from the industrial ministries and the State Planning Commission) were sent to the countryside, the state was weakened, as was its control over enterprises (Teiwes 2000). Nevertheless, annual plans continued to be produced and were more or less followed, although protagonists of the Cultural Revolution frequently interfered with the management and functioning of enterprises. Disruption was most serious in 1967 and 1968, but material incentives remained weak until the death of Mao Zedong. The Cultural Revolution, however, was not really directed at economic management, and the formal rules governing state enterprises were not revised in any significant way during this period.

On the eve of the major reform efforts of the post-1978 period, therefore, Chinese industry was largely state owned; but there was also a growing collective industry sector in both rural and urban areas, comprising mostly small firms. Allocation of inputs was according to plan (through administrative rather than market channels), but the planning and allocation were often done at the provincial and county levels rather than by Beijing. The mono-bank took deposits but otherwise did little else that a bank in a market economy would do. Mostly the bank helped enforce the plan. Prices were fixed by the state and bore little relation to the relative conditions of scarcity that existed at the beginning of the 1980s. Enterprises were mainly small shops or individual factories, and their decisionmaking authority was largely confined to the daily operations of the firm. They did not for the most part sell on the market, and they did not purchase intermediate inputs or factor inputs from a market. Except for some consumer goods, markets for other products were virtually nonexistent.

This was the situation that the reformers faced in 1978. They knew that this system was performing poorly, but they had few ideas about how to make it work better. However, on two matters, there was a high degree of consensus. It was clear to all that the per capita availability of foodstuffs had barely improved over the past 20 years, and that the lack of incentives for farmers probably was responsible for this weak performance that left so many millions in abject poverty. Deng Xiaoping and others certainly remembered how households and rural markets had helped to restore agricultural productivity in the early 1960s and ended the famine that took 30 million lives in 1959–61 (Becker 1996; Johnson 1998). Those in control in 1978 also understood that the bias of the leftist ideologues against foreign technology and foreign imports was disadvantageous for China.

Thus, the initial reform efforts emphasized agriculture and the opening up to foreign trade. In agriculture there was a movement back to household farming and rural markets that was as much a locally spontaneous grassroots affair (in Anhui, for example) as it was centrally led (Perkins and Yusuf 1984). With respect to foreign trade, there was a decision as early as 1977 to allow industry much easier access to imports, but the centralized system of controlling imports and exports under the monopoly corporations of the Ministry of Foreign Trade remained in place for a few years longer (Lardy 1992).

THE FIRST STEP TO INDUSTRIAL TRANSFORMATION

In early 1979, Chinese reformers faced a situation very different from that confronted by the Soviet, Russian, and East European reformers after 1989. The Communist Party was still very much in control in China, and while it rejected the utopian goals of the Great Leap Forward and the Cultural Revolution, it remained wedded to a version of socialism that included reliance on state-owned enterprises and some form of central planning.[6] There was interest in the various efforts in Hungary and Poland to make the socialist system work better, but even that level of reform was controversial. "Privatization" was ruled out. There was an emerging willingness to liberalize the price of some agricultural products and a few urban consumer goods on an experimental basis, but not grain or

---

6. Blanchard and Shleifer (2000) are of the view that it was the strength of the Chinese state relative to that of the former Soviet Union that accounted for the greater effectiveness of decentralized development in China. The regional and decentralized organization of production allowed for experimentation and permitted the entry of and competition from TVEs—if only on a local or regional basis—without capitalism formally having taken root (McMillan 1997; Qian and Roland 1998; Qian, Roland, and Xu 1999). The initially less complex production relations among Chinese producers also helped the country avoid the pain of "disorganization" when reform began to dismantle these tight linkages without immediately replacing them with alternative input-output relationships (Blanchard and Kremer 1997; Roland 2000).

intermediate industrial inputs. The term "socialist market economy" to describe the reform goal only surfaced at the 14th Party Congress in 1992.[7]

By the early 1980s, however, China enjoyed three advantages over the situation that emerged in Eastern Europe and Russia after 1989. First, most Chinese economic output was produced in small-scale units. Agriculture was based almost entirely on household farming, services were increasingly in the hands of small traders, and these two sectors, excluding large-scale finance and other large-scale state services, accounted for nearly one-half of total GDP. In industry, only 40 percent of gross output was produced by what the Chinese considered to be large- and medium-scale firms, and many of these firms would have been considered small in advanced industrial economies. Thus, roughly three-quarters of the Chinese economy was in the hands of units that did not need much ownership restructuring in order to become profit oriented. Households and small units are natural profit maximizers, because they directly benefit from an increase in profits and they exit the business if they make losses. If prices were freed up, these producing units could be counted on to respond appropriately.

The second advantage China enjoyed at the beginning of the reform period was a high degree of macroeconomic stability. Domestic retail prices had increased by just 1 percent between 1965 and 1978, and the degree of repressed inflation was modest. China had given generous pension and other benefits to workers in SOEs, but the number of people involved, unlike in Eastern Europe, was only 19 percent of the total workforce because of largely successful efforts to hold down the size of the urban industrial workforce; and most of these employees were not yet ready to retire (Putterman and Dong 2000). Large, unfunded pension liabilities would not become a macroeconomic problem for China until well into the 1990s, and even then the cost was not remotely comparable to the burden weighing on Eastern Europe. Nor was the banking system saddled with a large volume of nonperforming assets. State enterprises were rendered profitable by the planning system, for the most part, and had little trouble paying back the working capital loans that they received. If they did run deficits, these were financed directly from the government budget. China also had no international debt whatsoever. The country had run balance of trade surpluses in the 1970s through 1977, and then it incurred deficits aggregating to $5 billion in the 1978–81 period, but

---

7. Starting from the position "that the planned economy leads, the market economy supports," China's reformers adopted the term "planned commodity economy," which was followed in 1992 by "a socialist market economy with Chinese characteristics."

this multiyear sum was less than 2 percent of GDP in a single year. Thus, China, in the early 1980s, had no serious macroeconomic disequilibria.

Finally, China was surrounded by some of the most rapidly growing economies of the second half of the 20th century, and could benefit from the spillover effects of a dynamic neighborhood. Many of those responsible for the industrial achievements of these neighboring countries were ethnic Chinese who still had some ties to the motherland. The Chinese leadership reasoned that, if these people were allowed to play a role, they could provide Chinese industry with ready-made expertise in how to export manufactures to the markets of the United States and Europe.

Prior to 1984, for the state-owned industrial sector, these advantages were a long way from being realized. The state enterprise reform measures that unfolded from 1979 through 1983 were of several types. Perhaps most important was the increased emphasis on enterprise profits. This was essentially a continuation of experiments that had been tried in the first phase of central planning. First, the enterprises were allowed to retain and spend profits above a specified planned amount, a planned amount that had to be negotiated. This was combined with a formal tax on profits, but that, too, in practice had to be negotiated.

Negotiated profit retention in the Chinese context was not comparable to a situation where a firm keeps all profits after paying a profits tax, and where the profits tax applies equally to all firms or all firms of a certain type. This latter approach was not feasible in China, because enterprises even in a single industry had widely varying profit rates, and a uniform tax that yielded the desired amount of revenue would have pushed some enterprises into the loss column and left others with large retained earnings. Across industries, the distortions in prices further exacerbated the problem—starving some high priority sectors of profits while allowing others of lower priority to enjoy handsome profits.

As long as the level of retained profits is negotiable, however, enterprise managers will spend much of their energy on lobbying the government to increase their retained share, not on efforts within the firm to raise profits by cutting costs or increasing sales. If the negotiated retention rate changes frequently, firms will have little incentive to cut costs because they can always negotiate lower taxes. The scope for negotiating taxes was, and to a lesser extent is, one of the main factors responsible for the soft budget constraint.[8]

---

8. This early reform period is discussed at length in a variety of works, notably Naughton (1995); Tidrick and Chen (1987); and Otsuka, Liu, and Murakami (1998). Access to finance at subsidized rates from state-owned banks displaced negotiated taxes as a factor responsible for the softening of budget constraints on SOEs.

Another reform in the early 1980s, which also mirrored prior initiatives, was the attempt to simplify and reduce the administrative controls and reporting requirements impinging upon the individual enterprises. At the bottom of the hierarchy, there was an effort to consolidate several enterprises into industrial corporations, so that the higher bureaucratic organs would have fewer units to deal with; but these new corporations, instead of creating independent enterprises, introduced a new layer of bureaucracy. Attempts were also made to simplify the lines of authority over enterprises under city or provincial governments, by eliminating reporting requirements to both their provincial "owner" and the central government. Whatever the precise purpose, the changes did not simplify the reporting and control system significantly. In fact, administrative expenditures within these revised structures actually rose as a share of total expenditures.[9]

Other reforms in this period allowed for greater flexibility in the hiring of industrial workers. In addition, the scale of bonus payments was increased. Enterprises could also "sell" or otherwise dispose of output produced that exceeded plan targets; and enterprises could borrow from banks to finance their own investment plans, although retained earnings were a more important source of these enterprise investment funds than were bank loans (Naughton 1995). These reforms followed a common pattern. They would be tried first in a select number of firms or in a region of the country, and, if the outcome was deemed satisfactory, their use would then spread gradually to the rest of the country.

So prior to 1984, reform was similar to the measures tried in Eastern Europe before 1989, and even in the Soviet Union. The dominant economic policymaker in this period was still Chen Yun. Among the senior Chinese policymakers of that period, he was the one who believed most strongly that the market had a role to play in China—but mainly in agriculture, and with respect to the tens of thousands of small enterprises that central planners could not hope to track and control. At heart, however, Chen remained a planner; and for the larger state-owned enterprises, he firmly believed in central planning.[10] Chen also was a strong advocate of price stability, and this advocacy was to put him at odds with

---

9. For more discussion of these administrative reforms, see Chai (1997, pp. 36–50).

10. Chen Yun's views at the beginning of the reform period, on the role of the market versus planning, were given in a speech on March 8, 1979. Because the speech discussed the need for markets to supplement planning, it was reprinted in 1986 (see Chen 1986). For some of Chen Yun's earlier speeches on this subject in the late 1950s and early 1960s, see Lardy and Lieberthal (1983).

the post-1984 reformers who wanted to give local authorities greater leeway to expand investment in their regions (Shih 2003).

By the mid-1980s, another group of policymakers took the lead in reforming state-owned industry. Zhao Ziyang, as the first party secretary of Sichuan Province, had been a leader in experimenting with reforms in agriculture and enterprise autonomy (Riskin 1987, chapter 14). His success in implementing the first round of reform caught the attention of the leadership in Beijing and resulted in his being appointed as the premier, with overall responsibility for economic reform. The spread of these agricultural reforms and their dramatic success in raising farm output and incomes gave Zhao great credibility as a reformer—and gained him powerful allies elsewhere in the Communist Party leadership, notably Deng Xiaoping, who was not himself an economic policymaker but appreciated anyone who could deliver results.

China's rising export earnings, which helped to defray the costs of imports, further improved Zhao's standing with Deng and others. Exports in 1984 were more than two and one-half times the level of 1978, and such reforms as the opening of special economic zones, deservedly or not, were given some of the credit for this outcome. When Zhao came to office, however, neither he nor any of the group of reform-minded officials around him had a grand scheme for transforming China into a socialist market economy. But Zhao did have an open mind as to what might improve China's economic performance. He solicited ideas from an unusually wide range of people, including younger Chinese economists and many foreigners; and it was as a result of his initiative that SOE reforms took a major step forward with the introduction of management contracting that transferred some of the control rights to managers. Zhao's initiative was noteworthy because, at that time, SOEs were not under any stress. In fact, they were making large accounting profits, and the intellectual environment in China (or elsewhere) was not necessarily supportive of such reform.

THE INDUSTRIAL REFORM INITIATIVES, 1984–9

The year 1984 was the watershed year for reforms that would eventually redraw the entire Chinese industrial system, including the state enterprises—although this was not foreshadowed at the time in the main reform documents. On May 10, 1984, the State Council promulgated "Provisional regulations concerning the expansion of the autonomy for state-owned industrial enterprises," most often referred to as the

10 regulations for the transfer of power. These regulations further loosened the control exercised by the central government over state industrial enterprises—but on paper left intact the powers of the planners. The following list of some of the May 10 initiatives, most of which were implemented, illustrates how far the reformers were allowed to push enterprise autonomy, at least formally.

- Enterprises could sell their above-quota production at their discretion— and could even sell 2 percent of the planned production quota.
- Enterprises could, for producer goods that they were allowed to dispose of at their discretion, charge prices 20 percent above or below the state prices. However, consumer goods had to be sold at state prices.
- Enterprises could sell idle assets, but there were clear rules limiting how the funds realized could be used.
- Enterprises could use 70 percent of the money in their depreciation fund rather than turn it over to the central government for allocation.
- Enterprise managers had more latitude in determining the wages of their workers under the reforms, and the proportion of workers who could receive merit raises of this type was increased from 1 to 3 percent of the workforce. Over the next several years the size of the enterprise wage bill was linked to the growth in enterprise profits; and by 1988, the wages of 60 percent of industrial workers were linked to profits.
- The enterprise manager had greater authority to appoint and remove middle-level managers under the reforms; and, in principle, managers now had the power to nominate their deputy directors, although implementation of this latter measure was slow. Selection of the enterprise manager, however, remained—and still resides—in the hands of provincial, municipal, and central government organs. This is the case for the more senior appointments within the Communist Party as well.
- Enterprise managers could now make changes in the internal organization of their enterprises rather than simply implement organizational structures issued from above.
- Though not included in the 10 points document, after 1984 there was an effort to put the enterprise manager more firmly in charge of all business decisions—and to curtail the enterprise party secretary's involvement in these kinds of decisions. This measure proved difficult to implement, although progress was made.
- Another key measure not included in the 10 points document was the decision to move most of the enterprise workers away from lifetime employment to a contract system. Experiments with this measure began in 1983, and in 1986 an effort was made to apply this system to all new

workers.[11] By the 1990s, SOEs were hiring most of their new workers on a contractual basis; and in 2002, the majority of the industrial employees were subject to these terms.

On the surface at least, enterprise reforms were mainly designed to increase autonomy within a still centrally planned structure. The Chinese leadership viewed the reforms as a means of instituting a "planned commodity economy," and they served as the basis of the enterprise law passed in 1988. No doubt these measures, by relaxing control over the state enterprises, did give managers more flexibility in their efforts to improve the performance of their firms, but within fairly narrowly defined limits.

The document that is widely seen as formalizing the decision to reform China's industrial system, the "Decision of the Central Committee of the Communist Party of China on Reform of the Economic Structure," was approved a few months after the 10 regulations on October 20, 1984, at the Third Plenum of the 12th Central Committee. As the following excerpts make clear, this document gives even less of a hint of what was to come:

> Socialist society practices a planned economy on the basis of public ownership of the means of production. It can thus avoid the anarchy of production and cyclical crises characteristic of capitalist society. . . . At the same time, historical experience shows that the socialist planning system should be one that combines uniformity and flexibility. We must take into account China's vast territory and large population, the difficulty of drastically improving in a short period its poor transport conditions, its inadequate information facilities and the obviously uneven economic and cultural development of its various regions. . . . In view of all this, . . . if the actual conditions of our country are ignored and if we try to incorporate all economic activities into the plans and implement them by administrative orders alone in disregard of the importance of the economic levers and the market, then there will unavoidably be a discrepancy between the subjective guidelines for planning and objective conditions, with the plans seriously out of step with reality.

And a bit later in this document:

> Our present irrational price system finds expression mainly in the following: inadequate price differentials for a given product with diverse quality, irrational price ratios between different commodities, particularly the relatively low prices for some mineral products and raw and semi-finished materials . . . The irrational system of pricing is closely related to the

---

11. This discussion of the May 10 directive and of other similar measures implemented at this time is based on Hua, Zhang, and Luo (1993, pp. 101–3), and Naughton (1995, chapter 6).

irrational system of price control. In readjusting prices, we must reform the over-centralized system of price control, gradually reducing the scope of uniform prices set by the state and appropriately enlarging the scope of floating prices within certain limits and of free prices." ("Decision of the Central Committee" 1984)

The State Council also approved a decision to reduce the number of industrial products subject to mandatory planning from 120 to 60. The 120 figure was already lower than the 256 products subject to mandatory planning in 1979, but prices of those products subject to mandatory planning were still to be set by the state except for production by these enterprises over and above their plan targets (Hua, Zhang, and Luo 1993, p. 121; "Planning System" 1984). In principle, these new rules (including the 10 regulations) did not go directly against the views of such powerful conservatives as Chen Yun, since planning remained paramount and the use of the market was confined to above-plan products and sectors such as agriculture and small-scale industry that were difficult or impossible to plan.

What actually transpired in the next several years, however, was the beginning of a radical shift toward a market economy. These changes went well beyond what was envisioned in the 10 points regulation of May 10, 1984. Progress toward the goal of a full market economy proceeded on two levels: a practical level and a theoretical level. At a practical level, China introduced enterprise contracting and formalized and expanded a dual track pricing system that to some degree already existed. The people leading this effort were drawn from a group of young reformers who had the attention of Zhao Ziyang. The thinking of these advisers was outlined in a document, remarkable for its time, released by the China Economic System Reform Research Institute; it explored the possibility of state reform in a wide variety of areas as of 1984 or early 1985. These reformers also undertook a systematic survey, unheard of at that time, not only to assess the course of reform but also to explore attitudes of the population toward such questions as how they would feel if employment in enterprises were no longer permanent. The questionnaire administered for the survey also probed the attitudes of society toward living in an economy governed mainly by market forces. The official reform documents still assigned the key role to planning, but the researchers of the Economic System Reform Research Institute were clearly contemplating an economy governed increasingly by market forces.[12]

---

12. The Institute staff produced "A Summary and Analysis of the China Economic System Reform Research Institute Survey." For an English translation of this study, see Reynolds (1987).

Performance contracts—signed between the government and state-owned enterprises—began to be introduced in China from the mid-1980s, and were widely implemented after 1986.

After the 13th National Party Congress in October 1987, China adopted the principle of the "state regulating the market and the market conducting enterprises" (Wu 1997), and the government promoted the "contract responsibility system" (*chengbao zhi*). Under this system, the term of the contracts was extended for at least three years (to avoid annual bargaining), and more control rights were delegated to managers. These arrangements allowed SOEs to retain a larger share of their profits, and a variety of techniques were used to divide the cash flow between government and SOEs. By the end of 1987, about 80 percent of large and medium-size SOEs adopted performance contracts; and by 1989, almost all SOEs adopted contracts that continued through 1993, supplemented in the later years by leasing arrangements. Shougang steel is an example of a major SOE that entered into a long-term contract with the Beijing Municipality. This contract, which extended through 1995 and gave the enterprise considerable autonomy, required that profit paid to the state would increase by 7.2 percent per year, the SOE's wage bill would be related to profits, and the state would not provide additional financing (Nolan and Yeung 2001).

All performance contracts were negotiated, written agreements between governments and SOE managers, and specified explicit targets that management pledged to achieve within a given time frame. Before performance contracts were put into place, most governments had few criteria for evaluating the performance of their SOEs. And because good performers could not be rewarded and bad performers went unpunished, managers of SOEs had little incentive to improve efficiency and increase productivity. Thus, performance contracts offered a solution—by giving managers autonomy and incentives to improve efficiency and holding them accountable for the results.

Another change related to the use of contracts was that industrial inputs became readily available at market prices to enterprises outside of the state plan. Collective enterprises had existed in China since the 1950s, but up through 1969 they had rarely amounted to more than 11 percent of the gross value of industrial output (GVIO). It was in 1969 that the government began encouraging the formation of collective industries or workshops in the cities and the rural small-scale industry program in the countryside. Between 1969 and 1977 the share of collective industry rose rapidly—from 11 to 23 percent of industrial output—but thereafter slowly grew to only 26 percent in 1983 (National Bureau of Statistics 1990,

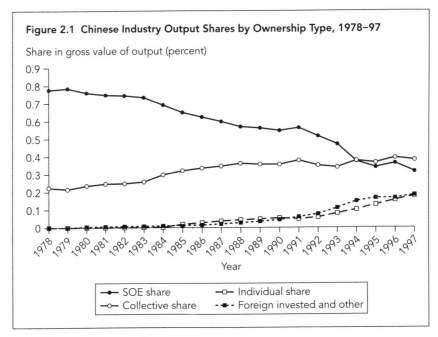

Figure 2.1 Chinese Industry Output Shares by Ownership Type, 1978–97

Share in gross value of output (percent)

Year

—●— SOE share   —□— Individual share
—○— Collective share   - ■ - Foreign invested and other

Note: SOE, state-owned enterprise.
Source: China Statistical Yearbook (National Bureau of Statistics, various years).

p. 416).[13] Inputs for these industries depended not on the market but on central planners allocating a share of the output of producer goods and intermediate inputs to the local governments for distribution to these enterprises. When not allocated for them by their planners, the enterprises had to make their own machinery; and a common sight in many of these small plants was a large machine tool shop set up to produce and repair much of the equipment the plants required (American Rural Small Scale Industry Delegation to China 1977).

Once enterprises were allowed to purchase what they needed on the market beginning in 1984–5, the result was the boom of TVEs. As the data in figure 2.1 make clear, the share of collective industries in total industrial output took a marked turn upward, and by 1988 reached over a third of all output—with TVEs alone accounting for a quarter of the industrial output. When one adds in "individual" and foreign-invested enterprises (which at that time were mostly small in scale and dependent on the market for

---

13. For a view of the rural small-scale industry program as it existed in 1975, see American Rural Small Scale Industry Delegation to China (1977).

their inputs), the share of SOEs in the total fell roughly 20 percent, to about 57 percent of all industrial output in 1988 (World Bank 1993).

The reform process in 1984 and 1985 at the government policy level was in response to a number of practical administrative and political problems, and was not guided by any coherent program to establish a market economy. The setting of prices for producer inputs is a good illustration of both the nature of the problems and the partial reforms introduced by the government in response. Prices of industrial inputs prior to 1984 were defined for the most part by the government, but "government" could mean Beijing, a provincial government, or a local government. As a result, state-set prices varied across and within provinces. When in the early 1980s enterprises were allowed to sell their above-plan output to buyers, prices had to be set that would make it possible to sell those products as well. Thus, there were many administered prices for a range of individual products. The principle that prices were to be determined administratively rather than by the market, however, was retained. But in reality there was wide scope for negotiating price adjustments at the enterprise level.

This realization prompted the next step, which was to free up the prices that were not controlled by the government. This was similar to what had already happened in agriculture, where the state determined the prices for grain but collective market prices were largely determined by market forces. Completely freeing up prices for industrial inputs, on the other hand, was not acceptable to many powerful groups, notably the managers of large state enterprises. And it was feared by some reformers as well as by Chen Yun and his allies that such a radical step would lead to chaotic changes in industrial structure and to inflation. Hence, the dual price structure was the compromise solution. The state would retain control of the prices of goods distributed through administrative channels in accordance with the plan—and would adjust the prices gradually to better reflect market conditions. The prices of goods produced outside the plan would be decontrolled, although in many instances freedom meant the right to negotiate prices within a certain band above and below the state-set price.

The dual-price system that arose out of this compromise over price reform came under vigorous criticism not long after it had been implemented, but it is useful to understand the intellectual context in which these changes were taking place. Six or seven years later, when reforms began in Eastern Europe and Russia, the dominant view among the economic reformers in those countries was that reform called for the decontrol of all prices, privatizing the ownership of all or most producing units, and maintaining a stable price level mainly through control of the money supply. Furthermore, in the eyes of some reformers, these changes were to be implemented across-the-board and as quickly as possible. No such intellectual framework existed in China in the mid-1980s, and it would have been politically unacceptable if it had existed. For China, ruled by a Communist Party that still believed in economic planning and in state ownership of industry, there had to be a different way. But was there another way? And if so, was it necessarily inferior to the path chosen six years later in Eastern Europe?

A third reform begun in 1984 also had an important bearing on the performance of state-owned enterprises. In that year, the government broke up the mono-bank into a central bank and four large commercial banks.[14] On paper, China then acquired a banking system that resembled the banking systems in advanced market economies. As will become apparent later in this chapter, however, changing the structure of the banking system did not necessarily modify the behavior of the banks. For many years thereafter, these commercial banks continued to lend money at the request of local politicians and planners rather than based on the commercial viability of the projects being financed; and two decades of reforms have failed to root out such practices.

The transition to an efficient market economy has five essential elements:[15]

1. Industrial inputs and other products must be available on a market. Such markets must either already exist or be created by the enterprises themselves or by the government. In the early 1980s, China began creating markets for intermediate and producer goods. Other markets sprang up spontaneously, and this process accelerated after 1984, going well beyond what was originally anticipated by the 10 regulations issued in May 1984.

2. Prices must be adjusted to reflect relative scarcities in the economy if products are to be distributed to their most efficient uses. At the margin the dual price system did, in fact, determine the allocation of marketed intermediate and producer goods—and did so in an efficient way (Byrd 1991). Inputs allocated administratively through the plan at state-set prices, of course, were not necessarily allocated efficiently.

---

14. See Riskin (1987).

15. This formulation of what a market requires, from Perkins (1988), was translated into Chinese and published by the journal of the Development Research Center of the State Council, *Guanli shijie* (*Administrative World*) in volume 6, number 21 (November 1988, pp. 9–29), and volume 1, number 22 (January 1989, pp. 59–73).

Furthermore, the existence of two prices for the same product created numerous opportunities for arbitrage, both legal and illegal.

3. For the market to promote both dynamic and static efficiency, there must be market competition. Planning, however, is easier if each firm has a monopoly of a particular market. China in the early 1980s rapidly dismantled the local and regional monopolies that existed up to that point, although some local governments tried to maintain control of certain markets.[16]

4. For the market to promote efficient allocation of goods, "getting prices right" is sufficient. The enterprises that purchase these goods must behave in accordance with the key rule of market behavior—profit maximization. In the eyes of the Russian and East European reformers, this objective was to be achieved by privatization—although they soon learned that privatization alone does not necessarily result in the desired behavior. For China in the latter half of the 1980s, privatization was not an option. In fact, the wave of privatization had barely begun in the Western countries (see chapter 4). So Chinese reformers had to generate the desired behavior through other incentives. This effort involved two closely related but separate types of activities. First, the budget constraint on most state enterprises had to be hardened.[17] Bank loans should not be made available on request to the state enterprises, taxes should not to be subject to negotiation, and administratively allocated inputs at low prices should not be increased to help out enterprises making losses. Where loss-making firms risked going out of business, managers needed to maximize profits—and to do so by cutting costs or increasing sales, not by lobbying for more subsidies. Second, enterprise management had to be separated from the government and the Communist Party. As long as appointments and promotions were decided by government ministries or by the Communist Party, managers would try their best to meet the objectives of those officials and party leaders; and rarely was profit maximization the only (or primary) goal of the government and the party. As chapters 3 and 4 of this volume make clear, the struggle to induce state enterprise managers to behave appropriately continues to this day; and the Party still retains its grip on managerial appointments.

---

16. As long as the state-set prices for raw materials such as cotton were kept low, local governments had an incentive to keep such raw materials for use by local enterprises. The high profits earned by a local cotton textile enterprise would, for example, rebound to the benefit of the local government.

17. The term is used here as defined by Kornai (1992, pp. 140–145).

5. Even if the above four conditions were met, efficient allocation guided by market principals would be difficult if there was a high rate of inflation or other forms of macroeconomic instability. In theory, an inflation rate of 20 or even 100 percent need not undermine the market. But in practice, this is almost never the case. Once prices begin rising at a level that is deemed politically unacceptable, the government comes under pressure to institute price controls; and price controls soon induce shortages. When the shortages become severe, governments often reinstate rationing—and the distribution of goods is once again in the hands of the planners. In China, there was little political tolerance for price increases, because of the hyperinflation experience of the 1940s and because the populace had grown accustomed (post-1949) to a regime of administered and almost perfectly stable prices. This stable macroeconomic situation changed in the latter half of the 1980s, and again in the mid-1990s; but unlike Russia or Eastern Europe, China did not have to make the transition to a market system in the context of severe inflation.

The absence during the 1980s of a coherent theoretical vision regarding transition to a market economy triggered a vigorous debate over the correct path to market reform. This debate has often been portrayed as a debate between two sides: one that advocated freeing up prices as rapidly as possible and another that believed the main issue was how to first change the state enterprise structure so that SOEs would respond appropriately to market forces. Both sides agreed that prices should be freed up as much as possible eventually—but the latter group argued for doing so only after enterprises had been restructured and their property rights more firmly established.

One well-known figure in the latter group was Li Yining, a professor at Beijing University and an adviser to Premier Zhao Ziyang, who argued that the key to reform lay in changing the behavior of enterprise management (item four mentioned earlier). Li's preferred method for accomplishing this was to establish state enterprises as shareholding corporations where the shares would be held by workers, other enterprises, and other state organizations. These new "owners" would presumably be interested in profits rather than the myriad social goals (including gross output) that were in the objective function of state enterprise managers and their government supervisors.[18] China did, in fact, begin introducing

---

18. Li Yining's views are discussed in Hsu (1991), pp. 157–61. See also Li (1992)—the original article reproduced in this volume was published in 1988 in *Jingji yanjiu cankao culiao*, number 128.

a shareholding system for a few state enterprises around this time. But, as the analysis in later chapters makes clear, that shareholding system has had only a modest impact on management behavior in what are still largely state-owned or state-controlled enterprises.

Those arguing for more or less immediate price and related reforms included Wu Jinglian, then a senior research economist and now senior fellow in the Development Research Center of the State Council in Beijing. Wu maintained that once macroeconomic stability had been attained, the prices of industrial inputs (among other products) should be liberalized within one or two years. Enterprises should at the same time be permitted to set their own prices, purchase inputs, determine the internal structure of the enterprise, and much else. But Wu did not specify how this enterprise autonomy was to be achieved, other than through the issuing of a government directive that would make the enterprise autonomous (Wu 1988). Directives of this sort are not unlike what the earliest socialist market theorists such as Oscar Lange and Abba Lerner advocated. They argued that even within a socialist economy, enterprises could be made to follow the profit maximization rule by passing a law to that effect. Seventy years of experience since these theories were put forth have made it clear that converting a centrally planned, state-owned enterprise into a market-oriented, profit-maximizing firm cannot be achieved by administrative fiat. Thus Wu, in the latter half of the 1980s, focused mainly on the first, second, and fifth of those components required to create an efficient market economy.

By 1988, this lively debate among policy-oriented economists had produced a reasonably complete picture of what a market economy would require, although there was little understanding then (as is true even now) as to how the various reforms could be implemented and sequenced (see chapter 4). There was a growing consensus, however, as early as 1986 that the dual-price system should be replaced by a single, market-determined price, although again, without much clarity with regard to how quickly this should happen.[19] The persisting stricture against even discussing privatization limited but did not preclude (as the work of Li Yining shows) at least some discussion of how to change the incentives facing state enterprise managers. There was also a general effort at this time to reduce the role of the party committees in operational decisions, both in enterprises and in the government more generally. And that, too, would have

19. One prominent economist who often reflected high-level economic policy thinking clearly stated the desirability of moving away from the dual-price system.

reduced political interference in technical decisions if it had been vigorously implemented.[20] As events over the next decade would demonstrate, these discussions of how to make enterprise managers respond appropriately to market forces fell far short of hardening the soft budget constraint and removing politics from the selection of high-level state enterprise management.

By 1988 and 1989, events in both the economic and political spheres were beginning to veer out of control in a way that was for a time to interrupt the reform effort. Inflation, as represented by the urban cost of living index and which had never risen much above 2 percent per year since the end of the famine in 1962, suddenly averaged 9 percent a year in 1985–7 and jumped to 20.7 percent in 1988. This spike in prices was partly the result of economic overheating—but also was linked to the loosening of central plan controls over state enterprises. This allowed liberal access to bank loans, which, in turn, encouraged high levels of investment. Local governments were particularly active in pressuring the local bank branches to increase lending to enterprises under their jurisdiction; and they were supported in the central government by Premier Zhao Ziyang, whose political base rested in part on party support at the provincial level (Shih 2003). Credit to industrial enterprises in 1989 was 65 percent above the level of 1986—an amount that Latin American economists might consider commonplace. But for Chinese reformers, a 20 percent increase in prices was political dynamite that might provide potent ammunition for those who opposed the move to a market system. One should remember that the party and government leader at this time still spoke of a planned commodity economy as the goal: There was no consensus that a market economy was even the long-term objective.

The other politically dangerous development in the late 1980s was the rise in corruption involving government officials. Much of this corruption should be attributed to the continuation of widespread discretionary bureaucratic controls over the economy, plus the gradual fading of official disapproval regarding the acquisition of luxury goods.[21] But the correlation between rising corruption and the expansion of the market economy led most to see a causal link between the two. The dual-price system lent more than a little credibility to the view that the reforms did, in fact, have something to do with increasing corruption. Those with the political

20. The decline in the role of the Party committee in SOEs is discussed by Ji (1998).
21. On the issue of corruption in China, see Manion (2004).

influence to gain access to goods sold at low state-set prices stood to make enormous profits if they could find a way to sell those same goods on the market; and many did find a way.

As the world knows, these economic trends reinforced the discontent with the reforms in China's urban areas. When the students began their sit-in protest on Tiananmen Square in 1989, they had many urban sympathizers. A split within the Communist Party leadership over how to handle the students led to the fall of Zhao Ziyang, by then Party Secretary, along with many of the young reformers who had surrounded Zhao in such organizations as the Systems Reform Institute, which was also abolished (Nathan and Link 2001).

With the introduction of martial law after the student demonstrations ended on Tiananmen Square, the debate over economic policy was temporarily stilled. Instead, there were official pronouncements by Premier Li Peng and by the new Party Secretary Jiang Zemin stating that privatization of state enterprises was out of the question. In a speech given at the 40th anniversary of the founding of the People's Republic, Jiang stated:

> Our socialist economy is a planned commodity economy based on public ownership. . . . In the past decade, while practicing guidance under the state plan, we also gave play to the positive role of regulation through the market and achieved marked success in developing the national economy, making the market prosperous and improving the living standards of the people. Of course, if we persist in weakening and totally negate the planned economy and try to create a completely market-oriented economy, it wouldn't work in China and would surely throw the economy and the entire society into confusion. . . . In China's economic growth, we shall persist in taking public ownership as the main body and developing diverse economic sectors, bringing into play the beneficial and necessary supplementary role of the individual economy, the private economy, Chinese-foreign joint ventures. . . . This doesn't mean in any way weakening or eliminating the position of public ownership in the main sector, much less do we want to "privatize" our economy. . . . (Jiang 1989)

Jiang, it should be noted, also made clear that the opening of the economy to foreign trade and foreign investment would continue uninterrupted. The thrust of his remarks (and of various statements of Premier Li Peng) was that the reform process would continue, but at a slow pace. Emphasis in the latter half of 1989 and in 1990 was on controlling inflation, and the rate of price increase was brought down to 1.1 percent in 1990. Prices again began to rise immediately thereafter, but at a slower pace than in 1988–9.

From the late 1980s through the early 1990s, performance contracting with SOEs also came under increasing scrutiny—and was largely abandoned after 1994: Although attractive in theory, actual practice proved disappointing, with few gains in efficiency. The chief reason that performance contracts failed to induce increased profitability or efficiency was because many of the targets were inadequate or flawed measures of economic performance.[22] For example, an enterprise could achieve its target and receive a high score under a performance contract, yet its total factor productivity could actually fall below precontract levels. Moreover, if a target was flawed, it could be achieved by increasing inputs, even if efficiency declined. Performance contracts also failed to meet expectations because incentives tended to be asymmetric with managers who were not consistently penalized for failing to achieve targets.

To achieve better results, performance contracts had to reduce the information advantage that managers enjoyed over the state, motivate managers to achieve the contract's targets through rewards as well as punishments, and convince managers that the promises contained in the contract were credible. Good contracts were those that strongly induced managers to meet objectives by way of sensible targets, stronger incentives, and longer terms. Unfortunately, there were too few good contracts.

The performance contract was a sound idea at that time and in the Chinese context. But SOEs are different from agricultural households; and the contract system, though very successful in agriculture, did not work well in the SOE sector. Given the complicated internal arrangements and external relations of SOEs, performance contracts would have required supplementary fiscal, financial, and other reforms. These proved intractable at that time, and so the contracts fell into disuse (Qian 1996).

During the late 1980s, Li Peng was critical of the TVEs, which he viewed as competing in illegitimate ways with the state-owned enterprises. TVEs were viewed as diverting low-priced raw materials away from the state sector and evading their proper share of enterprise taxes, or so it was believed. When the government moved to rein in the TVEs in 1990, these rural enterprises were made to bear the brunt of the anti-inflationary credit crunch, while the state industrial sector was allowed to continue borrowing. There was tighter central control of key inputs, a measure that

---

22. The empirical evidence on the effectiveness of performance contracts on actual performance is mixed. In their study, Shirley and Xu (2001) find that performance contracts improved productivity of slightly more than half of the sampled enterprises. They find that performance contracts alone are not enough to improve the performance of SOEs. Instead, they need to be coupled with increases in product market competition.

was also designed to favor state enterprises.[23] By 1991, the total number of TVEs had fallen to 675,200 (from 733,800 in 1988). But it soon became apparent to the Chinese leadership that during the 1980s, TVEs had provided most of the 10 million new nonagricultural jobs created each year. The state sector accounted for only around 2 million of these new jobs each year. To a government worried about political stability, new jobs outside of agriculture were critical. So the leadership soon reversed its attitude toward the TVEs.

Formally, relatively little was done to promote further price liberalization in the 1989–91 period, but the role of market-determined prices rose steadily nevertheless. By the early 1990s, only 17 agricultural products were subject to price control—versus 110 a decade earlier. The prices of well over two-thirds of all consumer goods had also been deregulated, as were those for 58 percent of industrial raw materials (World Bank 1993). Profits of state enterprises plummeted in 1989 and 1990, in part because the effort to stem inflation led to a sharp slowdown in industrial growth (particularly in the state sector), but also because state enterprises found it progressively more difficult to obtain industrial inputs at low, state-set prices. Whatever the formal regulations said, enterprises producing these inputs had a powerful incentive to sell them at the higher market prices, and they found many ways to do so. The dual-price system was being undermined in favor of a single market price, but state-set prices had not yet disappeared.

RENEWAL OF THE REFORM DRIVE, 1992–7

In early 1992, Deng Xiaoping made a trip to southern China that included visits to reform sites, notably the special economic zone in Shenzhen. Deng pronounced himself favorably impressed by what he saw. In particular, he was struck by the economic dynamism induced through FDI and economic opening; and this once again brought economic reform to the forefront of official and public debate. The need to revive a sluggish economy so as to generate more jobs and reverse political discontentment and the desire to catch up with China's rapidly growing neighbors were other factors that compelled the leadership to act. In October 1992, a renewed reform agenda was passed by the 14th Party Congress—and for the first

---

23. For a more complete description of the conservative backlash in 1989–91, see Naughton (1995, pp. 273–9).

time, the official stated goal of the leadership was to create a "socialist market economy" (Naughton 1995, p. 288). This was further elaborated by the 14th Central Committee in 1993. The word "planning" was no longer in the core phrase describing the reform goals. Instead, the main objective was to establish a socialist market economy.[24]

In 1989 and 1990, the government had tried to reduce the differential between state and market prices of industrial inputs by raising many state-set prices for key industrial inputs. But the government also attempted to place a ceiling on market prices, a move that could have reduced the role of market allocations of industrial inputs. But in 1992, the government completely freed up the prices of 600 industrial producer goods. By the end of 1992, the number of industrial goods and transport prices subject to state-set prices had fallen from 737 to 89 (Chai 1997, p. 99).

Between 1992 and 1997, a succession of reforms affecting industrial SOEs were instituted. Prices of industrial inputs and outputs continued to be liberalized; and increasingly, the government allowed the domestic price structure to reflect the international price structure. A new enterprise accounting system was issued in 1993 to replace the old system based on Marxist categories.[25] Or, more accurately, the new system was designed to replace the variety of accounting systems that had previously been used. Promulgating a new system proved far simpler than actually ensuring its adoption by firms throughout the country. Predictably, the implementation of the new system was a slow process.

In 1994, the government adopted a value-added tax (VAT) that was uniform across enterprises of all ownership types. This sought to reduce the state's reliance on enterprise profits as the major source of government revenue. This latter decision was not a particularly difficult one because SOEs were no longer making large profits. With the reform in the price system, many were actually making losses. Thus, the government had to introduce a new tax system if it wanted to reverse the sharp decline in government revenue that had occurred.[26] State revenue as a percentage of GDP had plunged from 31 percent of GDP in 1978, to 22 percent in 1985, to 16 percent in 1990, and 14 percent in 1992. Some of this decline

---

24. Wang Hui observes that "in contrast, to pre-reform socialism, while contemporary socialism is a type of Marxism as an ideology of modernization, it has already in effect been stripped of the anti-modern character of the prior socialism" (Wang 2003, p. 152).

25. Much of this discussion of the 1993–7 institutional reforms is based on Naughton (1995) and Chai (1997).

26. The fiscal problems that led to the reform introduced in 1994 are described in Zhang (1999), Lieberthal (1995, chapter 9), Xu and Ma (1995), and Gao (1995).

in revenue represented a change in the way investment was financed (from bank loans paid back out of SOE profits rather than grants from the government budget). But the entire decline was not for this reason. From the standpoint of the incentives available to SOEs, the significance of this change in the way profits were taxed was that it meant enterprises (at least in principle) faced a uniform percentage tax rate that was the same for all enterprises, no matter what the ownership. With hindsight, it is now apparent that this was only the beginning of what has proven to be a prolonged effort to reform the tax system and actually implement new rules. For quite some time payments continued, and even a decade later SOEs and COEs with a large supply of cash on hand could be subject to pressure to turn over some of the funds to a government bureau (Steinfeld 1998).

Other enterprise-related reforms gave firms greater flexibility in the hiring of workers. Lifetime employment with full enterprise-based pension rights, the right to enterprise-built housing, and other benefits came under attack. The "iron rice bowl" was increasingly seen as an obstacle to the efficient operation of the state sector. As mentioned earlier, in 1986 a decision was made to allow state enterprises to hire new workers for a fixed period of time rather than permanently—and to do so without providing the full range of benefits given to permanent workers. The number of contract workers in the state sector rose from 10.1 million in 1988 (when the reformers were still in charge), and then to 15.9 million in 1991 (an increase rate of 16 percent a year), even though the conservatives controlled the policy levers. With the reforms back on track, the number of contract workers climbed to 20.6 million in 1992 and to 55.5 million by 1996—an increase rate of 28 percent per year (National Bureau of Statistics 1997, p. 114). The total number of staff and workers in the state sector only increased from 99.8 million in 1988 to 106.6 million in 1991 and 109.5 million in 1996, which means that the number of workers in the state sector with the full benefits of the iron rice bowl rose slightly, from 89.8 million in 1988 to 90.8 million in 1991, and then sharply fell to 54 million in 1996. In state manufacturing alone, the number of workers with full benefits fell from 33.5 million in 1991 to 7.7 million in 1996.[27]

Another major change during this period was the expansion of the number of enterprises that sold shares and listed those shares on the Shanghai and Shenzhen stock exchanges. China began allowing stocks and bonds to be traded on the market on April 1, 1986. By the end of 1988 the value of

---

27. These data on noncontract workers, presumably those with permanent employment for the most part, had to be derived from the data on contract workers and total state sector employment from pages 108 and 114 of National Bureau of Statistics (1997).

enterprise shares issued amounted to only 3.5 billion yuan, but only 61 percent of those shares were in the hands of the public (Jiandong 1989). The boom in the number of listed companies on the stock exchanges and in the value of shares issued came in 1993. In that year there were 183 listed companies, and 9.6 billion yuan in shares were issued and sold. By 1997 there were 745 listed companies, mostly former SOEs, and the stocks issued and sold that year amounted to 26.8 billion yuan. The total value of issued shares by 1997 was 1,715.4 billion yuan, but only 520.4 billion yuan of those were tradable on the stock exchanges. Five years later the total market value of shares of listed stocks and the "negotiable" portion of those stocks was double the 1997 figures.

The listing of state-owned enterprises on the stock exchange and the sale of their shares, however, were not the beginnings of an effort to change the nature of corporate governance. The purpose of the sales was mainly to provide the enterprises with other avenues for raising capital both at home and abroad. At home these shares had the added advantage of providing the public with an alternative to putting their savings in the state banks or under their mattresses. This process did not affect governance, because shareholders had no right to select company management or influence the behavior of management in any other way. The state held the majority of shares in these enterprises, and the government along with the Communist Party retained complete authority over the selection of top enterprise management. The idea that a shareholding system would allow China to move toward a system of corporate governance where profit-oriented shareholders would select a board of directors—and that board would, in turn, select top management of the state-controlled enterprises—was not at this stage adopted, even as an experiment. This reflected the prevalent belief among key members of China's leadership that ownership was not a decisive influence on SOE performance, and that privatization was to be ruled out. In 1995, Jiang Zemin maintained that the fact that "some SOEs, lack vigor has nothing to do with the ownership system." The problems of SOEs could be traced to "the interior environment [to] residual problems of history [and could] be completely solved by deepening reforms" (Lam 1999, p. 61).

The final reform of significance in the mid-1990s that affected SOEs, and which should be considered here, is the rapid expansion of foreign direct investment in China. While increasing during 1989 through 1991, FDI was actually still at a modest $3 billion per year. Most of this was from Hong Kong and by overseas Chinese investors—and was channeled into small export-oriented firms in Guangdong and Fujian provinces.

Then in 1992, the total FDI utilized jumped to $11 billion; and in 1993, it rose further, to $27.5 billion. By 1996, the total of new FDI actually used had passed $40 billion and increasingly came from large companies in Europe, Japan, and the United States. The dollar figures for FDI, how-ever, do not fully capture the importance of the entry of foreign firms into China. Many companies signed agreements with existing large SOEs in China, to cooperate in the production of such major products as automo-biles. As noted in chapter 1, these companies brought with them access to foreign markets and management skills as well as money. Foreign firms acting on their own, and Chinese firms working in cooperation with these foreign corporations, competed directly with the rest of Chinese industry. Those unable or unwilling to compete were in immediate danger of falling far behind.

The changes that occurred in Chinese state-owned industry in the 1992–7 period, therefore, were profound. Many of the institutions of a modern market-oriented industrial economy were being put in place. On the surface, China appeared to be moving in a steady and fairly rapid way toward an industrial economy that looked much like its counterparts else-where in the world, albeit with a larger share of state ownership in indus-try. But in China in the mid-1990s, changes in enterprise behavior did not always follow changes in the formal structure of the industrial system. Of the five criteria needed to make a market work efficiently, four had been largely applied. But the fifth—enterprises with the principal objective of profit maximization through the enterprise's own efforts—was not yet in place.

The core of the problem that persisted can be seen in the relationship between the state-owned banks and the other state-owned enterprises. The banks, on the surface, were commercial banks making loans to proj-ects they deemed viable. But in reality, the banks lent mainly to SOEs and did so either at the request of the enterprises or at the behest of powerful political patrons of the state enterprises. There was little or no effort to determine whether the project for which money was being sought was a good project likely to produce a high rate of return, enabling the enter-prise to pay back the loan (Lardy 1998, chapters 3 and 4).

Although in the 1980s the State Planning Commission still had enough authority to direct investment in capacity expansion by the larger SOEs, this had weakened by the mid-1990s. The central bank, the People's Bank of China, was even weaker. It accommodated the commercial banks by providing them with whatever financing they required. Stated more formally, if the enterprises or their political patrons required loans, the commercial banks provided them. When the commercial banks were lent up to their limits, the central bank could be induced to raise the limit by creating more high-powered money.

If the expansion of the SOEs had been motivated mainly by profits, they would have been careful in their expansion plans to ensure that the contemplated projects were commercially viable. But a commercial calculus was rarely employed by such enterprises. Expansion was considered good whether or not it made a profit, so long as it helped raise employment, market share, or the bonuses of managers. Moreover, continued operation of a loss-making unit was also desirable—even if it meant taking on more loans that would drive the enterprise further into debt and into losses. Private firms usually did not have the option of going to the banking system for loans to cover their losses. In fact, many could not even go to the banking system for good projects.

That this was the case in the mid-1990s can be seen by the performance of bank loans, the money supply, and prices. The bank loan and money supply data are presented in figure 2.2. Bank loans during the mid-1990s continued to expand at between 20 and 25 percent per year. The money supply rose steeply as well, in part because of the continued expansion of bank credit, but also because this was a period when FDI was accelerating. In addition, the current account moved from a deficit into a growing

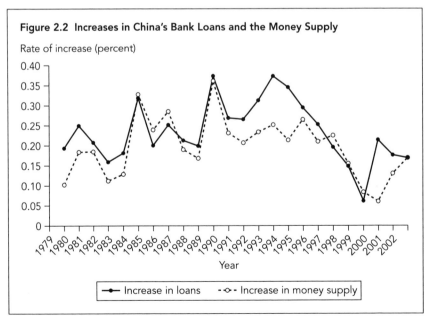

Figure 2.2 Increases in China's Bank Loans and the Money Supply

Rate of increase (percent)

Year

— Increase in loans   - -o- - Increase in money supply

Source: China Statistical Yearbook (National Bureau of Statistics 1997, 2002).

surplus after 1993 (National Bureau of Statistics 1999, p. 73). Thus, China was faced with a major inflationary problem, and consumer prices rose by an average of 19 percent per year in 1993–5. Interest rates on loans were raised twice in 1993, but remained well below the rate of inflation. So even if state enterprises had been profit oriented, these interest rates would not have restrained their borrowing. As it was, bank loans to the state enterprises grew at over 20 percent per year throughout this inflationary period.

Even though the political fallout from inflation was not as large as in 1988–9, price increases of this magnitude were still a political liability for the Chinese leadership. To deal with the problem, however, the government did not turn to market forces and further raise interest rates. Instead, the government appointed one of its most forceful senior officials, Zhu Rongji, to head of the central bank; he, in turn, set lending quotas for the commercial banks and made clear that there would be serious consequences for bankers who overshot their quotas. In short, to deal with the planned economy mentality that was still pervasive in both the state banks and the SOEs, Zhu Rongji, a former central planner himself, resorted to centralized administrative controls, even in the mid-1990s.

The steps taken by Zhu Rongji quickly brought down the rate of inflation. Allocation of credit in accordance with administrative controls set by a central government, however, does little to promote the efficient allocation of credit or induce the central and commercial banks to respond to market signals. For many enterprises it did not even choke off credit. Many SOEs, unable to obtain bank loans to cover their credit needs, resorted to stopping payment on their obligations to other state-owned firms. The result of this was the expansion of what has been called "triangular debt," with many state enterprises building up large accounts receivables that might never actually be realized. It became increasingly difficult under these circumstances to determine whether or not an enterprise was really viable in the long run. The efforts by Zhu Rongji to rein in inflation, therefore, may have contributed to a hardening of the enterprise budget constraint, but it is difficult to tell. Still, China under Zhu Rongji's leadership as premier after 1998 (with Jiang Zemin's support) was about to embark on an even tougher effort to change state enterprise behavior.

WHAT THE FIRST ROUND OF REFORMS ACHIEVED

Many reforms were introduced during the 1980s and again after Deng Xiaoping's Southern tour in 1992; but did these reforms achieve their objective of improving the performance of China's state-owned enterprises? The outcome of the reforms in the 1990s and into the 21st century will be analyzed at the end of chapter 3 and more systematically in chapter 5 of this volume. But what can be said about the reforms in the 1980s?

A number of efforts were made to measure total factor productivity (TFP) in industry in the 1980s, and these are reviewed at the end of chapter 3, along with the somewhat more reliable estimates of productivity for more recent periods. The majority of these estimates show that the TFP of state enterprises grew in the 1980s, although the TFP growth rate of these enterprises was lower than that among the TVEs and other collective enterprises. However, the available data do not allow one to estimate movements in TFP for state industrial enterprises prior to 1978. TFP for the economy as a whole rose in the 1980s as compared with the two pre-reform decades (when TFP for the economy was negative); but the data are not sufficient to attribute these gains to state enterprises as contrasted to nonstate enterprises, agriculture, and services. The 1980s estimates are also flawed by the need to make assumptions about the deflator used in generating estimates of the real growth rate of state sector capital formation, a problem that does not exist for the 1990s because the Chinese statistical authorities have published their deflator estimates for this latter period.

Even if quantitative estimates of productivity cannot answer the question of the size of the impact of the 1980s' reforms on state-owned industrial enterprise performance, these reforms were broadly positive. It is known, for example, that the level of competition facing SOEs rose dramatically in the 1980s, in contrast to the pre-1978 period, when most SOEs had a monopoly of their local markets. By ending the administrative allocation of a wide variety of industrial inputs and by freeing up the prices of many of those inputs, the government raised allocation efficiency in the state industrial sector. However, the limited nature of enterprise management autonomy for most SOEs, the transformation of a few firms into shareholding enterprises, and the introduction of performance contracts appear to have had only a limited effect on the technical efficiency of state enterprises. Or, that at least appears to be the conclusion reached by those who instituted much more thoroughgoing reforms in the latter half of the 1990s, a conclusion supported by some of the empirical studies such as those of the steel industry (Movshuk 2004; Wu 1997; Zhang 2004b).

CHAPTER 3

THE ACCELERATED CHANGE IN
ENTERPRISE OWNERSHIP, 1997–2003

B y 1997 the reform of state-owned enterprises (SOEs) in China had been ongoing for well over 13 years. Impressive progress had been made at reforming prices, with 86 percent of the prices of producer goods (calculated in terms of the value of producer goods transactions) set by the market in 1999, and only 10 percent set by the state (Lardy 2002, p. 25). Retail prices for consumers were even less regulated. Even certain energy prices and the purchase prices for grain that were still determined by the state were adjusted up or down to bring them more in line with world prices for those products. SOEs, by 1997, also had a considerable degree of autonomy over what they produced and the inputs used to produce goods. Centrally planned targets that had to be adhered to in the past no longer existed. Labor was increasingly being hired on short-term contracts and could, in principle, be laid off.

From the standpoint of the government leadership and the wider economic perspective, however, the state enterprises were still a problem. Profits in 1996–8 fell to an all-time low of less than 2 percent of the gross value of state enterprise industrial output; and the losses of SOEs rose in those same years, to over 3 percent of state sector gross industrial output (see figure 3.1).[1] This decline in profits, it should be noted, occurred in the nonstate sector as well. The cause of this decline was the freeing up of prices combined with the rapid entry of new firms that increased competition and hence put pressure on profits.

---

1. As one quantitative study has shown (using data extending through 1999), it was declining profitability—not declining productivity—that was the main driving force behind the government's decisions when outright liquidation or privatization of SOEs was under consideration (Li and others 2001). However, the findings reported here indicate that the government first transferred ownership of the better performing, to facilitate the reform process.

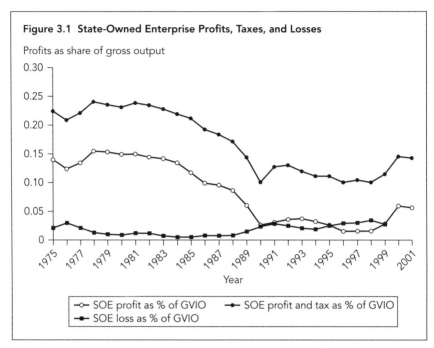

Figure 3.1 State-Owned Enterprise Profits, Taxes, and Losses

Note: GVIO, gross value of industrial output; SOE, state-owned enterprise.
Source: China Statistical Yearbook (National Bureau of Statistics, various years).

Low profitability, in turn, meant that nonperforming loans to the state enterprises continued to accumulate in the state commercial banks, as observed in chapter 1 of this volume. To counter this, the government created policy banks to relieve the commercial banks of having to make government-directed loans for policy purposes rather than commercial purposes. The jurisdiction of regional bank branches was also changed, so that these jurisdictions were not the same as the sphere of control of local politicians. The objective of both these measures was to reduce political influence on bank lending. The commercial banks, however, continued to make policy-driven loans, and their performance did not improve.

The East Asian financial crisis of 1997–8 brought a new sense of urgency to both banking and SOE reforms. China was largely insulated from the crisis, because by then the government had built both huge foreign exchange reserves and a considerable current account surplus, and benefited from a large inflow of foreign direct investment (FDI) that was unaffected by the crisis. No investor in China, whether domestic or foreign, had any rational reason to fear that China would be forced to sharply devalue its currency (as was the case in Indonesia, Korea, Malaysia, and Thailand), although investors in Hong Kong (China) and elsewhere spent much time speculating about a possible Chinese devaluation. Thus, in China there was no panic followed by a collapse of the banking system— even though China's banking system, measured by the share of nonperforming assets in total assets, was in worse shape than those countries hardest hit by the crisis.

While China avoided a financial crisis, the difficulties experienced by other countries in the neighborhood were a warning to the Chinese leadership that time could be running out on the weaker sectors of the economy, and that included the SOEs and state banks. In 1998 the government moved decisively to begin dealing with the bloated payrolls of the state sector, arguably the most difficult task of all from a political standpoint. Employment in state-owned units of all kinds was cut by 20 million in 1998. This figure fell by another 30 million by the end of the second quarter of 2003 (National Bureau of Statistics 2002, p. 120; National Bureau of Statistics 2003, p. 11; also see table 3.1). Thirty-six percent (50 percent if retirees are included) of the entire workforce in the state sector, the part of the workforce with the most capacity to create political trouble, was laid off over this five-year period, starting with the 15th Party Congress in September 1997 (Solinger 2002).

China, up to this point, had delayed the shuttering of SOEs and the dismissal or furloughing of workers until it had the beginnings of a national welfare system to replace the old enterprise system.[2] Unemployment insurance was introduced starting with a security fund for laid-off workers created in 1992. This was superceded by two funds: one providing unemployment insurance for two years and the second, an allowance for *xiagang* (furloughed) workers who were laid off but retained links with their SOEs. Enterprises were also required to set up unemployment centers with the help of public funds (Garnaut and others 2005). And efforts were under way to create a national health insurance system. But the crafting of national insurance programs (as compared to enterprise-based programs) was still in the experimental stage when the decision was made to cut state enterprise payrolls; and national insurance schemes thus applied to only a fraction of the total state labor force.

The central government at this time also indicated that it was less willing to sustain loss-making SOEs. Senior officials sometimes spoke about retaining central government responsibility for 500 state enterprises, and

---

2. If one accepts the idea that state enterprises have a social welfare obligation as well as a profit obligation, a model can be developed that explains the low profit drive of state enterprises and the delay in introducing full market-oriented reforms (Bai and others 2000).

Table 3.1 Share of China's State-Owned and State-Holding Enterprises

	1998[a]	1999	2000	2001	2002
Number of SOEs	—	50,651	42,426	34,530	29,449
Number of SOEs and state-holding enterprises	64,737	61,301	53,489	46,767	41,125
Number of state-holding enterprises	—	10,650	11,063	12,237	11,676
Total number of national enterprises[b]	165,080	162,033	162,885	171,256	181,557
Share of SOE of national total enterprises (percent)	—	31.26	26.05	20.16	16.22
Share of SOEs and state-holding enterprises of national total (percent)	39.22	37.83	32.84	27.31	22.65
Share of state-holding enterprises of national total (percent)	—	6.5	6.79	7.15	6.43
SOE output at current prices (billion)	—	2,221.59	2,015.63	1,722.92	1,727.11
SOE and state-holding output at current prices (billion)	3,362.10	3,557.12	4,055.44	4,240.85	4,517.90
State-holding enterprises output	—	1,335.53	2,039.81	2,517.93	2,790.79
National total industrial output	6,773.71	7,270.7	8,567.36	9,544.9	11,077.65
Share of SOE output of national total (percent)	—	30.56	23.53	18.05	15.59
Share of SOE and state-holding output of national total (percent)	49.6	48.92	47.34	44.43	40.78
Share of state-holding output of national total (percent)	—	18.37	23.81	26.38	25.19
SOE and state-holding enterprise employment	27.21	24.12	20.9	18.24	15.46
National total enterprise employment	47.53	44.28	41.02	38.38	37.29
Share of SOE and state-holding employment of national total (percent)	57.25	54.47	50.95	47.52	41.46

Notes: SOEs, state-owned and state-holding enterprises; — not available. The difference between the numbers for SOEs cited in the table and in the text reflects changes in the sampling frame of the Chinese statistical authorities. This reduces substantially the total number of SOEs.

a. Value-added and other performance data are mainly derived from various tables of Main Indicators of All State-owned and Non-state-owned Above Designed Size Industrial Enterprises (referring to enterprises each with an annual sales over 5 million yuan).

b. In 1998, the industrial statistics were adjusted to cover all state-owned industrial enterprises and enterprises with an annual sales of over 5 million yuan.

Source: China Statistical Yearbook (various years).

at other times for 1,000 state enterprises—but eventually settled on identifying 520 "key-point" enterprises, 514 of which were state owned or controlled. The remaining SOEs and even most of the 8,700 large and medium-size enterprises (mostly but not exclusively state owned) would have to fend for themselves or seek the assistance of subnational governments. In "grasping the large and letting go of the small," the state was not committed to privatizing the smaller state enterprises, because many (possibly most) were owned by provincial-level and county governments. But it became the responsibility of these local governments to bail the enterprises out of trouble.

In principle, provincial and local governments (unlike the central government) do not have the capacity to print money. Therefore, any subsidies to local state enterprises must come out of the revenue of these local governments. In practice, the issue is not so simple; and this explains, in part, why reform of the banking system must be coordinated with a hardening of the budget constraint of SOEs even at the provincial level, a point mentioned in chapter 1. It also reinforces the survey findings reported here—that SOEs and reformed SOEs do not yet confront a hard budget constraint. Formally, the money supply and the level of allowable bank credit are determined exclusively by China's central bank, subject to approval from the top leadership of the government and the Communist Party. In reality, the provincial authorities are still able to induce the local banks to lend to their favored enterprises, as evidenced by credit growth in 2003–4 and the composition of bank lending, which still favors the SOE.

As mentioned earlier, the Chinese government has made some effort to ward off the political pressure on the commercial banks but has achieved only modest success in this regard. Most of the discussion of banking reform has instead focused on how to get nonperforming assets off the books of the state banks. In 1998, the government issued 270 million yuan worth of special bonds to recapitalize the four principal banks. This was followed in 1999 by the formation of four asset management companies, one for each of the four large state commercial banks, to take over a portion of the nonperforming assets of these banks.[3] This approach to the problem has been standard ever since it was pioneered by the United

---

3. The four were Xinda for the China Construction Bank, Huarong for the Industrial and Commercial Bank of China, Dongfang for the Bank of China, and Changcheng for the Agricultural Bank of China. Together they received an initial capital endowment of 400 billion yuan from the state and raised an additional 1 trillion yuan through a state-guaranteed bond floatation. These funds were used to purchase 1.4 trillion yuan in bad loans (Lo 2004).

States in response to its savings and loan bank crisis in the 1980s.[4] The refinancing of the banks in this way, however, helps only if enough of the nonperforming assets are transferred off the banks' books to allow them to operate profitably without government support. It is also critical for the banks to see this refinancing as a one-time affair—with the government credibly committed to a stance that excludes periodic future bailouts.

Neither of these objectives was achieved by China's bank refinancing measures during 1999–2000. The amount of refinancing as of the end of the year 2000 was 1.4 trillion yuan, a sizable sum, but perhaps only around a third of all nonperforming bank assets. Furthermore, it is not at all apparent that this refinancing will be a one-time affair. As noted in chapter 1, the official figure for nonperforming assets of 16 major commercial banks was reported to be 13 percent of total assets in 2003. The four large commercial banks continue to accumulate new nonperforming loans, and the stock of nonperforming assets (shared among banks and asset management companies) may not have been reduced to any significant extent. In addition, the asset management companies have had modest success in selling off the assets they acquired from the banks; and what has been disposed of has fetched not more than 10 percent of its book value. Instead, given the absence of a market for most of these assets, China instituted a debt-for-equity swap that on the face of it, improved the books of the asset management companies, the SOEs, and the banks but had little effect on the behavior of either the banks or the SOEs. The budget constraint facing the SOEs and state banks was harder than it had been a decade earlier, but was still softer than what one finds in most advanced market economies.

THE DECISION TO JOIN THE WORLD TRADE ORGANIZATION

China's economic policymakers could not directly curb SOE access to bank and other financial resources, regardless of performance, because of the political power of the leaders of many of those enterprises and their allies in the government and the Communist Party. Economic policy reformers could, however, and did move to create conditions that would force the SOEs to reform or restructure (*gaizhi*) and which could not readily be undermined by domestic political resistance. The method

---

4. There is a large literature on the savings and loan bank crisis in the United States. The approach used of having an independent government organization take over the nonperforming assets of failed banks and then resell these assets to private investors was adopted in varying forms by a number of Asian countries after the 1997–8 financial crisis in that region.

chosen was to increase competitive pressures on the state sector by expos-ing the sector to more vigorous foreign competition. The mechanism for accomplishing this task was not a few select reductions in tariffs and quan-titative restrictions on imports that could be easily reversed at a later date. Instead, the vehicle was an international agreement that China could break only if it chose to alienate all of its trading partners and risk severing its ties with critical export markets, one of the main engines of rapid Chinese growth during the reform period.

China had been negotiating with Europe, the United States, and other nations to join the World Trade Organization (WTO) for over a decade, but progress toward an agreement was slow because of the stringent terms for membership. Where developing countries had in the past been able to join the General Agreement on Tariffs and Trade (the predecessor to the WTO) on relatively lenient terms that allowed them to restrict trade to promote local industry, that option was no longer open to countries attempting to join in the 1990s. The United States would not even permit China to be classified as a developing country when and if it were allowed to join the WTO. If China wanted to enter, it had to accept the abolition of all quantitative restrictions on trade, lower tariffs to levels that would give only limited protection to a few infant industries, and accept Western advanced-country definitions of intellectual property rights. In addition, it would have to open up its financial sector to direct competition from foreign banks, insurance companies, and other nonbank financial institutions.[5]

Given these stringent terms, there was every prospect that China would resist accepting them and that negotiations would drag on for another period of years until either the advanced industrial countries lowered the barriers to China's entry or Chinese industry reached a point where most firms could compete internationally. Instead, Premier Zhu Rongji visited the United States in April 1999 and placed before the Clinton administration a proposal to accelerate China's entry into the WTO, by accepting all of the more important conditions insisted on by the American negotiators. The Clinton administration first rejected Zhu's offer but reversed itself several days later—and opened negotiations with China on its entry into the WTO. When the United States published the terms being offered by China shortly after Zhu had presented them, many state enterprise managers and other high-level officials were shocked.

_____

5. For a more complete presentation of all the terms that China accepted when it joined the WTO, see Lardy (2002) and Rumbaugh and Blancher (2004).

These terms had been a closely held secret known only to some of the highest-level officials, and were a major departure from the trade policies of the immediate past. In effect, China was agreeing to dismantle many of the measures that had been used to protect SOEs from foreign competition. Despite this initial shock and the political problems it created for Premier Zhu, however, the negotiations moved forward; and following the completion of similar negotiations with other WTO members, China, in November 2001, formally joined the WTO.

Many of the terms of these accession agreements dealt with agriculture and with efforts by industrial countries to limit the disruptive impact of rapid increases in Chinese exports (antidumping procedures, for example). The provisions that affected Chinese industrial policy and the SOEs included an agreement to reduce the average tariff on imports of industrial products to 8.9 percent. By way of comparison, the 19th-century unequal treaties that successive Chinese governments objected to had a 5 percent ad valorem tariff that was seen as a purely revenue-generating tariff consistent with the free-trade principles then dominant in Britain, the main imperial power at that time. Most of these new lower tariffs were to take effect by 2004.

Probably more important than the proposed decline in tariff rates was China's agreement to eliminate all quantitative barriers on imports no later than 2005, including quotas, licenses, tendering requirements, and other similar measures (Lardy 2002, pp. 65–66). Foreign direct investment in manufacturing was further liberalized from the already favorable provisions in effect years earlier. China, in essence, agreed to give most FDI national treatment. In addition, and of potentially profound significance for SOEs—foreign banks and insurance companies were to be allowed into the country; and many of the restrictions that had confined these banks and insurance companies to the Shanghai or Shenzhen areas were abolished.

A number of attempts have been made to analyze the likely impact of these provisions on the various sectors of the Chinese economy.[6] While the conclusions drawn by these studies are hypothetical (since there has not yet been time to appraise the actual effects of the changes related to WTO accession), most of the conclusions that pertain to manufacturing and SOEs are not surprising. Large parts of Chinese manufacturing have long since become internationally competitive, and this includes most

---

6. In addition to Lardy (2002), there are studies such as the special issue of the *China Economic Review*, volume 11, number 4 (2000); Wang and Li (2003); and Bhattasali, Li, and Martin (2004).

labor-intensive manufactures, from textiles and shoes to toys and sporting goods. By 2002, China was also highly competitive in a wide range of electronic products. Exports of computer and communications products in 2002, for example, were $54.5 billion, up 51 percent from the year before (Wang and Li 2003, p. 113). And Acer, Hon Hai Precision, and Quanta, the large Taiwanese manufacturers of desktop and notebook computers and motherboards, had moved most of their assembly activities to China.

The areas where China must greatly improve its current performance, if these sectors are to compete with imports, include capital-intensive sectors such as automobiles, high quality steel products, and machinery—products that China can now produce but not at internationally competitive costs—and, of course, the financial sector. Here the SOEs will be under great pressure, as Premier Zhu and others had hoped. It is important, however, not to overstate the consequences for Chinese industry and financial services. There are two mitigating factors that apply to at least some industries. First, because China began liberalizing import regulations long before its accession to the WTO (aside from industries such as automobiles), many of these sectors have already adjusted to the competition from imports. Unweighted tariff rates, for example, had fallen from 43.2 percent in 1992 to 15.3 percent in 2001, and effective tariffs were in the 3–5 percent range before the WTO rules had introduced any changes whatsoever[7] (Lardy 2002, p. 34). The number of companies authorized to conduct foreign trade rose from the 12 Ministry of Foreign Trade monopoly corporations that existed at the beginning of the reform period to over 5,000 firms in 1988, and 35,000 firms in 2001 (Lardy 2002, p. 41). In a similar vein, as already mentioned, the rules governing foreign direct investment were steadily liberalized as well.

Second, in China (as in most transition economies), one must always distinguish between what the rules state and whether and how these rules are actually implemented. A casual reading of the accession agreements concerning the financial sector, for example, might lead some analysts to assume that foreign banks, large and small, would soon flood into China and cut deeply into the deposit and loan business of the state banks. But China has also issued a regulation stating that any bank wishing to open a new branch in any given city doing both yuan and foreign currency business must reserve 600 million yuan ($73 million) of operating capital for each new branch (Leung and Kueh 2002). Only the Hong Kong and

---

7. This is implied by the tariff revenues collected on imports.

Shanghai Bank, Citibank, and a few others are in a position to comply with this rule. The ministry of finance also levies a turnover or "business tax" (*yingye shui*) of 7 percent off the top of bank income before any deductions for costs. The effect of this tax is to make it extremely difficult for any bank to become more than marginally profitable. For the state banks this has been less of a problem, because ultimately the government is responsible for making up for any shortage in their capital. But the tax applies to private banks as well, and they have no government agency to ensure the adequacy of their capital base (Langlois 2004).[8]

More generally, the central government has agreed to provide national treatment to foreign investors in a wide variety of areas; but that does not mean that the local governments will cooperate with this effort if locally powerful companies are placed at a disadvantage. As mentioned in chapter 1 of this volume, local protectionism has been ubiquitous in China throughout the reform period, even when no foreign firms are involved (World Bank 1997). If competition in a local market requires a local commercial outlet with a physical presence in the locality, the local government, if it chooses, can interfere with any attempt to set up such an outlet by means of discriminatory implementation of myriad local regulations and licensing provisions. Nor can most outsiders resort to the courts to redress grievances of this sort; the courts do not have the power to overrule the local political authorities in most cases, an issue discussed later in more detail.

China's decision to join the WTO, therefore, was a courageous attempt to force the pace of enterprise reform; and to some degree, that decision will have its intended impact. Nevertheless, foreign competition alone, whether through trade or FDI, will not by itself complete China's transition to a market economy where state industrial and financial enterprises compete on a level playing field with all other enterprise ownership forms.

CORPORATIZING CHINESE STATE ENTERPRISES

Along with the central government's decision to "grasp the big and let go of the small" enterprises and to expose most industrial enterprises to international competition, China began to introduce other changes both in how property rights in industry would be defined and in the degree of emphasis given to different forms of ownership. The number of

---

8. Whalley (2003) believes that China will confront severe problems in implementing some of its trade agreements.

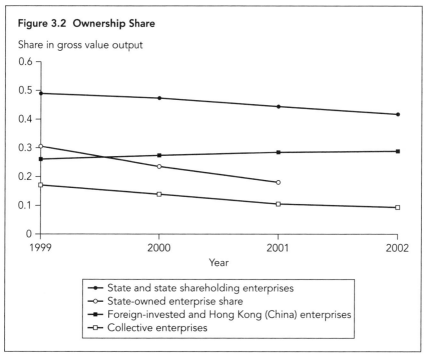

Figure 3.2 Ownership Share

Note: This chart does not include data on the share of private firms, and the collective share reported in this chart includes many firms that were really private—the so-called "red hat" firms.
Source: *China Statistical Yearbook* (National Bureau of Statistics 1997, 2002).

establishments has fallen rapidly since 1998 (see table 3.1). Mirroring the reduction in the number of state-owned industrial establishments, the share of gross industrial output accounted for by SOEs "owned by all of the people" is falling (see figure 3.2). The old system of state ownership, therefore, is receding rapidly. Foreign-funded enterprises are now the most rapidly growing sector, replacing the township and village enterprises (TVEs), although, as discussed later, many of the larger Western and Japanese foreign-invested firms are joint ventures with what were the better-endowed SOEs, albeit with indifferent management. Domestic private enterprises are also increasing their share. Even among the smaller SOEs, there has been a considerable amount of privatization in some regions (Gang 2002). Furthermore, the state has taken steps to level the playing field—for private enterprises and private entrepreneurs can now become members of the Communist Party.[9] The national constitution is also being

---

9. This was announced by Jiang Zemin on July 1, 2001, reversing a ruling passed in August 1998 (Dickson 2003).

revised to put the private sector on the same footing as the state sector— at least in a formal sense. Finally, there is a category of ownership referred to as limited liability companies (LLCs). In accordance with the company law passed in 1994, smaller SOEs were converted into limited liability companies and larger SOEs were commonly converted into limited liability shareholding corporations (LLSCs). Since then, the number of LLCs has increased dramatically (see figure 3.3) relative to SOEs and LLSCs. The intent behind the creation of limited liability companies was to increase the independence of these companies from the government and reduce the government's responsibility for their losses; but whether this change in business organization makes much difference to actual enterprise behavior remains to be seen, although the findings reported in chapter 5 suggest that it may.

In what follows, the changes made in each of the other ownership categories are examined (Zhang 2004a). It is important to bear in mind, however, that these ownership categories are not buttressed by well-defined property rights. There are differences in the control rights of the

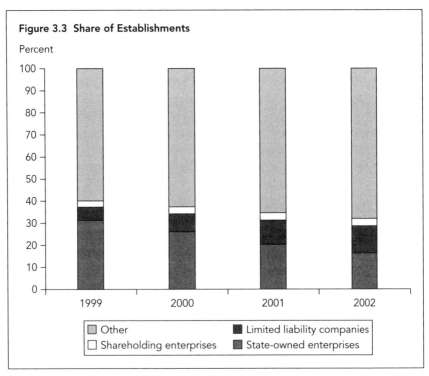

Figure 3.3 Share of Establishments

Percent

Legend:
- Other
- Shareholding enterprises
- Limited liability companies
- State-owned enterprises

Source: China Statistical Yearbook (National Bureau of Statistics 1997, 2002).

different ownership categories, and this may be more important than whatever the formal ownership documents say. But these control rights are imprecise and somewhat fluid (Grossman and Hart 1986; Hart and Moore 1990). Thus, control rights over SOEs have gradually moved from the planning commission and the industrial ministries to enterprise management, but this shift is far from complete. Control rights in the collectively owned TVEs are held by varying combinations of the local governments and the firms' management, with control gradually shifting toward the latter. Much the same can be said about formally private domestic enterprises.

One central question with regard to ownership and control rights is how to think about the shareholding enterprises, most of which were former enterprises "owned by all of the people." Of the total number of shares issued as of 2001, 65 percent were nontradable shares and 35 percent were tradable. The tradable shares were mostly held by domestic or foreign individuals. Of the 65 percent that were nontradable, 46 percent were held by the state, and the remainder (18.5 percent) mainly by "domestic legal persons." The number of shares held by the state, however, is not a good indicator of how many companies were actually controlled by the state. In one careful study of a sample of 1,105 listed companies (see Liu and Sun 2003), only 8.5 percent were directly controlled by government departments or agencies. Indirect control was another matter, however. Many of the nontradable shares of these listed enterprises were in the hands of state wholly owned holding companies or state-controlled nonlisted holding companies. When all of these indirect ways that the state ultimately controlled listed companies are combined, state control in 2001 came to 84 percent of the total. Only 16 percent of the 1,105 firms were not state controlled. The "state" in these cases, of course, includes many different governmental bodies, ranging from central government bureaus to provincial bureaus and many other types of state units.[10]

While ultimate state control does not mean monolithic direction of listed enterprises from the central government in Beijing, these

---

10. Because most of the holding companies are not listed on the Shanghai or Shenzhen exchanges, the authors of this study used a variety of methods to discern the ultimate control of this sample of 1,105 listed companies, including interviews, review of documents released by the holding companies, and so forth. The discussion in this paragraph is based on Liu and Sun (2003). Liu and Sun (2005) note that "the state is still the dominant owner of public corporations in China, enjoying ultimate ownership control of 81.6 percent of firms at the end of 2001. In other words, over a decade of stock market development, the market has managed to produce less than 200 private firms" (p. 120).

state-controlled firms do have a number of features in common. Most important, the ultimate state owners all refuse to award minority shareholders in these firms any control rights. The sole right of minority shareholders is to receive dividends when the management of the enterprise deems it appropriate to distribute them. These shareholders cannot bring a legal suit against management, no matter how egregiously management diverts resources to purposes that are not in the interests of the shareholders. Stated differently, if the minority shareholders do go to court, the courts are unlikely to find in their favor; and if the courts do find in their favor, the shareholders cannot enforce that judgment. In fact, the only real protection that shareholders currently have against asset-stripping or the diversion of profits by management is that the state does not want to see its profits and assets diverted to private uses. In addition, and unlike Russia in the early 1990s, the state in China still has the power to prevent some forms of profits and asset diversion.

Minority shareholders also have no effective right to elect boards of directors of these state-dominated shareholding enterprises. A few of these firms have appointed "outside" directors, but these directors appear to have little power over management, which is selected by the government and the Communist Party (Qian 1999, p. 39). Lower levels of enterprise management are, in turn, appointed by top management. Thus, success for a manager still entails adherence to the directions provided by the manager's political supervisors. One essential feature of a typical state-owned enterprise anywhere in the world, therefore, remains constant. Even the reformed SOEs are strongly influenced by politicians, and politicians have multiple objectives. Profit maximization is, at best, only one of those objectives. Until enterprise managers are free to concentrate on increasing the sales made by their firms, cutting their costs in order to raise profits, and pursuing longer-term strategies to enhance competitiveness by building innovative capability, these Chinese enterprises will not fully respond to market signals, a point taken up in chapters 4 and 5.

THE FORMATION OF BUSINESS GROUPS

Another development in the ways that enterprises in China are owned and organized does not show up in the ownership statistics—but has for some time profoundly influenced the business practices of SOEs. This change relates to the formation of business groups (*qiye jituan*) referred to in chapter 1, through mergers and acquisitions. These business groups are being formed all over the nation and across all sectors.[11] By the early 1990s there were many such business groups, and by 1995 the total assets of known business groups amounted to 1,120 billion yuan (Keister 2000). Since then, the numbers of such groups and their total assets have continued to grow. Most enterprises of any size are now part of business groups (*qiye jituan*). The structure of these groups varies considerably, but most probably fall somewhere between a highly integrated conglomerate and the more loosely related firms of a Japanese *keiretsu*.[12] The three biggest groups are the Donglian Petrochemical Group, the Qilu Petrochemical Group, and the Baosteel Group. Others include groups formed by Haier and Konka (Smyth 2000).

Foreign investors are also participating in this mergers and acquisitions movement (Norton and Chao 2001). Once detailed data on business groups become available, it might be useful to analyze the performance of Chinese industry using group data to supplement what has been learned from individual enterprise statistics. But for now, it is possible only to explain how these groups are being formed and how they are structured.

Prior to reform, Chinese state enterprises (as pointed out in chapter 2) were little more than bureaus of the industrial ministries and the State Planning Commission, although formally they were independent accounting units.[13] Accounting, however, was the only sense in which these enterprises were independent. They were the bottom level of an administrative hierarchy, and, as such, it was general practice for an enterprise to be a single factory or a grouping of workshops in a particular location. As noted earlier, there was some effort in the early 1980s to merge these individual enterprises or factories into corporations; but the motivation for this was administrative efficiency. There were just too many individual enterprises for the ministries and the planning commission to monitor.

Consequently, at the beginning of the industrial reform period in the mid-1980s, China had one of the least concentrated industrial

---

11. The emergence of industrial groupings is widespread in East Asia, but it is commonplace in many industrializing and industrialized countries as well.

12. The *jituan* were strongly championed by Jiang Zemin following a visit to Korea in 1995. He thought that China should learn from the experience of conglomerates in Korea and Japan. Jiang Zemin observed that the performance of the U.S. economy depended upon 500 multinational corporations, while in Japan and Korea a far smaller number played a critical role. Thus, China too should rely on a few of its biggest SOEs "for economic development, industrialization and raising quality of the whole economy" (Lam 1999, p. 60–61). For a systematic look at the way these business groups are organized, see Keister (2000), chapter 4.

13. See World Bank (1997) for a discussion of how the state-enterprise assets were organized and managed.

organizations in the world; and as mentioned earlier, the size of even the leading firms was not large by international standards. The data for the various Chinese industrial sectors in 1988 are presented in table 3.2.

In the breakdown of the 39 industrial sectors represented in table 3.2, in only 8 sectors (3 connected with petroleum and 1 the tobacco monopoly) did firms with output of over 100 million yuan constitute more than 50 percent of the total output of that sector. In 17 of these 39 sectors, firms with gross output of 100 million yuan accounted for less than 10 percent of total output. Of a total of 420,000 individual enterprises with independent accounting systems, only 1,558 had revenues of 100 million yuan (or $27 million at the dollar/yuan exchange rate at that time). A firm in an advanced industrial economy with $27 million in revenue would be considered a small firm. In China, this amount would place a firm within the top 0.4 percent of all firms in terms of size.

International comparisons with China are difficult because the data are not plentiful, and measures of industrial concentration have used varying breakdowns of industry by sector. A large country will also, other things being equal, tend to be less concentrated than a small country. Still, the comparisons presented in table 3.3 make the essential point.

In China, in only 13 percent of the sectors (those mainly connected with petroleum) did the top 18 to 100 firms control more than 60 percent of the total output of a given sector in 1988. Data on the largest four firms in these sectors in China reveal that they controlled more than 60 percent of the output in only 6 percent of the industrial sectors. In Malaysia, the top four firms in a given industry controlled 59 percent of the industrial sectors; and in the Philippines, after liberalizing reforms, the comparable percentage was 26. Even in Taiwan (China), where small-scale industries have been the drivers of growth, the top four firms controlled 60 percent or more of output in 23 percent of the industrial sectors.

There are no established normative standards for judging whether a particular level of concentration is more efficient than another. Countries with competition laws, of course, have legal standards for judging when concentration is excessive; and these standards are based, to some degree, on the presumed impact of a particular level of concentration on long-term efficiency. Whatever the ideal industrial organization structure may be, however, there is little doubt that Chinese industry is less concentrated than any efficiency standard would dictate, although this is changing in the energy and petrochemical sectors. It then follows, as indicated in chapter 1, that it appears desirable for Chinese enterprises to merge with each other in order to enhance their efficiency and competitiveness in domestic and international arenas.

Table 3.2 Number of Chinese Enterprises

Enterprise	Total number of Chinese enterprises	Number of industrial enterprises over 100 million yuan	Share of firms with over 100 million in output	
			(% total number)	(% gross output)
All industry	420,929	1,558	0.37	29.55
Coal mining	9,230	55	0.60	53.99
Petroleum and gas	30	17	56.67	99.87
Iron mining	1,264	4	0.32	25.74
Nonferrous metals	2,233	6	0.27	16.01
Construction	9,971	0	0	0
Salt	605	605	100	19.45
Other mining	24	0	0	0
Wood and bamboo	2,981	16	0.54	25.56
Food manufactures	42,755	43	0.10	5.10
Beverages	14,406	17	0.12	6.81
Tobacco	298	92	30.87	89.20
Fodder	3,878	5	0.13	5.67
Textiles	24,017	236	0.98	21.86
Sewn products	18,017	4	0.02	2.75
Leather shoes, etc.	7,929	1	0.01	0.37
Wood products	11,000	1	0.01	1.12
Furniture	10,891	0	0	0
Paper products	10,182	23	0.23	10.62
Printing	10,732	2	0.02	2.11
Education products	3,897	1	0.03	1.76
Arts and crafts	10,671	2	0.02	1.81

(Table continues on the following page.)

Table 3.2 continued

Enterprise	Total number of Chinese enterprises	Number of industrial enterprises over 100 million yuan	Share of firms with over 100 million in output (% total number)	(% gross output)
Electricity supply, etc.	11,293	101	0.89	52.53
Petroleum products	690	38	5.51	95.26
Coke gas products	2,235	5	0.22	25.52
Chemicals	17,864	118	0.66	29.02
Pharmaceuticals	2,802	27	0.96	16.58
Chemical fibers	494	26	5.26	59.97
Rubber products	3,740	34	0.91	29.72
Plastics	14,065	7	0.05	2.76
Construction materials	55,859	17	0.03	3.12
Ferrous metal products	3,015	134	4.44	79.15
Nonferrous products	2,158	68	3.15	59.03
Metal manufactures	29,841	7	0.02	2.38
Machinery	43,059	161	0.37	18.81
Transport equipment	10,368	79	0.76	43.20
Electrical machinery	14,118	102	0.72	30.57
Communications equipment	4,159	96	2.31	48.96
Instruments	3,460	4	0.12	6.18
Other industries	5,544	1	0.02	1.51

Source: National Statistical Office (1989).

Table 3.3 Industry Concentration Ratio in East Asia

Indicator	United States 1963	Japan 1963	Korea, Rep. of 1974	Taiwan (China) 1976	Malaysia 1990	Philippines 1983	Philippines 1995	China 1988	China 2002
Largest firms	Top 4	Top 4	Top 5	Top 4	Top 4	Top 4	Top 4	Top 18–100	Top 4
Sample size (number)	417	512	205	131	22	31	31	39	17
Percent									
80–100	12.2	5.6	26.9	10.7	18.2	25.8	9.7	7.7	5.9
60–80	9.1	7.8	17.9	12.2	40.9	41.9	16.1	5.1	0
40–60	19.6	27.9	27.3	24.4	31.8	16.1	29	12.8	0
20–40	39.3	25.4	21.9	35.2	4.5	16.1	35.5	17.9	11.8
0–20	19.8	33.3	6	17.5	4.5	0	9.7	56.4	82.4
	100	100	100	100	100	100	100	100	100

Source: The Chinese data are derived from table 3.2.

In China, mergers occasionally result from the initiatives taken by two or more firms. Much of the time, however, both the national and local governments play a major role in merging successful firms with others.[14] The precise nature of these mergers varies, but most of the resulting business groups involve cross-shareholdings, interlocking directorships, and typically a core or lead firm together with a number of specialized firms, plus several other firms in related lines of business (Keister 2000).

The majority of merger decisions are orchestrated by the government when government officials may not be well qualified to make such judgments. There are no well-established international normative standards that these officials can refer to. So instead, it appears that many promoters of business groups look to the Korean *chaebol* or the Japanese *keiretsu* and argue that China, too, needs large business groups with internationally recognized brand names. Proponents of such groups argue that the mergers reduce interenterprise transaction costs and assist with the enforcement of property rights, which remain ill-defined in China. Business groups can also make it easier to coordinate investment decisions and can create an internal capital market that substitutes for missing financial institutions (Yafeh 2002; and footnote 41 in chapter 1 of this volume). Ironically, while some Chinese are looking at the *chaebol* as a model, the Korean government is investing a good deal of energy and political effort to induce a restructuring of the *chaebol* in an effort to reduce the economic and political power of these entities.[15] Moreover, the ties among *keiretsu* members and to their main banks were apparently never particularly tight and are growing weaker (Miwa and Ramseyer 2002; Yafeh 2002). These developments in the two countries where groups were most directly associated with economic performance underscore the significance of findings that question the utility of groups. These findings indicate that group members are not more profitable than other groups, do not allocate resources more efficiently, and do not enhance the quality of governance.

THE EMERGENCE AND SIGNIFICANCE OF NONSTATE FIRMS

In the late 1990s and after the year 2000, the other ownership forms of importance in China were collective enterprises, foreign-funded enterprises (including those funded by companies or individuals in Hong Kong,

---

14. For an example of government persuasion to affect a merger, see Keister (2000, p. 150).

15. See Graham (2003) on the efforts under way to restructure the *chaebol* and Westney (2001) on the changing nature of Japanese *keiretsu*.

China), domestic private firms, and limited liability corporations. There is more than a little overlap in these categories, but they have distinct definitions in the "Regulations on the Management of Registration of Corporations" and elsewhere. The rise and decline of the collective sector are among the more interesting phenomena in China during this period— and say a great deal about how the environment surrounding industrial enterprises was changing at that time.

The largest component of the collective sector comprised township and village enterprises that, as explained in chapter 2, grew (in part) out of the rural small-scale industry program that dates back to proto-industrialization in the early decades of the 20th century and the growth of rural collectivized industries from the 1960s onward. As a number of writers have pointed out, TVEs were not really collectives in the sense that most were owned and managed by their employees (Byrd and Lin 1990; Oi 1999); but they had close ties to and were often effectively controlled by the township and village governments where they were located. To Duckett (2001), they were the outgrowth of state entrepreneurialism spearheaded by local bureaus; but as described by Gore (1998), the state-sponsored TVEs often resulted from the entrepreneurship of individual bureaucrats. Local governments provided essential services to these enterprises and received a significant portion of their profits in return.[16] Among the services provided were protection from predation by elements of those same governments, access to capital from local credit institutions that were controlled by the state, and other forms of support in dealing with higher government officials. Firms that were really owned by an individual or a group of individuals frequently classified themselves as collective rather than private (wore the "red hat") because of the protection, support, and *guanxi* (connections) that could be garnered from such a classification. Firms that were formally private also had close ties to the local government for similar reasons (Dickson 2003). SOEs in cities such as Shanghai helped promote some of these TVEs through subcontracting arrangements and the provision of second-hand equipment, or as a way for the SOEs to circumvent government restrictions on the ability of state enterprises to hire more workers or to gain access to land needed to expand their operations (Ho 1994).

Many of these incentives for the formation of collective enterprises had begun to disappear by the latter half of the 1990s. Labor could migrate easily to the cities, even if most of that labor could not attain regular urban

---

16. For many purposes, given the central role of the local governments, it makes more sense to see the enterprises of an entire township as a single firm than to treat each enterprise as an independent decisionmaking organization. See Che and Qian (1998).

resident status (*hukou*), for example. More important, the state began to extend to private enterprises legal standing comparable to that possessed by state and collective enterprises. Large numbers of bank managers in the local branches of rural credit cooperatives and the Agricultural Bank became supporters of privatization and no longer depended so much on local government guarantees of loan repayment by the collective firms. Profitability mattered more, and the private firms (on average) were more profitable (Brandt, Li, and Roberts 2001; Park and Shen 2003).

Therefore, by 1996, and in some cases as early as 1993, a widespread if little noticed movement had begun to privatize many of the TVEs.[17] In a sample of 390 collectively owned firms in the two coastal provinces of Jiangsu and Zhejiang over the period 1993–9, 157 TVEs were completely privatized, usually by selling the firm to an individual or group of individuals; 111 became shareholding companies, with the township retaining majority control in only 31 of these cases; and 64 were declared bankrupt and closed down. In another 68 cases the township government sold off their shares to private parties.[18] This privatization was little noticed, in large part because the process was endogenous in the sense that it was driven by the localities responding to pressures to improve firm efficiency and competitiveness. Managers appointed by local governments to run local enterprises gradually evolved into TVE managers on fixed-payment contracts, who increasingly saw themselves as independent entrepreneurs and were hired on that basis by the local governments. As these managers gained increasing control rights over their firms, they performed better than their appointed counterparts—and the system spread to other localities across the country.[19] Partial confirmation of the positive impact of these changes can be found in a study of garment and metal casting enterprises in the Yangtze River area, which shows that privatization, at least in these industries, led to significant improvements in enterprise productivity (Sonobe and Otsuka 2003).

As TVEs declined in importance, firms owned and to a large degree controlled by businesses in Hong Kong (China) and in foreign countries rose both in number and in their share of total industrial output. The basic data on actually realized foreign direct investment are presented in figure 3.4. Entrepreneurs from Hong Kong (China) were the first to

---

17. On this, see the papers in Oi and Walder (1999).

18. These numbers and this paragraph are based largely on Brandt, Li, and Roberts (2001). The numbers add up to slightly more than 390, presumably because (in a few cases) a firm went through more than one ownership change during this period.

19. This theme is developed at length in a study of TVE management by Hongyi Chen (2000).

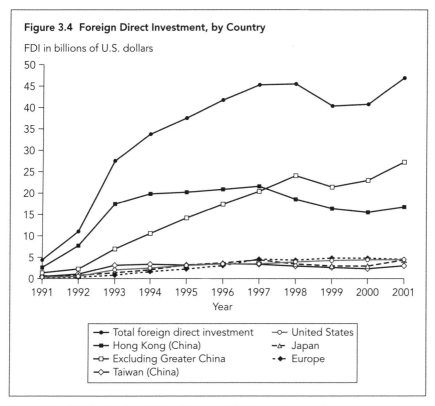

Figure 3.4 Foreign Direct Investment, by Country

FDI in billions of U.S. dollars

Legend:
- ●— Total foreign direct investment
- ○— United States
- ■— Hong Kong (China)
- △— Japan
- □— Excluding Greater China
- ◆— Europe
- ◇— Taiwan (China)

Source: China Statistical Yearbook (National Bureau of Statistics, various years).

take advantage of the opportunities to invest in China. They had the connections and understanding of how to operate in an environment where the legal institutions of a fully developed market economy were missing. However, as China gradually liberalized the terms under which foreign investment could enter the country, and as the legal framework supporting foreign investment began to develop, Japan and the more advanced market economies of the West began to invest more and more. By the year 2001, FDI from outside the greater China region accounted for half of all such investment. FDI took various forms, but it was all private in nature even when it involved a joint venture with a state enterprise. An unknown share of this investment involved "round-tripping" by domestic Chinese investors hoping to take advantage of the favored tax and regulatory treatment received by foreign investors through most of the 1990s. Round-tripping may also have increased management control rights over these enterprises, since it was harder for the government to interfere with a foreign-owned firm than a domestically owned enterprise. No doubt, there were other motives for round-tripping as well. Bermuda, the Cayman Islands, and the British Virgin Islands, for example, account for virtually all of the FDI coming to China from Latin America and the Caribbean ($6.9 billion in 2003); and there are many reasons why companies choose to channel their funds through offshore havens of this type ("China: Circulating Capital" 2003).

Much of the analysis of FDI in China and elsewhere emphasizes the motivations of multinational corporations in deciding to invest in one country or another and the advantages, or the disadvantages, that those multinational corporations bring to the recipient country. This analysis typically stresses the multinationals' search for cheap labor in order to remain competitive in labor-intensive industries, for reliable supplies of natural resources, and for access to the domestic market of countries with high trade barriers against foreign imports. From the FDI recipient-country point of view, the standard explanations for receiving FDI are the need to gain access to foreign technology and foreign management skills, the desire to increase capital formation by importing capital from abroad, and the desire to become a part of international production networks and gain access to foreign markets controlled by the multinational corporations. All of these considerations are present in the case of China, but they do not fully explain why FDI in China has grown so rapidly.

China, for example, has accepted large amounts of foreign direct investment in industries where there was little advanced technology to be accessed. The boom in FDI also occurred when China was itself in the process of becoming an exporter of capital. The import of $50 billion to $60 billion of FDI each year may seem like a large sum, but China's total gross investment in 2003 was 5,190 billion yuan (or $627 billion at the official exchange rate). Official Chinese outward FDI was $7 billion, and the "errors and omissions" term in the balance of payments was another $4.9 billion, most of which was probably caused by capital outflow.[20] In addition, there was, no doubt, a great deal of underinvoicing of exports and overinvoicing of imports to add another 10 or 20 billion dollars to the capital outflow total. Furthermore, there are many ways to gain access to foreign markets without allowing foreigners to acquire a major ownership stake in local industries, as demonstrated by Japan, the Republic of Korea, and Taiwan (China) in the 1960s through the 1980s, before their own companies gained direct access to foreign markets.

---

20. For more details, see "China Round Tripping" (2003), where the Hong Kong Connection is emphasized (the source of 200,000 of China's 389,549 foreign-funded enterprises). Also, it is noted that errors and omissions have run as high as negative $10 billion—but that this figure was a positive $7.8 billion in 2003—possibly in anticipation of a change in parity.

To fully understand the reasons for the rapid rise in FDI in China, one must go beyond these standard explanations and consider why many SOEs and local governments aggressively sought more FDI—unlike some of their East Asian neighbors. Much of the FDI, for example, involved foreign firms buying into the assets of shareholding firms which, as discussed earlier, were mostly SOEs. From the point of view of the SOEs, particularly the state enterprise that was in financial difficulty, transfer of their assets to an enterprise with partial but controlling foreign ownership was a way of effectively privatizing some of the more valuable assets of the firm. Ownership of the state portion of the shares of these firms might rest with a holding company; and that holding company often continued to be responsible for such liabilities as unfunded pension obligations of past employees, and bank loans in arrears. The new joint venture with the foreign company, however, often was able to avoid taking on these liabilities.

FDI in China did involve some green field investments that were wholly owned and controlled by foreign multinationals. But the official FDI total included much else, ranging from domestic Chinese funds round-tripping through Hong Kong (China) and the Cayman Islands, to privatization schemes involving both foreign firms and domestic state enterprises, to Hong Kong (China) and overseas Chinese ownership arrangements that were little more than subcontracting structured to reap the tax and regulatory advantages available to foreign investors. In most cases, the transformation to foreign ownership did involve some foreign management and could lead to complete foreign control. New technology not available on the international market was made available in some instances, although this was not generally the case. A large portion of China's manufactured exports were marketed through Hong Kong (China) to the rest of the world; at times this resulted in Hong Kong ownership of the producers, and sometimes it did not.[21] Therefore, in analyzing the effects of FDI on the Chinese economy and findings on the relative performance of foreign-invested firms (reported in chapter 5), it is important to take these varying forms of foreign investment into account and not just assume that one is dealing primarily with foreign multinationals that have complete control of the operations of the firms that they own.[22] Instead, there was a complex array of business relationships between Hong Kong (China), foreign, and domestic firms.

---

21. Hong Kong's share of Chinese goods imported into the territory for reexport rose from 5 percent of total Chinese exports in 1975 to 41 percent in 1989, well before the large-scale boom in FDI (Sun 1991, p. 136).

22. This discussion of FDI draws heavily on the works of Yasheng Huang (2003a, 2003b, 2004).

Finally, a few words should be said about the officially registered domestic private enterprises. Most analysts, when discussing the private sector, lump TVEs and foreign-invested firms into this category, but the Chinese government also recognizes individually owned enterprises and formally private domestic enterprises.[23] The latter now includes private shareholding enterprises as well as firms owned privately through other mechanisms, such as partnerships and sole proprietorships. The category "individually owned and managed enterprises" (*getihu*) is by definition very small, with seven or fewer employees. The category became formally of significance in the central government's statistical reports after 1984, and may now account for as much as 10 percent of the gross value of industrial output. Domestic enterprises formally registered as private are larger in scale, and in 2001 accounted for 9 percent of the gross value of industrial enterprises produce by firms "above a designated size" (excluding individual firms and other very small enterprises).[24] The rapid expansion of this latter category (up from only 6.1 percent of gross industrial output value in 2000) presumably reflects, to a significant degree, the re-registration of firms as private. Many of these small, private firms may have previously been registered under some other category, such as "collective." Given the absence of a consistent time series for either the individual or the private firms above a certain size category, these ownership categories are not analyzed further in this chapter.

MISSING MARKET INSTITUTIONS: THE WEAK LEGAL SYSTEM

In a true market economy where private businesses dominate, most decisions concerning enterprises are made without the executive branch of the government becoming involved, even for such major restructuring issues as bankruptcy and mergers and acquisitions. In a market economy, it is usually the firms themselves and their creditors that decide when a bankruptcy filing is appropriate—and if a bankruptcy should lead to restructuring or outright liquidation. Also in a market economy, it is the firms and their shareholders that decide whether to buy out another firm

---

23. For a discussion of the size of the private sector in China using various definitions of "private," see Garnaut and Song (2000).

24. See Wiemer and Tian (2001) for a discussion of how small-scale firms are included in the national accounts.

in either a friendly or hostile takeover. If the country has a competition or antimonopoly law, the executive branch may make a ruling on whether or not the proposed merger is consistent with maintaining a competitive market. But that is usually as far as it goes. When minority shareholders have evidence that management is diverting company resources for their personal use, these shareholders can go to court to obtain redress.

Such matters concerning corporate organization and governance can be handled without the involvement of government ministries, because there are rules governing bankruptcy, mergers and acquisitions, and minority shareholder rights, for example. Enforcement of those rules is not in the hands of a government ministry with the discretionary authority to decide whether or not it wants to enforce a specific rule in a particular situation. Enforcement of the rules is in the hands of either the courts or a regulatory agency that is largely independent of the executive branch of the government. In either case, the court or the regulatory agency has little discretion over the rules themselves—although findings of fact and the like do involve judicial or regulatory judgment.

In China, by contrast, most decisions of this type are at the discretion of senior officials in the executive branch of the government. China has had a bankruptcy law on the books since 1986; and in the second half of the 1990s, several thousands of state enterprises were declared bankrupt, involving the write-off of 126.1 billion yuan in bank loans (Mu 2003; Zhang 2004a).

Neither the creditors of the bankrupt enterprises nor the courts, however, played much of a role in deciding the fate of those enterprises. Government ministries and higher authorities typically ordered a healthy enterprise to absorb a poorly performing competitor. When that was not feasible, government ministries could order the closing of the enterprise. In 2003, the government created the State-Owned Assets Supervision and Administration Commission (SASAC), a super ministry directly under the State Council authorized to lay down the rules for the restructuring of SOEs. This agency brought together under one roof administrative functions previously performed by a half-dozen bodies (Green and Ming 2005). Some of the largest firms were directly supervised by the central offices of SASAC, while smaller firms were supervised by local state asset management agencies under its control (Mu 2003). The relevance of this approach to the management of state assets and supervision of the performance of state enterprises in general (not just the bankrupt enterprises) is that enterprise managers know their ultimate fate is in the hands of government supervisors. That fate might be decided strictly in accordance with the rules of bankruptcy on the books; but it will more likely be a negotiated solution in which management's relationship with higher government officials will play an important role.

In a market economy well furnished with institutions, the executive branch of the government also would not have much say in merger decisions, except where there was an indication that a merger would reduce competition to below some acceptable level determined by the competition laws of the country. The companies would work together and chart out a friendly merger on their own, or one company would merge with another in a hostile takeover. The decisions would be made by the business managers most familiar with the situation, and if they were wrong, those same managers would bear the consequences of their mistakes. All of this would take place in accordance with a set of legislated rules monitored and enforced by the judiciary or a regulatory body that was independent of the executive branch of the government. No such monitoring and enforcement mechanism yet exists in China.

In the absence of an independent judiciary or regulatory agency governed by detailed rules determined by the legislature, the executive branch perforce must intervene in merger decisions. But when local governments, government ministries, and higher-level officials play this kind or role, the enterprise is no longer an independent actor responding to market forces. The enterprise or the business group is, in part, a creation of the government; and the future of that enterprise or group is likely to depend critically on those same government officials. The distinction between what is private and what is public becomes blurred.

Bankruptcy, mergers and acquisitions, and minority shareholder rights are but three areas of corporate governance among many where a well-functioning market economy requires a key institution—an independent judiciary or independent regulatory body—to operate in consonance with market forces, not in response to the discretionary authority of government executive branch officials. But China (much like some of the other transition economies whose efforts to develop such institutions are discussed in chapter 4) both historically and currently has no tradition supporting an independent legal system. Historically, Chinese county magistrates, the lowest rung of the executive branch of the imperial government, doubled as judges in criminal trials. Commercial disputes rarely came before these magistrates and were usually settled through guild rules or other more informal procedures established by the merchants themselves. And during the Cultural Revolution (1966–76), Mao Zedong abolished the legal profession altogether. So when the reform period began, the government not only had to restore the legal system as it had previously existed but also had to fundamentally alter most of its commercial laws to make them consistent with the new market-oriented conditions.

Writing new laws is the easier half of the task, however. The real challenge is to create a judiciary that is technically competent, can render judgments based on the law without interference from other branches of the government, and can use bailiffs or the police force to enforce those judgments against parties in various commercial disputes.[25] In China, as in some of the other transition economies discussed in chapter 4, the reality is that the judges are not well trained, they are not independent of the politicians who rule the country, and they have limited powers or mechanisms by which to enforce their decisions. Government ministries and even powerful state enterprises can overrule or simply ignore their decisions.[26] Regulatory agencies in China are even less independent of the politicians—and are really little more than bureaus of the executive branch of the government. This situation is gradually changing, and in major cities on the coast the judiciary is beginning to play a more active role in commercial affairs. But China has a long way to go before most commercial disputes can be taken out of the discretionary hands of government officials and turned over to an independent body that follows the rules. Until this happens, even the most private of firms will have some of the same characteristics as state enterprises—they will be as much concerned with signals from government officials as they are with signals from the market (see Dickson 2003).

THE CONSEQUENCES OF REFORMS DURING 1997–2003

Reforms introduced through the early 1990s and since 1997 have changed the way Chinese enterprises are owned, managed, and organized, at least in a formal sense. But what differences do these many reforms make for the performance of enterprises? To appraise the overall performance of state enterprises during the first two decades of reform, one must look at the various estimates that have been made of total factor productivity

---

25. See Berglof and others (2003) on the Russian experience.
26. There is a large literature on Chinese legal reform. See, for example, Lubman (1999) and Clarke (1996).

(TFP) in Chinese industry in general and the SOE sector in particular. As indicated in chapter 1, there have been a great many efforts to estimate TFP in industry and in state-owned industry during the 1980s. Some of the early estimates were controversial, primarily because assumptions had to be made about how to deflate intermediate goods used in industry reported in current prices (Jefferson, Rawski, and Zheng 1992; Woo and others 1993). Since the publication of these earlier works, however, the statistical authorities in China have released to the public the relevant deflators, making it possible to arrive at somewhat more rigorous estimates.

The more credible industry TFP results for the 1980s suggest that TFP in Chinese state-owned industry grew at a little over 2 percent per year, while that of collective industry rose at a higher rate, perhaps over 4 percent per year. Later estimates of Jefferson and others, for the period 1980–92, give figures of 2.5 percent per year for state industry and 3.43 percent per year for the collective industrial sector (Jefferson and others 1999, pp. 138–140). Given that the state industrial sector grew at 7.7 percent per year in the 1980s, and the collective industrial sector at 18.7 percent per year, increases in inputs (capital, labor, and intermediate) accounted for roughly three-quarters of the growth of output in both the state and collective sectors and TFP for the remaining one-quarter.[27] The variation in TFP across industries was pronounced, ranging from negative TFP growth of 4 and 5 percent per year in such sectors as electric power and petroleum and natural gas, to positive figures of 5 and 6 percent per year, respectively, in machinery and automobiles (Li and others 1993, p. 69).

To assess the full impact of reforms in the 1980s on productivity, one would need estimates of TFP in SOEs for the pre-reform period as well. Unfortunately, the quality and availability of data for this earlier period are not adequate for the kinds of calculations that economists find convincing. The estimates that have been made for industry in the pre-reform period suggest that TFP growth was either near zero or negative (Jefferson and others 1999, pp. 138–9). Estimates of TFP for the economy as a whole in this earlier period also indicate that changes in TFP were

---

27. These figures are for the rate of increase in gross output of these sectors over the decade ending in 1990, which would have been somewhat higher than for the growth rate of value added in these sectors. The rate of increase in value added of all industry was 9.5 percent over this same period, but a breakdown of industry value added by ownership was not readily available. The gross value growth rates are appropriate to use in these TFP calculations, if the calculations include intermediate inputs as well as capital and labor.

negligible or negative.[28] There appears to be little doubt, therefore, that the reforms of the 1980s had a positive impact on the productivity performance of Chinese industry in general, and the state-owned industrial sector in particular. Further evidence that this was the case is the fact that real wages and urban incomes rose rapidly after 1978 but hardly at all during the pre-reform period, while the rate of investment as a share of GDP remained much the same. It would take extreme assumptions to attribute all of this rise in living standards to developments in the nonstate sector alone.

When assessing the more recent period, it is important to note that there is a major problem of selection bias in all of the comparisons made here. For example, in initial public offerings (IPOs) the China Securities Supervisory Commission in 1997 gave preference to state firms that had taken over loss-making SOEs (Zhang 2004a). Therefore, whatever the long-term impact of being able to sell shares on the stock exchanges, the short-term impact was probably to lower the profits of these state enterprises. Similarly, some of the SOEs that converted into foreign-invested enterprises often did so because they were in financial trouble (Huang 2003b). However, the reported profitability of these new enterprises would depend on which liabilities of the former state-owned firm the "new" foreign enterprise had to acquire. Foreign firms that could leave many of these liabilities behind in a state holding company presumably registered a large jump in profits, although not necessarily a rise in TFP. And some researchers reported that state enterprises making losses were the most likely to be privatized or liquidated through bankruptcy or merger.[29]

Data presented in figures 3.1 and 3.5 indicate that profits of state enterprises as a percentage of gross output bottomed out during the recession of 1990, having fallen rapidly in the preceding reform years. With economic recovery, the profit rate rose slightly through 1993, and slowly fell again through 1996.[30] Measured as the return on assets rather than as a percentage of gross value output, profits in the state sector were lower

---

28. Crude estimates of TFP growth are easier to make for the economy as a whole than for subsectors of industry, largely because one can work with the aggregate capital stock and labor force data that are available (or can be readily derived for this earlier period, and, at least in the case of value added, can be deflated in a way that removes the massive relative price distortions of the 1950s through the 1970s). See Perkins (2001, p. 282).

29. See, for example, Li and others (2001).

30. The size of the losses by enterprises that made losses rose during the first part of the 1990s. Zhang (2000) speculates that this may be due to the fact that many firms at that time were unable

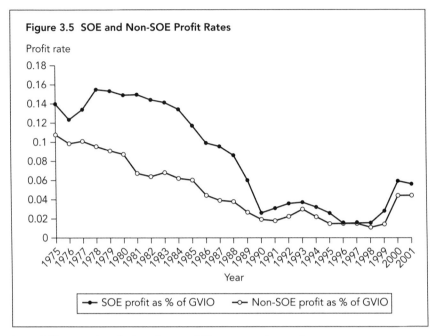

Figure 3.5 SOE and Non-SOE Profit Rates

Note: GVIO, gross value of industrial output; SOE, state-owned enterprise.
Source: China Statistical Yearbook (National Bureau of Statistics, various years).

than in the other sectors; but the difference is narrowed if one includes sales or value-added taxes (VATs) in profits. State industries were more concentrated in sectors with higher VATs, and these cut more deeply into profits (Holz 2002).[31] However, some of the sectors with high sales or value-added taxes also earned high monopoly profits, notably tobacco.

Profits rose sharply in 1999 and continued to rise rapidly through the first half of 2003.[32] Because the profit rate in private and other nonstate

to take advantage of the economies of scale that existed in many of these industries at that time, and so operated at a high cost. This was a period of increasing concentration of industrial organization, at least in some sectors, as firms attempted to take advantage of these scale economies.

31. Holz measures profit relative to assets, while in this study profit is related to gross value output. Assets and net assets in the Chinese system are calculated at their value at the time of purchase or installation. Thus, given the high level of inflation in this period, assets as reported should significantly understate the true value of those assets at the prices in 2000 or 2001. Whether or not this would be equally true for the assets of nonstate enterprises would depend on when those assets were acquired relative to when state sector assets were acquired. See also Cheng and Lo (2002).

32. State enterprise profits in the first half of 2003 rose by 77.4 percent over the comparable period in 2002 ("Industry Profits Jump" 2003).

enterprises behaved much the same as in the state sector during this period, it seems to be a reasonable presumption that profit rates were driven more by general economic conditions in China than by factors unique to the state sector. As noted at the beginning of this chapter, with prices freed up, the entry of new firms mainly in the nonstate sector drove down final product prices and drove up input costs, for both state and nonstate enterprises. But to attribute the decline in state sector profits entirely to external events beyond that sector's control would be misleading. It was the state sector that benefited from state bank loans; and state enterprises gained the most when China began making an effort to clean up the books of the state banks. In the 1996–8 period, China's state banks wrote off 120 billion yuan in state enterprise debt; and in 1999 the government converted 350 billion yuan in state enterprise debt of these banks (or of the asset management companies) into equity shares (Lin and Zhu 2001). But the leap in profits in 1999 through 2004 occurred in the nonstate sector as well, and the nonstate sector did not benefit significantly from these efforts to clean up the books of the state banks. Something else was going on, but what?

A partial answer to this question can be found in the data for profits by sector. Of the total profits of enterprises with independent accounting units in the state sector, including shareholding firms with majority state control, 72.1 percent of those profits in 2001 came from four sectors: petroleum and gas extraction, tobacco processing, ferrous metal smelting, and the processing and supply of electric power. Total state enterprise profits in that year were 239 billion yuan, with 172 billion yuan accounted for by sectors where the state still had an effective monopoly of most production. In 1998, before the large run-up in the profits of state enterprises, total state sector profits were only 52.5 billion yuan, but the main sources of those profits were the same four sectors. By contrast, the main sources of profits of foreign-funded enterprises in 2001 were electrical and telecommunications equipment and machinery, transport equipment, and electric power supply sectors.[33] The rise in state sector profits after 1998, therefore, was largely unrelated to major improvements in overall state sector profitability—although six loss-making sectors did move into the profit column. The main increase in profits instead came from sectors where the Chinese government could charge monopoly prices (tobacco,

---

33. These data are from the *China Statistical Yearbook* (National Bureau of Statistics 1999, 2001). The 1999 yearbook breaks down profits by industrial sector—not by both industrial sector and ownership. But most of the profits came from the four sectors where state ownership was total or dominant.

ferrous metal processing where the government controlled most of the iron mines and iron ore imports, and electric power) or from petroleum (where China benefited from the rise in world oil prices).

Other sets of data that have some bearing on state enterprise perfor-mance are the various indicators of the productivity of individual factors of production. The rate of return on capital valued at the original pur-chase price of that capital, for example, fell from 24.8 percent in 1978 to 7.7 percent in 1999 (Industry and Transport Department of the National Bureau of Statistics 2000, p. 54). But this reflects the same forces at work discussed earlier, where profits were reported as a percentage of the gross value of industrial output.

Labor productivity data are even more revealing. In the state industrial sector, labor productivity in constant 1990 prices rose from 32,304 yuan per worker in 1991 to 85,876 yuan in 1999. But labor productivity in the collective sector increased even more rapidly, from 20,664 yuan in 1991 (two-thirds of that in the state sector) to 114,490 yuan (a third higher than in the state sector). State industrial sector labor productivity thus rose at 13 percent a year. In contrast, labor productivity in the collective sector (if the data can be believed and are truly in constant prices) rose at 24 percent per year. Labor productivity in "other" enterprises, mainly those involving FDI, rose at 12 percent a year (Industry and Transport Department of the National Bureau of Statistics 2000, p. 55).

Before leaving these partial productivity figures, it is useful to look at the relationship between energy use and industrial output. The data presented in figure 3.6 are for all industry, not just the state sector, but state sector performance is likely to be quite similar.

During the era of central planning, state industrial enterprises were profligate users of energy and electric power, despite the fact that plants often had to be shut down for long periods each day because of the short-age of electricity.[34] By the end of the 1970s, Chinese industry was using twice as much electric power per unit of value added as in the 1950s. With the reforms, in contrast, the use of electricity per unit of industrial value added fell back to the level of the 1950s. In this one area, at least, there was a dramatic improvement in efficiency; and the pace of improvement in the efficient use of electric power was more rapid in the 1990s than in the previous decade.

Partial productivity figures are a weak guide to the overall performance of industry, however. To appraise overall performance one must return to

---

34. By 1985, Smil (1993, p. 74) estimates that China's energy intensity was comparable to that of the Soviet Union and Poland, but twice that of Japan.

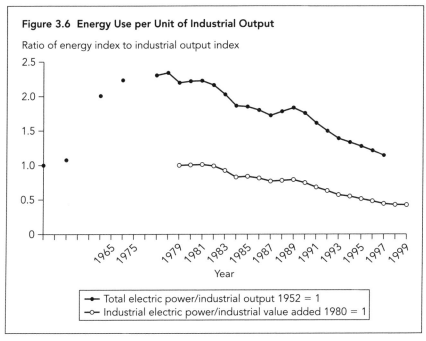

Figure 3.6 Energy Use per Unit of Industrial Output

Source: *China Statistical Yearbook* (National Bureau of Statistics 1997, 2002); National Statistical Office Industry and Transport Bureau 2000.

estimates that have been made of total factor productivity or of other measures of the efficiency of Chinese industry in general and the state-owned sector in particular. The estimates of TFP or of other methods of enterprise efficiency for the 1990s and the first years of the 21st century are not yet as plentiful as those for the 1980s, but some careful estimates do exist.

One estimate of "technical efficiency" of Chinese industrial enterprises by ownership type in 1995 (briefly noted in chapter 1) makes use of the data in the Third Industrial Census of China.[35] Because of the large size of this dataset, there are enough observations to evaluate six major industrial sectors separately. The concept of technical efficiency refers to the deviation of each enterprise's production function from a frontier production function for that industry. State enterprises in this study consistently have the lowest technical efficiency of all the ownership types in each of the six industrial sectors.[36] Collective enterprises perform

---

35. The discussion in this paragraph is based on Wen, Li, and Lloyd (2002).

36. The six sectors studied are textiles, garments and other fiber products, transport equipment, original chemical medicine, chemical medicine preparation, and cement manufacturing.

better than state enterprises across the board, but below the level of foreign joint ventures. Wholly owned foreign firms actually perform less well than foreign joint ventures in textiles and garments, but better in transport equipment. Joint ventures with overseas Chinese firms did as well as foreign joint ventures in textiles, but less well in transport equipment. Data for domestic private firms were available only for the textile sector, but in that sector these enterprises outperformed all other ownership categories. Shareholding enterprises did as well as foreign joint ventures for the most part, which probably should not be surprising since most of the firms allowed to list on the stock exchanges in 1995 were from among the more successful state enterprises.[37]

A second set of estimates makes use of firm-level accounting data for the years 1995 through 1998.[38] The sample size ranges from 66,544 to 84,359 depending on the variable selected. The study examines both profitability and total factor productivity. Among the findings of relevance in this study are that 36.2 percent of the enterprises were making losses over this period, and 51.9 percent had negative total factor productivity. Of these firms, 4.2 percent actually had negative value added; they took more out of the economy than they put back in. When enterprises are weighted by the size of their assets or the number of employees, loss-making enterprises account for 26 to 35.2 percent of the total, and negative productivity enterprises for 43.5 to 47.9 percent of the total. As these results indicate, larger firms performed somewhat better than smaller firms. Unfortunately, this study was unable to assess the effects of ownership on the performance of the firms in this sample.

A third set of estimates is that by Jefferson and Su (2002) for the years 1995 through 1999.[39] They find that TFP was positive for all state enterprises in their sample of 2,489 firms, but that state firms consistently performed below the levels of all other kinds of ownership, with foreign-invested firms from OECD countries performing the best. Total factor productivity in the various nonstate sectors was, in most years, 50 to 100 percent higher than in the state sector.

Within the SOE sector, firms wholly owned by the state performed less well than firms where the state share was more than 50 percent but less than 100 percent; and these latter firms had a lower level of TFP than firms where the state share was less than half. It is tempting to conclude from

37. These data are from table 8, adapted from Wen, Li, and Lloyd (2002, p. 725).
38. This paragraph is based on Xiao and others (2002).
39. The discussion that follows is based on Jefferson and Su (2002).

these figures that the shareholding system improved SOE performance. But it is also possible that the better-performing enterprises sold a higher percentage of their shares to the nonstate sector, which is supported by the authors' survey findings.

Finally, the Jefferson-Su paper compares TFP between the coastal and interior provinces and finds that large and medium-size enterprises (LMEs) in the former outperformed those in the latter. China's interior, of course, has fewer foreign-invested enterprises and fewer collective enterprises. It is a region still dominated by SOEs, which is now struggling to catch up but showing some signs of performance gains that are captured by the authors' survey findings.

These productivity estimates, therefore, are broadly but not entirely consistent with the qualitative discussion in this chapter. There have been real reforms of the ownership, management, and organization of SOEs that have affected productivity in the state-owned industrial enterprise sector, but these reforms have fallen well short of transforming these enterprises into independent market-oriented firms that behave much like their counterparts in the private or collective sectors. The "halfway house" of corporatization has released the potential of a few reformed SOEs, such as TCL and Changhong, but has not stimulated performance more widely. Neither has the formation of groups. And experience elsewhere in East Asia offers little support for the efficacy of such groups—and certainly does not justify government efforts to deliberately create groups through directed mergers. The overall impression is that the reform process is incomplete and needs to be followed through. Restructuring of SOEs without relinquishing state control of the LMEs has been tried, and the results have been fairly meager. Full privatization seems to be the logical next step, but the experience of other transition economies has raised many questions. Hence, before proceeding with our own analysis, we provide a review of the literature on SOE privatization, contrasting the results from Eastern Europe with those of China to date.

CHAPTER 4

CHINESE OWNERSHIP REFORM
IN THE EAST EUROPEAN MIRROR

The discussion in chapter 1 briefly noted the scale of privatization worldwide since the mid-1980s, along with principal outcomes. Chapters 2 and 3 traced China's gradual move away from the socialist pattern of industrial ownership and its piecemeal adoption of the institutions of a market economy. This transition was accomplished by increasing export orientation, expanding foreign direct investment (FDI), and by the unexpected success of township and village enterprises (TVEs) through the mid-1990s. As the relative advantages of autonomously managed firms operating in a competitive market environment have become increasingly apparent, China's reform-minded policymakers have sought to realize the potential gains from furthering the transformation of enterprise ownership within their perceived social and political parameters.

Evidence to date on privatization efforts (see tables A4.1–A4.3 in the annex to this chapter) indicates that permitting the divestiture and full privatization of the vast majority of state and collective industrial enterprises would help the Chinese government better come to grips with an array of economic and social challenges.[1] These include problems related to the quality of management, the weakness of corporate governance, the ineffectiveness of enterprise groups, the suboptimal size and geographic

---

1. Contrary to the findings of most other empirical work is Aussenegg and Jelic's (2002) study of 154 privatized firms from the Czech Republic, Hungary, and Poland that were listed on their national stock exchanges during 1991–3. Data for the period through 1998 show that these firms experienced a reduction in profitability and efficiency, regardless of whether the firms were subject to voucher or case-by-case privatization. One possible explanation for this result may be the large government shareholding in most of the firms in the sample. However, the authors maintain that partially privatized firms did better than fully privatized ones.

location of many enterprises, excess capacity in certain subsectors, and a lack of readiness on the part of most business entities to operate in a competitive free market environment. Further reforms are needed if China's business enterprises are to adopt the structure, strategies, incentives, and networking arrangements of the modern international corporations that will increasingly be their competitors. Ownership reform would also constitute a major step toward resolving the flow of nonperforming loans into bank portfolios.[2] Finding strategies to address these problems is vital for future competitiveness, and will depend upon the implementation of policies that first, facilitate the transfer of the ownership of most industrial state-owned enterprises (SOEs) into private hands and second, embrace the development of market institutions and the dismantling of barriers to a competitive environment and, in turn, facilitate entry and exit and induce efficiency and promote innovation. Future enterprise reform in China inevitably will be path-dependent and imbued with "Chinese characteristics." However, the design and implementation of policies, and the crafting of institutions, can be informed by decades of international experience on using privatization to advance business profitability, productivity, and growth.

INDUSTRIAL REFORMS IN EASTERN EUROPE

The industrialized countries took the lead in redefining the role of the state with respect to the market, by scaling back industrial policies and transferring publicly owned productive assets to the private sector beginning in the 1980s.[3] Since the early 1990s, developing and transition economies have also embraced privatization in an effort to enhance industrial performance, raise efficiency, or—as in the case of Brazil—defuse a fiscal crisis arising from budget and public sector deficits (Baer and Bang 2002). In most cases countries have been able to overcome the practical difficulties posed in valuing the assets and liabilities of firms, given the inadequacy of accounting statements. They have also coped with the limited scale of financial markets and the small pools of capital at the disposal of potential domestic

---

2. For instance, Cull and Xu (2000) find that bank employees were better able to assess the credit risks of the SOEs in the 1980s than were bureaucrats in China. However, they report that the quality of credit assessment deteriorated during the 1990s, contributing to the further accumulation of nonperforming loans by banks in China.

3. The onset of privatization in Western Europe dates back to 1984, when the British government sold off British Telecom. This was followed by the privatization of public corporations in France, beginning in 1986, a trend that continued through the 1990s.

buyers (Brada 1996). For these countries, privatization constitutes a fundamental step toward a market-directed and faster growth path over the longer term.[4] From a comprehensive survey of the literature, Megginson and Netter (2001) conclude, "Privatization increases profitability and productivity of firms: This consistency is perhaps the most telling result we report—privatization appears to improve performance in many different ways in many different countries" (p. 347). This sentiment is echoed in the Chong and López-de-Silanes (2005) review of the Latin American experience, in which privatization has raised profitability and productivity, improved the fiscal situation, and on balance benefited the poor. Countries that have ventured down this path have reduced the size of the public sector, and, in most cases circumscribed the scope of direct public involvement in productive activities. By and large, divestiture has allowed governments to reduce the budgetary costs imposed by loss-making public firms and derive large, one-time fiscal benefits from the sale of assets. Well-designed and effectively implemented privatization programs have expedited the orderly exit of failing firms and, in the majority of cases, enabled survivors to raise productivity and financial performance by exposing them more fully to competitive pressures and allowing them to enhance pecuniary incentives for management and other employees.[5] Where the design or execution was seriously flawed, however, privatizations have imposed large costs as a result of asset-stripping by the new owners, a sharp skewing in the distribution of national wealth, substantial medium-run disruption in industrial production, and few if any longer-term gains in corporate performance. Through the 1990s, privatized Russian firms generally performed little better than SOEs with respect to labor productivity and total factor productivity (TFP), and engaged in limited restructuring (Radygin and Entov 2001; Bhaumik and Estrin 2003).

Transition economies have employed a variety of schemes, including voucher privatizations (in Albania and the Czech Republic, and initially, in Poland), loans for shares, leasing and buyout (in Russia), and share-offering asset sales (Eastern Germany and Hungary) (Brada 1996).

---

4. The message of the "fundamental theorem of privatization" is that neither private nor public production provides the ideal solution to the problems that arise from the delegation of responsibilities when the available information is imperfect (Stiglitz 1994, p. 194). To those who believe that privatization is a solution to the ills of public ownership, Sappington and Stiglitz (1987) point out that private ownership would have to satisfy a number of restrictive conditions before the public objectives of equity and efficiency were met.

5. Following privatization of public enterprises in the United Kingdom between 1984 and 1991, financial incentives for managers improved significantly, which appears related to gains in company performance (Cragg and Dyck 2003).

Essentially, the modes of privatization were grouped into two categories: nonequivalent privatization and equivalent privatization. Both mass (voucher) privatization, which at one stroke transferred all ownership rights to citizens, and employee privatization, which gave majority or full ownership of an enterprise to employees, fall into the first category. Under equivalent privatization, the value of state industrial assets was first evaluated as a prelude to the creation of joint stock companies in which employees were given a portion of the equity, a portion was sold to the public, and the balance remained with the state. Although initially nonequivalent privatization enjoyed popular support because of its egalitarian stance, equivalent privatization subsequently came to be viewed as more supportive of stock market and financial development.

A major drawback of voucher privatization, for example, was that it flooded the market with equity for which demand in the early stages of transition was modest. This imbalance allowed well-placed insiders and others with access to liquid assets to buy large volumes of shares at low prices. In the case of Russia, 23,000 firms were privatized in one swoop—with about 20 percent of the shares going to managers, 40 percent to workers, and the government retaining about 20 percent of the shares (Aslund 2002). Thus, the majority of firms affected remained under the control of insiders. In 1995, the government accepted a proposal by a group of bankers to lend to the state in exchange for shares in 12 strategic firms. When the loans were not repaid during a stipulated period, the shares were then auctioned—and the bankers, well connected with the Yeltsin regime, were able to acquire control of key firms in the resource-based industries.

The message from these varied approaches, summarized by Megginson and Netter (2001), is that "where possible, firms should be privatized for cash in as transparent a method as possible and through an auction or sale process that is open to the broadest possible cross-section of potential buyers (including foreigners)" (pp. 358, 364). In hindsight, although the voucher-based privatizations in Albania, the Czech Republic, and Russia during 1992–4 did succeed in transferring state-owned assets into private hands, they sharply changed the distribution of wealth, inflicted some avoidable costs—economic and political—during the transition process, and did not, at least initially, lead to significant gains in economic outcomes.[6] For this reason, according to Goldman (1997, p. 43), "the general

---

6. Brada (1996) voices the earlier expectations that the use of vouchers would bring able outsiders into the ranks of management. And Dlouhy and Mladek (1994) voice the earlier positive views of Investment Privatization Funds in the Czech Republic. Ellerman (2001) provides a more recent and critical assessment of voucher privatizations in the Czech Republic and Russia.

public felt cheated . . . . In the vast majority of cases, the managers ran off with the proceeds or the funds simply evaporated. In the end, the average citizen ended up with nothing."[7]

The situation, however, has begun to change since the late 1990s. Following privatization and a period of adjustment, some aspects of company performance, especially unit costs and labor productivity, have started to show signs of improvement (Perevalov, Gimadii, and Dobrodei 2000). In Russia, at least, growth of GDP has averaged 6 percent per year since the late 1990s, led by the large, generally outsider-controlled, privatized corporations such as Sibneft, Lukos, and Norilsk Nickel. These firms have begun restructuring and are now performing far better than the state-owned firms, although their productivity and profitability are on par with that of other smaller, privately owned businesses (World Bank 2004b). The later experience of Poland partially validates the belief that drove Russian reformers to pursue rapid privatization. By deferring the privatization of larger firms and the networked industries, the Polish authorities permitted insiders to become more firmly entrenched and to mobilize stronger political resistance to privatization. In fact, at a lecture in November 2003, Leszek Balcerowicz observed that with the benefit of hindsight, it was a mistake for Poland to have delayed the privatization of its larger firms. This process has slowed to a crawl since 2001, primarily because of political opposition ("Pivotal Privatisation" 2004). Rapid and more widespread reform would have been a more effective strategy (Balcerowicz 2003). Balcerowicz's remarks echo the views of other Polish researchers on the design and pace of privatization. The realization that state ownership continues to hamper efficiency and restrain the development of financial intermediaries prompted the Russian government to embark on a further round of privatization. This is overdue, because the state's share of industry remains large. There are 9,860 state-owned companies, 718 incorporated companies where the state has a majority share, and 3,500 companies in which it has a minority share ("Russia: Government Aims" 2003; "Russia: Government Plans" 2003). However, the de facto renationalization of the Yukos petroleum empire in 2004 has

---

7. For an earlier and relatively optimistic assessment of privatization in Russia, see Boycko, Shleifer, and Vishny (1995). For a far less positive evaluation that dwells on the looting of state assets, the negligible gains in enterprise efficiency in spite of the potential for doing so with modest effort (McKinsey Global Institute 1999), and the small increase in revenue generated by the first round of privatization, see Goldman (2003). Even as recently as 2003, the majority of the population remained skeptical about the benefits from privatization, and 58 percent of those polled felt that a criminal investigation of the privatization in the 1990s was warranted ("Russia: Government Plans" 2003).

raised questions regarding the commitment to privatization—at least in the energy sector.

The methods and pace of privatization efforts in Eastern European countries provide a rich source of knowledge on the effectiveness and consequences of various privatization policies. The next section briefly reviews the specific aspects of the Eastern European experience that may provide the Chinese policymakers with insights on the privatization of state-owned enterprises.

LESSONS FROM EASTERN EUROPE

For purposes of ownership reform in China over the near term, the experience of the transition economies in Eastern Europe can offer some valuable lessons, most of which reinforce current thinking in China with regard to the direction that change should take, although there are areas of divergence. These lessons cover a range of pertinent issues including the speed at which enterprises are divested, the sequencing of reforms, the concentration of ownership, the mode of disposal employed, and several others (see, for example, Green 2005).

Pace of Reforms

One of the most important issues mentioned in chapter 1 of this volume concerns the speed of privatization. Unlike China, which adopted a cautious approach to reform, some of the transition economies (such as the Czech Republic and Russia) chose to move forward quickly so as to sustain reform momentum by harvesting early economic gains.[8] When these attempts faltered, the "Big Bang" approach to ownership reform acquired an undeserved, negative reputation among policymakers. In fact, the speed of privatization apparently has less bearing on its success than does the design of the program and parallel efforts at institution-building. Russia's reforms initially foundered, primarily because the institutional

---

8. Every step toward reform was preceded by debate, disagreements, and experiments to test the concept. Guthrie (1999, pp. 103–4) notes, "Price reform followed the course of gradual reform laden with politics, experimentation, and piecemeal implementation," which began in 1979 and continued through the late 1990s. Until recently, the state remained wary about enlarging the scope of the private sector. The emergence of TVEs was not premeditated—and took the Chinese leadership by surprise (Becker 2000, p. 68). While one school of researchers sees a "substantial ex post coherence to the Chinese reform process" (Naughton 1995, p. 309) and views the Chinese reform through experimentation as a successful strategy, others believe that "gradualism results primarily from a lack of consensus over the proper course with powers still divided between market reformers and old-style socialists" (Woo 1999, p. 117).

infrastructure of a market economy had been obliterated, and in its place a stultifying and pervasive network of controls and subsidies emerged. As Goldman (2003, p. 38) observes, when reform ensued, newly privatized firms did not deliver better results than the state-owned entities they displaced, because market and other institutions supporting financial development and governance were slow to materialize. But as Aslund states, Russian reformers may not have been wrong in grasping for opportunities as they arose. He observes,

> The main consideration for the timing of privatization should be if and when it is politically possible. Russia proved that mass privatization was possible immediately after the collapse of communism, when the expectations of various social strata were vague. It facilitated privatization politically. Poland, by contrast, illustrates the difficulties inherent in privatizing large enterprises later. Each privatization has to be negotiated for years truncating choices, because vested interests have been activated and hardened and have to be paid off. (Aslund 2004, p. 26)

China chose to defer privatization based on calculations made by the leadership at various times during the 1980s and 1990s, calculations that were influenced by the decentralized nature of controls over SOEs.

At this point, issues of sequencing are somewhat moot. More than a decade after the start of reforms in the Commonwealth of Independent States (CIS), it appears that those at the forefront of liberalization and privatization did better with respect to a number of economic and social indicators compiled for the period 1991–2001.[9] Growth was higher in the Czech Republic, Hungary, Poland, and Slovenia than in the gradual reformers, as was income equality, labor productivity, and ecological efficiency.[10] Conditions prior to reform undoubtedly had a hand in this, but policy surely played a bigger role.

Sequencing of Reforms

Much analytic effort has been devoted to delineating the sequence of reforms in transition economies; but it does not appear that optimal phasing of the privatization process has yet been achieved, although some of the building blocks of a successful privatization program are now better understood. When transition economies confronted the prospects of

---

9. The CIS countries are Armenia, Azerbaijan, Belarus, Kazakhstan, the Kyrgyz Republic, Moldova, the Russian Federation, Tajikistan, Turkmenistan, Ukraine, and Uzbekistan.

10. Havrylyshyn (2004, p. 41) finds that of the "nine rapid reformers eight have done very well. Most of those that choose a more gradual path have had fewer economic benefits and surprisingly higher costs." See also Balcerowicz (2003) and Green (2005).

large-scale privatization in the early 1990s, the questions of pace and sequencing were widely debated—as there were few rules to guide reformers. Policymakers and academic specialists alike were caught unprepared. In the absence of empirically verified guidelines, observers relied on their beliefs. One widely voiced belief was that mass privatization was the nettle to be grasped; a gradual, step-by-step reform risked being derailed by political resistance to privatization from affected employees of SOEs (Baltowski and Mickiewicz 2000; Aslund 2004).[11] A contending belief was that mass privatization rapidly implemented was the only way of quickly introducing decisive change. But its utility was questionable and its effectiveness could be compromised by the absence of the institutions needed to strengthen corporate accountability, focus management attention on profitability and efficiency, and increase access to new finance. A sequencing of reforms was also favored in some instances because of the cost and uncertainties of mass privatization. A sequence of sales was seen as a way to pace the availability of managerial talent, which came to be viewed as a vital ingredient for the success of newly privatized firms.[12] Sequencing provided information on SOEs to prospective buyers, and (by lessening the bunching of transactions) could raise the price received by the government for the average enterprise sale (Gupta, Ham, and Svejnar 2001).[13]

Experience has shown that the appropriate course of action for privatization is by no means straightforward—and depends upon country-specific circumstances. The Hungarian and Polish experiences now suggest that prior opening of the economy to competitive pressures can prepare SOEs for the conversion to private ownership and shorten both the length and severity of post-privatization adjustments. SOEs can be exposed to competition from foreign companies through a lowering of trade barriers or through FDI in local ventures. Competition can also be generated through a lowering of barriers to new firms, and by incentives that assist in the development of a private—or at least a nonstate—domestic sector that contests markets dominated by SOEs.

---

11. Stiglitz (1994, p. 192) sums up the concerns about timing as follows: "Much of the debate on timing is based on a balance of political judgments concerning the political consequences of an excessively slow privatization and the possibility that in the interim, the commitment to privatization and markets may be weakened."

12. Research by Boycko, Shleifer, and Vishny (1995) on the privatization of 452 small-scale Russian commercial establishments showed that improved performance was related to the infusion of new managerial talent brought by outsiders who acquired the shops.

13. From their study of two waves of privatization in the Czech Republic (in 1992 and 1993), Gupta, Ham, and Svejnar (2001) concluded that the more profitable downstream enterprises confronting more volatile market conditions were the ones privatized first—in the interest of revenue maximization by the government.

These pressures, if combined with a hardening of the budget constraints on SOEs and a signaling of impending privatization, can initiate the changes in organization, production methods, and customer orientation needed to enhance efficiency.

In both Hungary and Poland, commercialization and corporatization (through employee ownership in Poland) of smaller enterprises, and some large firms, began creating a competitive environment in the 1980s (Bornstein 1999). In the lead-up to privatization in the 1990s, governments also attempted to harden budget constraints on public sector utilities. Ten years after privatization commenced in Poland in 1991, the share of SOEs had gradually been reduced to about 20 percent of GDP. Ownership reform had raised efficiency by introducing changes in management and by ensuring that equity holders invested in the companies they acquired. Privatization, although long drawn, served the useful purpose of depoliticizing the allocative process and subjecting firms to market-based rather than politically motivated decisions (Baltowski and Mickiewicz 2000). By contrast, economic reform in Russia resulted in a fourfold increase in small and medium-size enterprises (SMEs) to 800,000 between 1992 and 1994. Since then, however, the sector has stagnated because of entry barriers, regulatory constraints, and lack of financing. And the 886,000 SMEs (in 2003) have contributed relatively little to the emergence of a competitive market ("Russia: Small Businesses" 2003). Among the reasons for this are the ownership stakes of regional governments in the older large and medium-size enterprises (LMEs). While partially or largely privatized, these firms retain close links with subnational governments, are easier to tax, and hence continue to receive favors as well as a degree of protection from new entrants (Slinko, Yakovlev, and Zhuravskaya 2003; Gehlbach 2003).

The preparatory institution-building has been ongoing in China for much longer than was the case in Europe, and on a much larger scale. Most prices in China are now determined through the market mechanism, trade and FDI have both expanded enormously, the nonstate sector now dwarfs state-owned industries, and the various levels of government have been hardening budget constraints—first, by largely eliminating fiscal support for the SOEs and forcing them to turn to banks and the financial markets, then by stepping up the pressure on banks to increase the stringency of their lending practices (most recently through the terms of China's accession to the WTO). Furthermore, the state in China has repeatedly engaged in piecemeal reform of SOEs and, through its actions since 1997, signaled a willingness to consider ownership reform that had been largely ruled out until recently. Many elements of an open and competitive market are now in place in China, including numerous industrial federations, associations, and guilds that are gradually acquiring the capacity to represent the interests of their member firms (Kennedy 2005). Thus, the utility of prolonging the reform efforts for other elements to fall into place seems to be rather modest.

Biases of Privatization: Sector and Size

Transition economies and developing countries have found it easier to begin by privatizing the smaller retail and manufacturing enterprises, for a number of good reasons.[14] First, it is less politically contentious to privatize small factories, retail outlets, and service providers than some of the pillars of the industrial establishment. Second, even when capital markets are virtually nonexistent, buyers can readily be found. Third, markets for the products of small manufacturing firms already exist, which means that the risks for buyers are manageable and performance benchmarks can easily be established. Fourth is the modest scale of the adjustment required. If there are layoffs, the numbers involved are relatively few; if additional investment is called for in plant and equipment, the amounts needed are within the capacity of the owners, aided by their networks of families and business associates. Last, with manufacturing firms, the government is not faced (to the same degree) with the regulatory issues that need to be addressed simultaneously when networked industries and natural monopolies are being privatized.

Ownership reform in Albania, which commenced with the passing of a privatization law in August 1991, succeeded in transferring three-fourths of small retail and service establishments into private hands by 1992 (Hashi and Xhillari 1999). Throughout Eastern Europe, privatization of small and medium-size manufacturing establishments has proven to be a positive sum activity, with gains in economic dynamism, in productivity, and the supply of new products resulting in higher political approval ratings.

After testing the effectiveness of other management and incentive mechanisms that stopped short of privatization, China also eventually chose to begin divesting its small and medium-size state-owned enterprises (SMSOEs) in the mid-1990s. This and other lessons from the European transition economies are being assimilated by China. The transfer of ownership in China could have begun earlier, and it could be implemented faster. But it is now emerging at the level of the small-scale manufacturing sector.

---

14. Countries have used both auctions and a case-by-case approach (Kalyuzhnova and Andreff 2003).

Market Institutions

Typically, the transition economies have embarked upon the process of reform without most of the institutions that are responsible for the effective functioning of market economies. Reformers initially lacked a full appreciation of the importance of such institutions, as well as the knowledge, the instruments, and the political will to put them into place. But the role institutions play in mediating reforms and supporting the difficult transformation of SOEs is now better understood, and the politics of institution-building are better appreciated. The driving force behind market institutions is a political vision—and a widely shared political commitment that acknowledges the costs in terms of political capital and material resources.

In the 1990s, it was much less obvious than it is today that large-scale privatization was unlikely to yield the desired results over a short political horizon, in the absence of a range of interlinking market institutions. Institutions are needed to monitor market participants and generate information, define and sustain rights to property, and promote effective corporate governance and the rights of minority shareholders (the new owners of privatized SOEs). In addition, institutions mediate bankruptcy, promote creditor rights, facilitate the orderly exit of failing companies— and assure a transparent and fair disposal of firm assets. Until recently, few proponents of privatization were ready to acknowledge that market institutions would need the backing of an autonomous legal system with the ability to implement the market rules without undue political interference. Recent empirical research on transition economies, as well as industrialized and developing countries, has gone a long way toward establishing the fundamental role of institutions in the reincarnation of SOEs as privately owned and efficiently functioning corporate entities. In particular, strong corporate governance exercised through a board of directors, banking and nonfinancial bodies, and the media, and by the rights afforded to minority shareholders of privatized companies strongly influences economic and financial performance. Such oversight also influences the degree to which companies adopt the accounting techniques and conduct the audits that are critical to corporate health. Commenting on privatization in Russia, Moers (2000, p. 329) remarked, "Stronger competition and better institutions may be necessary conditions for more restructuring . . . the best restructuring figures are obtained with a better quality of laws."

Experience has shown that institutions generally cannot be perfected in advance of privatization—and it may be costly to forego reform until all the rules are in place and working. That is a recipe for indefinite delay.

The better course of action is to recognize the endogeneity of institutions, begin the process of institution-building, and (based on the workings of the nascent nonstate sector) move forward with privatizing publicly owned enterprises—all while relying on the feedback process to shape and strengthen the requisite market institutions.

The accumulation of findings from numerous countries affirms the advantages of proceeding with privatization, even as market institutions are being developed.[15] Privatizing SOEs and banks can help accelerate the process and create the conditions that allow a hardening of budget constraints (Frydman and others 1999; Havrylyshyn and McGettigan 2000). Such hardening is difficult to enforce, however, until governments sever the ties of ownership. Where governments do curtail or eliminate direct support via the budget, they sometimes continue to permit or encourage financing of SOE deficits by publicly owned banks, as in the Czech Republic, Romania, and Slovakia—but also in China (Claessens and Djankov 1999). In effect, the efficient and market-directed functioning of SOEs is not fully achieved until the state has divested its ownership of both banks and firms (Megginson and Netter 2001, p. 331).

By coordinating ownership reform with institutional development, each can reinforce the other. Institution-building will also most likely garner the needed political backing when exigencies generated by privatization compel governments to focus on market rules.

Institutional development, in turn, stimulates the emergence or the more active participation of other market participants, which can contribute to the enforcement of rules. The monitoring of company performance and the enforcement of disciplined governance are primarily the responsibility of the board of directors, shareholders, and major bank and nonbank investors. But a host of other interested parties gather, analyze, and disseminate information on companies. These include rating agencies, brokerage houses, the business-oriented media, and companies engaged in market research.[16] Together, these entities help to create a competitive market environment that drives firms to innovate and efficiently utilize their resources. Building institutions and privatizing SOEs can thus have a galvanizing effect in the economic milieu of an economy in transition. It helps to create the niches for the many specialized

---

15. A cross-country study of the banking system by La Porta, Lopez-de-Silanes, and Shleifer (2000) found that resource misallocation by nationalized banks costs countries a few points of TFP growth.

16. Dyck and Zingales (2002) assess the degree to which the media can influence corporate decisionmaking.

players whose individual pursuit of profits contributes in the aggregate to the deepening and dynamism of markets.

The contrasting experiences of the Czech Republic and Poland, both of which started on the road to privatization with weak legal infrastructure and poorly developed financial systems, illustrate how subsequent institutional changes can affect outcomes. The Czechs used voucher privatization to expedite the entire process, whereas the Poles relied more on direct sales and share transfers. By the early 1990s, the Czech Republic had many more publicly held companies than Poland. But by the mid-1990s, it was clear that privatization in Poland was enhancing the performance of firms, whereas many privatized firms in the Czech Republic were the victims of tunneling by insider managers who had expropriated and spirited away the assets of minority shareholders (Johnson and Shleifer 1999).[17] Johnson and Shleifer maintain that Poland was able to avoid the problems that beset the Czech Republic by instituting and enforcing stringent securities regulations that averted the expropriation of minority shareholders and served to strengthen corporate governance. A broader cross-country analysis of securities law by La Porta, Lopez-de-Silanes, and Shleifer (2003) suggests that the value of securities laws derives as much from a lowering of the costs of private contracting and litigation as from public enforcement. But effective private action depends equally on equipping the courts with the personnel and procedures needed to adjudicate securities laws and enforce their decisions.

Competitive Markets

Economic theory shows that competition in product markets will lead to an efficient allocation of resources. It gives managers the incentives to maximize profits and generates information on the productivity of resource utilization by firms, information that allows owners to monitor managerial effort (Hart 1983; Yarrow 1986). In a competitive milieu with an active market for corporate control, firms that do not meet the market test of productivity and cost competitiveness are forced to exit or are taken over by other firms. The threats of bankruptcy or takeover credibly

---

17. The term "tunneling," coined to describe the situation that prevailed in the Czech Republic, refers to "the transfer of resources out of a company to its controlling shareholders . . . through self-dealing transactions . . . or the controlling shareholder [increases] his share of the firm without transferring any assets through dilutive share issues, minority freeze-outs, insider trading, creeping acquisitions, or other financial transactions that discriminate against minorities" (Johnson, Lopez-de-Silanes, and Shleifer 2000, p. 3).

discipline firm behavior; and when these are weakened or removed, market functioning is compromised, leading to a suboptimal allocation of resources and diminished productivity.

From the standpoint of theory, the financial performance of firms that are owned or controlled by the state is likely to be handicapped by political interference which, at best, compels them to pursue a variety of social objectives, and at worst, saddles them with narrow political concerns. The frequency of failure in political markets, of lack of transparency, and of distorted information means that social goals often lack clarity; and their costs are rarely assessed fully or realized in an efficient manner by SOEs (see Zhang, Zhang, and Zhao 2002). Although it has been asserted that SOEs should be able to match the performance of private firms (including TFP growth) under competitive conditions—in practice, this has been demonstrated in those cases where the management (and possibly the governance) has been transformed through public listing, joint ventures with foreign firms, and increased market competition (Brown and Earle 2000; Yudaeva and others 2003).[18] In fact, a number of studies in Eastern Europe (Carlin and others 2001), Russia (Yudaeva and others 2003; Brown and Earle 2000; Radygin and Entov 2001), and China acknowledge the significant effect of market competition on the performance of privatized (or reformed) SOEs (Li 1997; Shirley and Xu 2001; Sonobe and Otsuka 2003).

Competition Policy

The government can further the effectiveness of institutional development by way of competition policy that spells out the ground rules for newly privatized SOEs, other firms, and market participants in general. The ground rules define acceptable pricing practices and interaction among firms so as to contain unfair collusion. They also seek to limit the concentration of market power and reduce barriers to the entry and exit of firms. In transition economies such as Russia, competition policies must also tackle a host of administrative barriers that impede the start-up of a new business and protect incumbents.[19] In the Russian case, for example, many enterprises prior to and after privatization manage to exercise substantial market power as a result of the privileged relationships of insider managers with national and subnational agencies (these can also impose burdens on firms, as noted earlier in the case of China). These

---

18. See, for example, Ray and Zhang (2001).

19. On the plethora of subsidies and regulations in Russia during the early 1990s, see Vasiliev (1994).

relationships affect the pricing, investment, and marketing strategies of the favored firms and disadvantage existing and potential competitors. Competition is further curtailed by restrictions on access to transport, distribution, warehousing, and telecommunications services—many regulated and owned by subnational governments (Broadman 2002).[20]

The worth of competition policy is only partly a matter of the laws, however. As noted earlier, it depends upon enforcement as well. The parallel strengthening of the legal system not only enables reformers to implement ownership reform and new owners to restructure firms; it also sustains the enforcement of contracts that are critical to the functioning of competitive markets. As Blanchard and Kremer (1997) have observed, in the CIS countries, competitive pressures increased the nonfulfillment of contracts, in large part, because the legal system was ineffectual. This was mainly responsible for the sharp drop in production during the early stage of transition. The capability of the legal system in Russia has been conspicuously weak. And although the Russian constitution does provide a measure of judicial independence, the legal system remains hamstrung by the lack of transparency of the judicial process and limited accountability to higher courts. Moreover, as Berglof and others (2003, p. 83) point out,

> The very high level of effort required on the part of judges to uphold justice in Russia combined with the lack of incentives for judges to rule impartially that is imbedded in the design of the Russian judiciary, have created substantial room for corruption in the judiciary and resulted in the unreliability of the Russian legal system. Under-financing of the courts has exacerbated the problem. One common example of the subversion of justice in the Russian judiciary is the interference of local and regional government in the judicial process.

Role of Management and Restructuring

Before privatized companies are likely to register significant improvements in a range of performance indicators, there is usually a need for changes in the management and organization of the company, often involving considerable restructuring and layoffs. Such changes are more likely if privatization results in an ownership structure that is relatively concentrated, allowing strategic outsiders to exert their influence.[21]

---

20. This was noted in comments offered by Ksenia Yudaeva on a draft of this study.

21. See Kornai (2003) and the findings surveyed by Blaszczyk and others (2003). Radygin and Entov (2001) identify a weak relationship between the concentration of ownership in privatized Russian firms and performance. A broader cross-country study by La Porta and others (1998) suggests that in countries where shareholders' protection is weak, the major shareholders play a more active role in governance.

Companies have to reconsider their overall strategy, the product mix, the way production is organized, and their personnel policies. Changes of this magnitude are difficult to introduce in the closed world of state-owned enterprises, where the decisionmaking purview of managers can be limited and substantial authority continues to reside with public supervisory bodies. Workers often enjoy lifetime tenure, and the incentive systems rarely encourage or reward initiative. Where the management structure and corporate governance remain intact, and privatization does not affect the labor force or work practices, the reform of ownership will not change performance. Improving performance can require either sharing control with outsiders or transferring complete control to outsiders.[22] In other words, the distribution of ownership should empower a group of outsiders to exert the influence needed to bring about as much restructuring as is demanded by market circumstances. Where ownership is monopolized by insiders or external ownership is so diffuse that outsiders cannot change the management and organization of the firm, neither SOE reform nor even a rise in competitive pressures will improve outcomes.[23] Berglof and others observe that the impact of mass privatization in Russia in the short term was "small or even non-existent. When Russian firms were privatized, most were sold to insiders who did not bring with them new capital, technologies, or human capital. Instead, insider privatization often locked firms into far-reaching economic and social responsibilities to their employees who also owned substantial stakes, resulting in massive hoarding of labor and little restructuring" (2003, p. 20). Interestingly, the large corporate groups that are emblematic of Russian privatization were mostly formed by outsiders, which may explain some of the ire these groups have aroused.[24]

The design of ownership reform is, therefore, at least as important as complementary institutional development and the nature of the competitive environment. While control of a privatized firm by insiders or outsiders affects performance, so does majority (or substantial) ownership by the state and by foreigners. Where the state retains control rights, it is

---

22. The positive effects of ownership transfer to outsiders is consistent across countries and was recently reaffirmed by a study of Romanian firms using panel data for 1992–9 (Earle and Telegdy 2002). However, a study of 645 Czech firms privatized in 1991–3 showed that performance in 1996–9 was not greatly affected by the type of owner (investment fund, portfolio fund, bank, individual, and so forth) (Kocenda 2002).

23. The weakness of corporate governance in Poland tended to neutralize the effects of increased competition (Grosfeld and Hashi 2003).

24. According to some surveys, up to 80 percent of the Russian population questions the fairness of the privatization process (comment by Ksenia Yudaeva on a draft of this study).

likely to continue to determine the selection of management and influence the nature of restructuring, but not necessarily to the detriment of firm performance, as suggested by the experience of quasi-public firms in Singapore and Europe.[25] A joint venture with a foreign party or a takeover by a foreign company can lead to radical changes in management and organization as well as widening participation in overseas markets. But much depends on the ownership stake of the foreign partners and their intentions with respect to the joint venture (Guthrie 1999, pp. 62, 82).

Foreign ownership can entail a major reshuffling of management, with foreigners brought in to fill key positions, changes to both the organization and work practices, and a downsizing of the workforce (Kalyuzhnova and Andreff 2003). This was evident in the Czech auto industry once the government permitted privatization through FDI in 1998 (Pavlinek 2002). Studies also show large gains in value added by firms taken over by foreign companies relative to firms subject to employee buyouts (see, for example, Dyck 1997; and Smith, Cin, and Vodopivec 1997).[26] Such positive effects of foreign management are also apparent from the research on China (Cheng and Wu 2001; Zhang and Zhang 2001). Purchases of SOEs by foreign companies (especially the large multinational corporations) can also link the newly privatized firm with international production networks, thereby exposing them to competition in global markets, providing opportunities for exports, and multiplying the avenues for technology transfer. According to Djankov and Murrell (2002, pp. 758–9), "Privatization to workers is detrimental; privatization to diffuse individual owners has no effect, and privatization to investment funds or to foreigners has a large positive effect. Loosely speaking, privatization to funds is five times as productive as privatization to insiders, while privatization to foreigners or blockholders is three times as productive as privatization to insiders."

WHAT CHINA CAN LEARN FROM OTHER TRANSITION ECONOMIES

In China, realizing full gains from the ownership reforms to date is complicated by three factors. First, for the SMSOEs, ownership has been transferred mainly to managers and workers, which has constrained

---

25. A study of Czech firms by Hanousek, Kocenda, and Svejnar (2004) also offers support for the view that, in a competitive environment, the exercise of control rights by the state can lead to restructuring that enhances profits without requiring large layoffs.

26. That privatized firms in which foreign owners have acquired a majority share do better than other firms is further supported by the research on Czech firms by Kocenda and Svejnar (2003).

restructuring efforts.[27] However, to the extent that privatized SMSOEs must now respond to harder budget constraints and face the full brunt of a competitive environment, changes are being introduced that will enable the newly reformed firms to survive. The analysis in chapter 5 of this volume suggests that at least a substantial subset of the SMSOEs is taking positive steps to improve their performance. Greater and more widespread improvement is certainly possible. But until a second round of privatization brings outsiders to the helm of surviving firms, it is likely that the carryover of management, employee shareholding, and existing personal relationships and commitments with local government agencies could limit efforts by the new management (see chapters 1 and 5) to reshape the organization and trim the workforce and thereby risk displeasing powerful state agencies. Thus, while it is hard to establish empirically that much more could be achieved through reform that severs many of a firm's links with its past and with local regulatory agencies, the cross-country evidence argues for this.

A second factor that diminishes the benefits from ownership reform in China is the dominant stake of the government in the larger, newly formed limited liability companies (LLCs), which is now being transferred to the State-Owned Assets Supervision and Administration Commission from the various ministries and commissions. The possible effect of these factors is discussed in chapter 6 (also see "China Lays Out Business" 2003).[28] Although the significance of *guanxi* (connections) is waning, the larger SOEs derive many advantages from direct contacts with decisionmaking ministerial bodies. These direct dealings, which are frequent and increasingly complemented by the lobbying efforts of industrial associations, can lead to measures that reduce taxes (as with the software industry), contain competition in the domestic market (as with consumer electronics), or curb imports (as with steel).[29]

Using an unbalanced panel dataset of 903 to 1,284 firms, they found that foreign-owned companies did the most restructuring and achieved both growth of sales and a reduction in unit production costs.

27. In line with an emphasis on the role of management in chapter 1 of this volume, the experience of transition economies convincingly relates to gains in performance, to enterprise restructuring, and to substantial strengthening of incentives offered to managers who must transform SOEs into competitive firms (Djankov and Murrell 2002; McMillan 1997).

28. This is part of a wide-ranging reform of China's administrative and regulatory bureaucracy ("China: Government Restructuring" 2003).

29. See the discussion of industrial lobbying and direct dealings with industrial bureaus and ministries by Chinese firms in Kennedy (2005). Kennedy points out that the larger SOEs have better access and hence less interest in participating in industrial associations.

Chinese and foreign researchers have frequently remarked that China stands apart from other transition economies (Sachs and Woo 1997). Its size, history, current state of development, and specific institutional characteristics are distinct and in some respects unique. This is plausible up to a point, and few would disagree that adapting ownership reform to China's current circumstances would be desirable or that imbuing the process with "Chinese characteristics" would speed implementation. Still, the weight of theory and empirical evidence from a wide spectrum of countries argues for adherence to the guidelines presented in chapter 2 and this chapter. However, nearly 20 years after enterprise reform was initiated in China, the case for persisting with gradualism is losing credibility. Delay only compounds the losses from past inaction; and the survival of loss-making SOEs and the continuing investment in capacity by barely profitable enterprises compound the pressures on healthy and efficient firms by worsening the overhang of excess supply.[30]

An open and competitive market environment is now partially in place in China, as are the pools of capital and some of the institutional architecture needed for privatization to yield the results that other transition economies have begun to register. Even so, further institution-building should be pursued alongside privatization as a matter of priority. Indeed, there is no evidence to suggest that institution-building needs to be completed in advance; but now is the time for formulating a competition policy and creating a regulatory agency to implement that policy, as privatization builds momentum.

Although research does not in all cases convincingly endorse privatization across the board, it does, on the whole, underscore the case for privatizing industrial enterprises that compete in product markets. And it suggests, almost as strongly, that certain structures of ownership are better at delivering results. This is as likely to be true in China as it has been in Chile and Poland, for example. How the various forms of ownership affect performance of reformed SOEs is explored in chapter 5.

So what might be the best medium-run reform strategy for China? It appears that the process should be less about how the state holding company operates, and more about the institutions that China needs in order to build a competitive market economy where former SOEs can flourish. This strategy is explored in chapter 6.

---

30. This has forced firms to pare their prices during 2004–5 in the face of rising raw material costs and accept even lower profits on each unit of output ("Chinese Manufacturers" 2005).

ANNEX

Table A4.1 Selected Literature on Transition Economies

Authors	Methodology	Main findings
Kocenda and Svejnar (2003)	Examines the effect of ownership type and concentration on firm restructuring efforts after privatization, using an unbalanced panel of 1,540 Czech firms from 1996–9.	Finds that firms with concentrated ownership outperform firms with dispersed ownership structure. Furthermore, firms with foreign majority ownerships are the only ones that increased both profitability and sales revenue without changing the rate of increase of labor cost. Firms with majority domestic ownership kept the profitability constant, but by reducing the rate of growth of revenue and labor cost. Overall, the study finds that foreign majority ownership leads to superior economic performance in the Czech Republic.
Zalduendo (2003)	Examines the firm performance with different forms of ownership, using the financial data of 823 firms in 1994, 1997, and 2000.	Finds that firms with private ownership, a hard budget constraint, and operating in a market-based institution have higher profitability. Furthermore, consistent with the previous literature, insider sales and diffused ownership are both detrimental to restructuring efforts after privatization.
Aussenegg and Jelic (2002)	Examines the operating performance of 153 firms in Poland (43), Hungary (28), and the Czech Republic (82), using financial data from 1990–8.	Finds that privatized firms in the sample failed to increase profitability and saw productivity and output decline. Furthermore, firms privatized through mass privatization scheme (Czech firms) performed more poorly than firms privatized on case-by-case basis. Many of these firms are still partially owned by the state, and these firms outperform pure privately owned firms.
Cull, Matesova, and Shirley (2002)	Examines, using panel data from 1993 to 1996, the effect of looting and soft budget constraints on the performance of 392 Czech firms.	Finds that firms privatized through vouchers perform significantly worse than with publicly owned shares. Authors attribute this

Study	Description	Findings
Earle and Telegdy (2002)	Examines the impact of privatization on labor productivity in Romania, using a panel data of 2,354 firms in Romania from 1992–8	difference in performance to the abilities of managers, looting (excessive borrowing from banks), and soft loans. Finds a 1 to 1.7% increase in labor productivity with each 10% rise in private ownership. This productivity gain is most pronounced with sale of shares to outsiders; sale to insiders has smaller effect. Furthermore, concentrated private shareholdings are more productivity enhancing than in a dispersed ownership structure.
Kocenda (2002)	Examines the relationship between forms of ownership and firm performance, using financial data on 722 Czech firms from 1996–9.	Finds that, overall, there is no clear pattern between type of ownership and firm performance. However, specific types of ownership affect specific financial variables (for example, individual ownership has negative impact on the fixed asset growth).
Pavlinek (2002)	Examines the effect of FDI on privatization and restructuring of the motor vehicle industry in the Czech Republic during the 1990s, using 20 in-depth interviews with managers conducted in 2000 and 2001.	Finds that, overall, the large inflow of foreign investment resulted in a substantial increase in labor productivity, more effective organization, and better managerial control. In addition, infusion of foreign capital led to access to global markets and increased opportunities for technology transfer.
Gupta, Ham, and Svejnar (2001)	Empirically examines several competing government objectives for privatization, using firm-level data on 1,121 Czech firms in 1992. Firms in samples were privatized in two different periods, enabling authors to test their hypotheses.	Finds that firms that are more profitable in downstream industries and face demand uncertainty are privatized first, suggesting that selection for privatization by the Czech government was strategic, not random. Implication of this result is that most studies of privatization may suffer from selection bias.
Pivovarsky (2001)[a]	Uses data from 376 medium and large Ukrainian enterprises to investigate the relationship between ownership concentration and enterprise performance.	Finds that ownership concentration is positively correlated with enterprise performance in Ukraine; and that ownership by foreign companies and banks is associated with better performance over domestic owners.

(Table continues on the following page.)

Table A4.1 continued

Authors	Methodology	Main findings
Sachs, Zinnes, and Eilat (2000)[a]	Examines the empirical evidence across 24 countries to determine if change-of-title alone is sufficient to achieve economic performance gains, or if other factors (such as institutions to address agency issues, hardening of budget constraints, market competitiveness, depoliticization of firm objectives, and the implementation challenge of developing institutions and a regulatory framework to address them) are relevant.	Finds that privatization involving change-of-title alone is not enough to generate improvement in economic performance. While reforms directed at prudential regulation, corporate governance, hardening of enterprise budget constraints, management objectives, and developing capital markets contribute to economic performance on their own, the real gains to privatization come from complementing them with change-of-title reforms. The higher the level of prerequisite reforms, the more positive is the economic performance impact from an increase in change-of-title privatization. The study finds a threshold level of reforms in order for change-of-title privatization to have a positive economic performance response. Concludes that institutions matter as much as ownership.
Frydman, Hessel, and Rapaczynski (2000a)[b]	Examines whether the imposition of hard budget constraints alone is sufficient to improve corporate performance in the Czech Republic, Hungary, and Poland. Employs a sample of 216 firms: state-owned (31%), privatized (43%), and private (26%).	Finds privatization alone added nearly 10 percentage points to the revenue growth of a firm sold to outside owners. Most important, finds that the threat of hard budget constraints for poorly performing SOEs falters, since governments are unwilling to allow these firms to fail. The brunt of the lower creditworthiness of SOEs falls on state creditors.
Frydman, Hessel, and Rapaczynski (2000b)[b]	Examines whether privatized Central European firms controlled by outside investors are more entrepreneurial (ability to increase revenues) than firms controlled by insiders or the state. Study employs survey data from a sample of 506 manufacturing firms in the Czech Republic, Hungary, and Poland.	Documents that all state and privatized firms engage in similar types of restructuring, but that product restructuring by firms owned by outside investors is significantly more effective (in terms of revenue generation) than that by firms with other ownership. Concludes that the more entrepreneurial behavior of outsider-owned firms is due to the incentive effects of privatization (not human capital effects, specifically greater readiness to take risks).

Harper (2000)[b]	Examines the effects of privatization on the financial and operating performance of 174 firms privatized in the first wave and 380 firms divested in the second wave of the Czech Republic's voucher privatizations of 1992 and 1994. Compares results for privatized firms to those that remain state owned. Employs Megginson, Nash, and van Randenborgh methodology and variables to measure changes.	Finds that the first wave of privatization yielded disappointing results. Real sale, profitability, efficiency, and employment all declined dramatically (and significantly). However, second-wave firms experienced significant increases in efficiency and profitability; the decline in employment—though still significant—was far less drastic than after the first wave (−17% versus 41%).
Kornai (2003)[a]	Examines the privatization process in Hungary.	Suggests that hard budget constraints are as important as privatization, liberalization, and stabilization; and argues that harder budget constraints act as a selection process. Firms that are profitable can be sold, while those that are not must be allowed to go bankrupt rather than be given away.
Perevalov, Gimadii, and Dobrodei (2000)	Examines firm performance after privatization, using panel data of 189 Russian firms from 1992–6.	Finds that even though privatization does not yield improvement, on average, it led to a reduction in costs per unit of revenue and improvement in labor productivity. However, the positive effect of privatization highly depends on the methods used to privatize the firms and ownership concentration.
Djankov (1999)[c]	Investigates the relation between ownership structure and enterprise performance in the CIS, using detailed survey data from Georgia, Kazakhstan, the Kyrgyz Republic, Moldova, Russia, and Ukraine. Documents the changing pattern of ownership in 960 privatized manufacturing companies across the six countries from 1995–7.	Finds that state ownership is always associated with less restructuring (asset sales, renovations, and labor productivity), although the result is statistically insignificant.

(Table continues on the following page.)

Table A4.1 continued

Authors	Methodology	Main findings
Frydman and others (1999)[b]	Compares performance of privatized and state-owned firms in transition economies of Central Europe, and asks, "When does privatization work?" Examines the influence of ownership structure on performance, using a sample of 90 state-owned and 128 privatized companies in the Czech Republic, Hungary, and Poland. Employs panel data regression methods to isolate ownership effects.	Finds that privatization "works," but only when firms are controlled by outside owners (other than managers or employees). Privatization adds over 18 percentage points to annual growth rate of firm sold to domestic financial firm, and 12 percentage points when sold to a foreign buyer. Privatization to an outside owner also adds about 9 percentage points to productivity growth. Gain does not come at the expense of higher unemployment; insider-controlled firms are less likely to restructure, but outsider-controlled firms grow faster. Shows the importance of entrepreneurship in reviving sales growth.
Djankov and Pohl (1998)[c]	Examines 21 case studies of firms based on detailed financial information, from 1991–6, and interviews with top management using a structured questionnaire.	Finds that privatization is associated with improvements in restructuring (such as labor shedding, spinning off social assets, or finding new markets and products) and performance indicators (such as productivity and profitability performance).
Weiss and Nikitin (2002)[b]	Analyzes effects of ownership by investment funds on the performance of 125 privatized Czech firms during 1993–5. Assesses these effects by measuring the relationship between changes in performance and in composition of ownership at the start of privatization. Uses robust estimation techniques, in addition to ordinary least squares (OLS), since data strongly reject normality.	Finds that ownership concentration and composition jointly affect the performance of privatized firms. Concentration in the hands of a large shareholder, other than an investment fund or company, is associated with significant improvements for all measures of performance. Concentrated ownership by funds did not improve performance. Preliminary post-1996 data suggest changes in investment fund legislation may improve performance.
Claessens, Djankov, and Pohl (1997)[b]	Examines determinants of performance improvements for 706 Czech firms privatized during 1992–5. Using Tobin's-Q, tests whether concentrated ownership	Finds that privatized firms do prosper, primarily because of the resulting concentration in ownership structure. The more concentrated the post-privatization ownership structure, the

Study		
	structure or outside monitor (bank or investment fund) improves Q more than dispersed ownership.	higher the firm's profitability and market valuation. Large stakes owned by bank-sponsored funds and strategic investors are particularly value-enhancing.
Dyck (1997)[b]	Develops and tests an adverse selection model to explain Treuhand's role in restructuring and privatizing the German Democratic Republic's SOEs. In under five years, Treuhand privatized more than 13,800 firms and parts of firms and, uniquely, had resources to pay for the restructuring itself (but almost never chose to do so). Instead, this emphasized the speed and sales to existing Western firms over giveaways and sales to capital funds. Paper rationalizes Treuhand's approach.	Finds that privatized firms in the German Democratic Republic (GDR) were more likely to put Western (usually German) managers in key positions than were companies that remained state owned. Treuhand emphasized sales open to all buyers rather than favor those in the GDR. Shows that privatization programs must carefully consider when and how to affect managerial change in firms, and that plans open to Western buyers (and which allow management change) are most likely to improve firm performance.
Earle and Estrin (1997)[c]	Analyzes the ownership structure emerging from the Russian privatization process, using information from a sample survey of 439 state and privately owned manufacturing companies conducted in July 2004.	Finds evidence of positive effects of private ownership on enterprise performance, with managerial and institutional investor ownership having the strongest impact. Results also show that the privatization process may have contained a negative selection bias with respect to ownership by outside investors.
Smith, Cin, and Vodopivec (1997)[b]	Uses a sample with 22,735 firm-years of data drawn from a period of "spontaneous privatization" in Slovenia from 1989–92 to examine the impact of foreign and employee ownership on firms.	Finds that a percentage point increase in foreign ownership is associated with a 3.9% increase in value added; for employee ownership, a 1.4% increase. Firms with higher revenues, profits, and exports are more likely to exhibit foreign and employee ownership.
Earle, Estrin, and Leshchenko (1996)[c]	Analyzes the effects of the massive Russian privatization program on the ownership of firms and on the behavior of former state-owned enterprises.	Finds that privatization results in somewhat greater depoliticization and better enterprise performance, although the pace of restructuring (in the areas of production, marketing,

(Table continues on the following page.)

Table A4.1 continued

Authors	Methodology	Main findings
	A large random sample was drawn from a list of industrial firms, with a number of predetermined *de novo* firms added.	employment policy, and investment) is not significantly different across ownership categories.
Belka and others (1995)[c]	Examines the relationship between different emerging forms of ownership and the extent and nature of enterprise level adjustments taking place. A qualitative and quantitative survey was administered to 200 Polish firms from the manufacturing sector between November 1993 and March 1994.	Finds that privatization is associated with higher profit margins and investment than in state-owned firms, although all enterprises face a considerable increase in competition, which led to a restructuring of input purchases and marketing strategy across all firms.

a. From Kikeri and Nellis (2002).

b. From Megginson and Netter (2001).

c. From Havrylyshyn and McGettigan (2000).

Sources: Adapted from Megginson and Netter (2001), Kikeri and Nellis (2002), and Havrylyshyn and McGettigan (2000), with authors' additions.

Table A4.2 Selected Literature on Nontransition Economies

Authors	Methodology	Main findings
Barnett (2000)	Investigates the impact of privatization on fiscal and macroeconomic performance.	Finds that privatization proceeds transferred to the budget are mainly used to reduce domestic financing, with little evidence they are used to finance a larger deficit. The privatization process is strongly correlated with improved macroeconomic performance (via higher real GDP growth and lower unemployment rates). The estimates suggest that a 1 percent of GDP privatization corresponds to a 0.5 percentage point increase in contemporaneous real GDP growth and a further 0.4 point increase the following year. The point estimates also suggest that a 1 percent of GDP privatization is associated with a decline in the unemployment rate of just less than 0.25 of a percentage point in the year of privatization and a further 0.5 point the following year, resulting in a total impact of around 0.75 of a point.
Richardson and Barnett (2000)	Separates the possible fiscal and other macroeconomic impacts of privatization.	Finds that receipts of privatization are saved, not spent. Over time, the fiscal situation is improved by privatization, with positive effects on revenue and (for some countries) large declines in deficits. In terms of growth, private firms are more efficient than those run by the state, especially in competitive industries. The strong correlation between growth and privatization may be because privatization is a proxy for the more general factor of "favorable regime change." Also finds that unemployment falls after privatization, but may have detrimental impacts on particular groups of workers. Overall, the positive effects of privatization on growth and employment hold for all countries studied, though to a lesser extent in transition economies.

(Table continues on the following page.)

Table A4.2 continued

Authors	Methodology	Main findings
Jones, Jammal, and Gokur (1999)	Covers the welfare consequences of 81 privatizations in Côte d'Ivoire—not just infrastructure firms but a range of firms already operating in competitive markets (in agriculture, agro-industries, and tradable and nontradable sectors).	Finds (for the entire privatized sector) substantial benefits: (1) firms performed better after privatization; (2) firms performed better than they would have had they remained under public ownership; and (3) the set of transactions as a whole contributed positively to economic welfare, with annual net welfare benefits equivalent to about 25 percent of predivestiture sales. These results stemmed from a number of effects, including increases in output, investment, labor productivity, and intermediate-input productivity.
Boubakri and Cosset (1998)	Examines post-privatization financial and operating performance of 79 companies in 21 developing countries and 32 industries between 1980–92.	Concludes that there are economically and statistically significant post-privatization increases in output (real sales), operating efficiency, profitability, capital investment spending, dividend payments, and employment, as well as significant decreases in leverage. About 60 percent of sample firms showed an increase in employment of 5–10 percent after privatization. Real sales per employee increased by 27 percent. Unadjusted net income per employee increased (on average) by 63 percent.
Dewenter and Malatesta (1997)	Uses data from eight countries (Canada, France, Hungary, Japan, Malaysia, Poland, Thailand, and the U.K.) to compare initial returns for 109 companies with national average returns. Also tests whether PIPOs are more or less underpriced than private sector IPOs.	Finds that results vary by country: the U.K. shows significantly higher initial returns on PIPOs than private sector IPOs, while Canada and Malaysia point to the opposite case. Also, PIPOs in unregulated industries tend to be less than those for regulated industries. There is, therefore, no evidence that governments systematically underprice PIPOs. Relatively primitive capital markets (in this case Hungary, Malaysia, Poland, and Thailand) lead to a tendency for higher initial returns than offers in countries

142

		with more developed capital markets. Suggests that this is due to increased uncertainty about the value of privatization offers leading to lower offer prices. Also suggests that those countries with relatively primitive capital markets may try to broaden private share ownership by decreasing the initial offer price.
La Porta and López-de-Silanes (1997)	Criticizes privatization based on the possibility that the observed higher profitability of privatized companies comes at the expense of the rest of society. Focuses on two of the most likely channels for social losses: increased prices as firms capitalize on the market power, and layoffs and lower wages as firms seek to roll back generous labor contracts. Uses data for all 218 nonfinancial privatizations that took place in Mexico between 1983 and 1991.	Finds that privatized firms quickly bridge the pre-privatization performance gap with industry-matched control groups. For example, privatization is followed by a 24 percentage point increase in the ratio of operating income to sales. Those gains in profitability are roughly decomposed as follows: 10 percent of the increase is due to higher product prices, 33 percent represents a transfer from laid-off workers, and productivity gains account for the residual 57 percent. Transfers from society to the firm are partially offset by taxes that absorb slightly over half the gains in operating income. Also finds evidence indicating that deregulation is associated with faster convergence to industry benchmarks.
Majumdar (1996)	Examines the performance of SOEs, mixed ownership enterprises, and private firms in India during 1973–89.	Finds that industry-level survey data reveal efficiency scores averaging 0.975 for privately owned firms, which is significantly higher than both mixed ownership firms (0.912) and SOEs (0.638). Any state sector improvement is caused by concerted "efficiency drives," but quickly declines afterward.
Galal and others (1994)	Measures the effects of divestiture by comparing actual post-privatization performance of 12 large firms (in aviation, energy, telecommunications,	Finds that divestiture substantially improved economic welfare in 11 of the 12 cases. The gains were mainly due to a dramatic increase in investment, improved productivity, more rational

(Table continues on the following page.)

143

Table A4.2 continued

Authors	Methodology	Main findings
	transportation and shipping) in Chile, Malaysia, Mexico, and the U.K. with their performance prior to divestiture.	pricing policies, and increased competition and effective regulation. Despite assuring that public managers would adopt new technology and more rational procedures, also concludes that privatized firm performance was superior to the alternative of state ownership.
Boardman and Vining (1989)	Compares the performance of the 500 largest non-U.S. industrial firms in 1983. Results are compared for private corporations, mixed enterprises, and SOEs. Comparison is made on the basis of four measures of profitability: return on equity, return on assets, return on sales, and net income. Also includes two measures of X-efficiency: sales per employee and sales per asset.	Finds that state-owned and mixed ownership firms are significantly less profitable and productive than privately owned companies. To gain efficiency, full privatization is needed, because mixed ownerships firms are no more profitable than those wholly owned by the state.

Notes: IPO, initial public offering; PIPOs, privatization initial public offerings; SOE, state-owned enterprise.

Source: Adapted from Kikeri and Nellis (2002).

Table A4.3 Selected Literature on China

Authors	Methodology	Main findings
Jefferson and others (2000)	Uses a Cobb-Douglas production function and simple regression model to investigate Chinese industrial productivity from 1980–96. Examines differences in marginal factor productivity across ownership types, and considers the impact of business cycles on the interpretation of productivity trends.	Finds that long-term productivity increased, with growth rates declining during the 1990s. While capital productivity declined, labor productivity showed consistent rapid growth. Outcomes outside the state and collective sectors are modest, with shareholding enterprises suffering productive declines. Finally, finds consistent evidence of a rising trend in TFP of the entire industrial sector and for each of three major ownership categories.
Sonobe and Otsuka (2003)	Examines 78 garment and 89 metal casting TVEs across 52 counties in the Great Yangtze River Region from 1995–8, to see if (and to what extent) privatization has improved resource allocation and productivity. A modified growth function is estimated using 3SLS and OLS.	Finds that productivity was significantly enhanced by the recent privatization, with a time lag of a few years. The productivity effect of privatization was greater in an industry where products and materials were more efficiently transacted at free markets. The short-run incentive effect of privatization is significantly positive, which strongly indicates that privatization can be a driving force leading to the continued improvement of productivity over long periods, so far as privatization enhances market competition among enterprises across wide areas.
Cull and Xu (2000)	Investigates whether bank finance flowed to SOEs with higher productivity compared to direct government transfers from 1980 to 1994. The datasets are a survey of Chinese SOEs: 1980–9 and 1990–4. A production function, OLS, and fixed effects are used.	Finds that bank employees assessed SOE credit risks substantially better than the bureaucrats responsible for allocating direct transfers, at least in the 1980s. Banks imposed harder budget constraints on SOEs than bureaucrats, but those constraints softened as the 1990s progressed. As a result, bank finance did not flow to relatively productive SOEs later in the period.
Holz (2000)	Focuses on the impact of the liability-asset ratio on profitability in China's industrial-owned enterprises in	Finds that the perceived negative impact of the current level of the liability-asset ratio on enterprise profitability does not hold up

(Table continues on the following page.)

Authors	Methodology	Main findings
	the 1990s. The dataset covers 38 industrial sectors from 1993–7. A system of two equations and 3SLS is used.	in regression analysis. Low-profitability SOEs do tend to have a high liability-asset ratio (due to government-ordained support); but once the endogeneity of the liability-asset ratio is controlled for, a high liability-asset ratio tends to imply a high level of profitability. Thus, debt alleviation policies can be misguided.
Hu (2001)	Examines the relationship between R&D expenditure and productivity in China's enterprises. An empirical model that contains a system of three equations (the Cobb-Douglas production function, a private R&D equation, and a government R&D equation) is estimated using a cross-sectional dataset for Chinese enterprises of various ownership types, using data from a survey of 813 all high-tech firms in the Haidian District of Beijing in 1996.	Finds a strong link between private R&D and firm productivity. Although its direct contribution to firm productivity is insignificant, the government contributes indirectly to productivity by promoting private R&D. Therefore, incentives for enterprises to invest in R&D may be a better alternative than direct R&D grants. Besides, reallocation from the state sector to the nonstate sector of innovation R&D resources may yield social welfare gains.
Jefferson and others (2003)	Focuses on China's 22,000 LMEs, which collectively account for one-third of the nation's total industrial output. Using a panel of 1994–9 data for these enterprises, investigates changes in ownership, productivity, profitability, and innovation. A derived Cobb-Douglas production function is used.	Finds that a rapidly diversifying ownership structure in which the role of the state is steadily retreating. Also finds both considerable variation in measures of performance across ownership types and emerging evidence of high-intensity R&D performers that exhibit substantial innovation capacities.
Cheng and Wu (2001)	Attempts to uncover the key determinants of the performance of FIEs in China. The data are from a survey of 350 FIEs located in the Guangdong and Hainan provinces, conducted between July 1996 and February 1997. An ordered probit regression model is used.	Find that cash contributed by foreign parent companies had a significantly positive impact on current profitability, but not on subjective performance. Also finds some evidence that foreign management improved subjective performance. The duration of operation was a consistently positive factor. FIEs that sold more

Groves and others (1994)	Examines whether managerial decisionmaking autonomy and incentives of reforms were effective when the responsibility for deciding output levels was shifted from the state to the firm that benefited from the reforms. The dataset covers 769 enterprises from 1980–9. A program-evaluation model, loglinear production function, and OLS are used.	output to the domestic market (and which had comparative advantages) performed better. Find that when the responsibility for output decisions was shifted from the state to the firm, and when firms were allowed to retain more of their profits, managers of SOEs strengthened workers' incentives, and those incentives were effective in raising productivity (with increases in bonus payments for contract workers). The increase in autonomy raised workers' income and investment in the enterprise, but tended not to raise remittance to the state.
Li and others (2001)	Focuses on testing two alternative theories (efficiency theory and revenue theory) to explain why governments chose to dump state enterprises by privatization or liquidation. The dataset includes three surveys of several hundred Chinese state enterprises from 1980–99. A probit regression is used.	Finds that testing based on data from China rejects the efficiency theory and yields support for the revenue theory. In addition, finds evidence that the concerns for unemployment and for losing political benefit of control to the government are important obstacles to privatization or liquidation decisions.
Perotti, Sun, and Zou (1999)	Attempts to present a comprehensive survey of the comparison issue between SOEs and TVEs in China.	Finds that, although TVEs have important advantages (such as ownership and corporate governance structures) that enable them to outperform SOEs, SOEs may not have performed so badly if their broad social contributions (other than reported profits) are taken into account. Both SOEs and TVEs need to reform their ownership and governance structures.
Li (1997)	Investigates the effectiveness of China's incremental industrial reform between 1980 and 1989. Uses a panel dataset of 272 state enterprises covering 321 detailed variables. Develops and applies a method	Finds that there were marked improvements in marginal productivity of factors and in TFP between 1980 and 1989. More important, shows that over 87 percent of the TFP growth during this time frame was attributable to improved incentives,

(Table continues on the following page.)

Table A4.3 continued

Authors	Methodology	Main findings
	that measure marginal products of factors and changes in TFP.	intensified product market competition, and improved factor allocation.
Shirley and Xu (2001)	Investigates whether and how performance contracts signed between the government and state enterprise managers affect the productivity of SOEs, using a panel dataset consisting of 769 firms from 1980–9, located in four provinces of China (from *A Survey of Chinese SOEs: 1980–1989*). A Cobb-Douglas production function and the fixed-effects two-stage least squares (FE2SLS) are used.	On average, performance contracts did not improve performance and may have worsened it. But finds that China's contracts were not uniformly bad: In fact, they improved productivity in slightly more than half of the participants. Also finds that contract provisions mattered a great deal, and that contracts can improve productivity when they provide high-powered incentives, use sensible targets, and signal commitment through longer terms and managerial bonds—especially when implemented in a competitive environment. Good contract features were observed most often in smaller SOEs operating under local government oversight in a competitive environment with positive previous performance.
Wei and others (2003)	Examines pre- and post-privatization financial and operating performance, including profitability, output, employment, operating efficiency, and leverage. The dataset covers 208 privatized firms from 1990 to 1997. A general OLS is used.	Finds significant improvements in real output, real assets, and sales efficiency and significant declines in leverage following privatization—but no significant change in profitability. However, privatized enterprises experienced significant improvements in profitability compared to wholly state-owned SOEs during the same period. Firms that convey more than 50% of voting control to private investors experienced significantly greater improvements in profitability, employment, and sales efficiency compared to SOEs.
Lin and Zhu (2001)	Examines the initial organizational changes (including ownership restructuring) brought about by economic	Finds that the state retained a predominant ownership stake in over half of the restructured enterprises; that financial and

Study	Description	Findings
	reform in China. The data, from a questionnaire survey on the restructuring of industrial SOEs conducted by the State Statistical Bureau in 1998, include 40,238 samples. An OLS and Maximum Likelihood estimates for logistic regression are used.	personnel liabilities were not significantly reduced among restructured enterprises; and that there were widespread inconsistencies between the blueprint of reform and the actual organizational features of restructured enterprises.
Li, Li, and Zhang (2000)	Focuses on how product market competition induces institutional change through the interaction between bureaucrats and managers in regional government-controlled economies. Develops a theory of institutional change and applies it to analyze China's transition toward capitalism. The dataset of China's industrial census of more than 400,000 firms and OLS are used.	Submits the theory that, in general, intense product competition stimulates the rise of a private property system to a vigorous empirical test. Finds that the test supports the authors' postulation that cross-regional competition is the driving force behind China's transition to capitalism.
Zhang, Zhang, and Zhao (2002)	Assesses the reform of SOEs by examining the effect of ownership on the profitability and productivity of Chinese industrial firms. Identifies and discusses several methodological issues concerning profit measurements of enterprises under different ownership structures. The dataset includes all industrial enterprises located in Shanghai, over the period 1996–8.	Finds that capital structures, taxes, and welfare burden have a significant effect on the financial performance of Chinese enterprises. After adjusting for these effects, SOEs still show poor financial performance, which is attributable to the effect of "soft loans." In addition, although SOEs grew faster in productive efficiency during 1996–8, their growth rate in profitability lagged behind that of firms with other ownership structures.
Wen, Li, and Lloyd (2002)	Applies the stochastic frontier production function approach to examine the technical efficiency differentials among enterprises of different ownership types in Chinese industries. The data are unit records drawn from the Third Industrial Census of China, conducted in 1995.	Finds that enterprises with ownership types other than state ownership, domestic collective ownership, and joint domestic ownership are (technically) more efficient, on average, than these types. This may indicate that, after 20 years of market-oriented reform, an appropriate operating environment and institutions for

(Table continues on the following page.)

Table A4.3 continued

Authors	Methodology	Main findings
		enterprises of non-state or collective ownership types are coming into existence.
Zhang and Zhang (2001)	Attempts to quantify the effect of ownership and market competition on the productive efficiency and efficiency growth of Chinese industrial firms. A data envelopment analysis (DEA) model and OLS are used. The dataset includes all industrial enterprises located in Shanghai and covers the period 1996–8.	Finds a strong effect of ownership on efficiency, with foreign-owned enterprises exhibiting the highest efficiency scores and SOEs exhibiting the lowest. The degree of competition in the export market is positively associated with enterprise efficiency, but no such association is found between domestic competition and productive efficiency. Finally, SOEs showed (on average) a higher growth in technical efficiency than collective-owned enterprises during 1996 to 1998.
Ray and Zhang (2001)	Examines changes in levels of technical efficiency over time in China's SOEs. The panel dataset is from a survey of activities of 769 SOEs in four provinces (Jiangsu, Jilin, Shanxi, and Sichuan), with 10 annual observations for 321 variables from 1980–9. A DEA and Tobit regression are used.	Estimates a Tobit regression model, using the technical efficiency score as the dependent variable and a set of reform variables and firm attributes as regressors. Finds that technical efficiency can be improved without large-scale privatization, and that appropriate reform can successfully improve technical efficiency of SOEs.

Notes: DEA, data envelopment analysis; FE, fixed effects; FE2SLS, fixed-effects two-stage least squares; FIEs, foreign-invested enterprises; OLS, ordinary least squares; IPOs, initial price offerings; LMEs, large and medium-size enterprises; R&D, research and development; SOEs, state-owned enterprises; TFP, total factor productivity; TVEs, township and village enterprises; 3SLS, three-stage least squares.

Sources: Authors' summaries.

CHAPTER 5

ASSESSING THE EFFECTS OF OWNERSHIP REFORM IN CHINA

A review of the history and achievement of state-owned enterprise reform in China, and of privatization in the transition economies, suggests that ownership reform, particularly of industrial enterprises, can lead to gains in the profitability of firms and to increases in productivity. However, the effectiveness of the reform can depend upon the design of the reform process, the new ownership and governance arrangements, and the changes made in the institutional environment to support industrial organization and competition. The importance of some factors, such as the quality of corporate governance post-reform and the degree of competition, underlies the success of reforms in most countries, whereas other factors have differential effects on the performance of firms. In this chapter, the discussion is intended to extend and deepen understanding of the factors influencing the outcome of state-owned enterprise (SOE) reform in China. Using survey data collected specifically for this study by China's National Bureau of Statistics, the analysis in this chapter tests how institutional and managerial factors contribute to improvements in the performance of the reformed SOEs.

The survey was conducted in the latter half of 2002 and focused on seven manufacturing subsectors: consumer products, electronic components, electronic equipment, garments, general machinery, textiles, and vehicles and vehicle parts. Broadly speaking, these subsectors are drawn from the high-, medium-, and low-technology segments of the industrial spectrum. Among them, three subsectors—electronic components, garments, and vehicles and vehicle parts—will be critical to the growth of manufacturing in China over the medium term. The garment industry has been a driver of growth for the past two decades, and following China's accession to the World Trade Organization (WTO) and the elimination of these quotas by 2005, China's share of world textile exports may increase from the current level of 20 percent to as much as 50 percent by 2010, assuming that no new long-term measures are introduced to restrict the flow of trade ("Is the Wakening" 2003).[1] Exports of electronics from China increased at an astonishing rate of 36 percent per year between 1990 and 2000 (Lall and Albaladejo 2003), reflecting China's cost competitiveness, investment in manufacturing capacity, and the relocation of production from other countries. The explosive growth of domestic automobile demand and the associated rapid increase in production, as well as strong government support for this strategic industry, are likely to keep the automotive sector at the forefront of industrial development over the next several decades.[2]

REFORM IN THE CHINESE URBAN CONTEXT

The sample of firms in this study was selected from five cities: Beijing, Chongqing, Guangzhou, Shanghai, and Wuhan. These are the major industrial cities in China, and their outputs accounted for about 15 percent of China's GDP in 2003 (see table 5.1), and their share is increasing over time. Furthermore, the geographical distribution of these five cities provides a window on the differences reform has made to the performance of the sampled firms drawn from coastal and inland cities. Chongqing, for example, initiated reforms as early as 1983, yet it lags behind some of the coastal cities in terms of output per capita, wages, and foreign direct investment (FDI).[3] In spite of the divestiture of public assets after 1995, the state sector still accounted for 80 percent of industrial fixed assets in 2000 (Han and Wang 2001). Even in Shanghai the share of state-controlled enterprises amounted to 52 percent of GDP in 2002, having fallen from 86 percent in 1978, to 72 percent in 1990, and then 60 percent

---

1. Although the quota set by the WTO Agreement on Textile and Clothing (which replaced the Multifiber Agreement in 1995) was phased out by the end of 2004, this still leaves other protective measures such as tariffs, nontariff barriers, and anti-dumping (Li 2002; Mallon and Whalley 2004). However, these practices will be subject to the regular WTO discipline (Oxfam International 2004). In anticipation of such protectionist measures, China briefly imposed an export tax on textiles ("China Buys" 2004; "Unquotable" 2004) and has taken other measures to contain the explosive growth of exports in 2005.

2. China produced 5.07 million autos in 2004, an increase of 15.5 percent over 2003.

3. Chongqing was elevated to a provincial-status city much like Beijing, Shanghai, and Tianjin in 1997 ("Chongqing Takes Great Leap" 2003). With this upgrading in status and the government's "develop-the-west" policy, the future performance of Chongqing will be an important guide to how this policy will affect the future fortunes of the western region.

Table 5.1 Share of City GDP to National GDP, 1999 and 2003

City	1999 (%)	2003 (%)
Beijing		
Share of city GDP to national GDP	2.64	3.12
Share of city industrial output to total national	1.84	2.68
Share of city industrial employment to total national	1.99	1.40
Chongqing		
Share of city GDP to national GDP	1.81	1.92
Share of city industrial output to total national	1.41	0.54
Share of city industrial employment to total national	1.82	1.86
Guangzhou		
Share of city GDP to national GDP	2.42	2.93
Share of city industrial output to total national	2.63	2.33
Share of city industrial employment to total national	1.09	1.25
Shanghai		
Share of city GDP to national GDP	4.92	5.33
Share of city industrial output to total national	4.97	7.92
Share of city industrial employment to total national	3.28	1.97
Wuhan		
Share of city GDP to national GDP	1.32	1.42
Share of city industrial output to total national	1.35	1.40
Share of city industrial employment to total national	2.54	0.90

Note: GDP, gross domestic product.

Source: Data are derived from Beijing, Chongqing, Guangzhou City, Shanghai, and Wuhan City statistical yearbooks (2004). National statistics are from *China Statistical Yearbook* (National Bureau of Statistics 2004).

in 1995 (Shanghai Statistical Bureau 2003).[4] The actual share of the SOEs is much smaller in Shanghai compared to Chongqing (see table 5.2). Unlike the state-owned enterprises in Beijing, SOEs in Chongqing and Shanghai are larger than other firms and are relatively inefficient considering the gap between the share of employment and output. The SOEs in Beijing are just as inefficient.

Of the three other cities, Wuhan is a large, diversified industrial center that shares many of Chongqing's characteristics and is representative of cities in China's interior heartland. In the past it enjoyed a strategic location, situated on the Yangtze River linking Chongqing and Shanghai and the railroad line linking Beijing and Guangzhou (Han and Wu 2004). It has a large SOE sector, and the industrial composition is weighted toward the

---

4. These include SOEs and state shareholding enterprises, where the state holds the majority of shares.

Table 5.2 Share of SOEs in Beijing, Chongqing, Guangzhou, Shanghai, and
Wuhan, 2003

Share of SOEs in	Beijing (%) 2003	Chongqing (%) 2003	Guangzhou (%) 2003	Shanghai (%) 2003	Wuhan (%) 2003
Establishments	22.44	11.77	6.48	4.46	12.34
Output	13.45	8.09	4.98	8.99	40.35
Employment	23.48	16.52	—	8.89	46.12

Note: SOE, state-owned enterprise; — not available.
Source: Data are derived from Beijing, Chongqing, Guangzhou City, Shanghai, and Wuhan City statistical yearbooks (2004).

transport, engineering, and textile industries.[5] The reform process started in 1987, although the state retained ownership until 2000, when more serious efforts to divest state ownership began (Han and Wu 2004). The remaining cities, Beijing and Guangzhou, are more akin to Shanghai. Both are "coastal" cities with a strong outward orientation. Much like Shanghai, these two cities have been at the leading edge of the reform effort and have experienced rapid development—with producer services and high-tech manufacturing providing much of the impetus. Sizable flows of FDI into industrial subsectors have contributed to the transformation of SOEs in both cities.

By virtue of their size, the scale of the state-owned sector, the burgeoning market environment, and their location in the strategic economic regions of China, the five cities provide a representative perspective of how reform is changing the industrial landscape. A survey of firms in these cities also allows comparison of the survey findings presented in this chapter with those of other studies reported in other chapters.

The chapter is divided into three parts, with the data description in the next section followed by empirical analysis and then a discussion of the survey findings.

DATA DESCRIPTION

The survey of firms in China administered for the World Bank by the China National Bureau of Statistics Enterprise Survey Organization (NBS-ESO) was divided into two parts. The first part of the survey

---

5. The automotive sector accounts for 50 percent of output from the Wuhan Economic and Technological Development Zone ("China: On the Right Tracks" 2004).

Table 5.3 Distribution of Firms across Sectors, 1996–2001

Indicator	Total	Beijing	Chongqing	Guangzhou	Shanghai	Wuhan
Sample size (number)	736	136	150	145	150	155
Electronic equipment	142	25	12	33	33	39
Electronic components	157	36	22	35	33	31
Consumer products	45	4	4	18	14	5
Vehicles & vehicle parts	242	41	82	29	40	50
Garments & leather goods	88	23	8	19	29	9
General machinery	47	7	14	11	1	14
Textiles	15	0	8	0	0	7

Source: Authors' survey data.

instrument, completed by each firm's accountant, presents the basic company profile—with quantitative information on ownership, revenues, cost, and the labor force. It provides a comprehensive description of performance based on a number of selected indicators. The second part, based on a face-to-face interview with the general manager of each firm, elicited information on restructuring and associated layoff of workers, as well as the welfare costs, management structure, and the role of the general manager after restructuring. The interviews also sought information on factors affecting each firm's competitiveness, such as innovation capacity after restructuring.

The survey collected annual data for the period of 1996–2001, drawn from 736 firms in five cities and from seven sectors (see table 5.3). Samples were first drawn by the location and the ownership status of firms (SOE, reformed SOE, and non-SOE), then with reference to the industrial subsectors. Therefore, the sample is not random.

Sample firms are distributed nearly evenly across cities; however, because of difficulties encountered in locating enterprises with the appropriate ownership characteristics, there is some bunching across sectors. The largest number of firms is from the vehicles and vehicle parts sector (242 firms), while there are only 15 firms from the textile sector (see table 5.3). In the sample, there are 406 SOEs, of which 266 firms were transformed mainly into joint ventures, limited liability companies (LLCs), or limited liability shareholding companies (LLSCs) (see table 5.4).[6] In this chapter, an SOE is defined as having a 100 percent state

---

6. In order to register as an LLC, a firm must have a minimum registered capital of 100,000 yuan, with at least two shareholders. For an LLSC, the requirement is 10 million yuan in registered capital, with at least five shareholders (Zhang 2004b). This survey sample does not include employee shareholding cooperative enterprise. Often, small SOEs and township and village enterprises (TVEs) were privatized through insider buyout to take this form (Liu 2005).

Table 5.4 Distribution of SOEs by City and Sector, 1996–2001

Indicator	SOE (reformed)					SOE (not reformed)
	Subtotal	Joint venture	LLC	LLSC	Other	
Sample size (number)	266	73	130	45	18	140
By city						
Beijing	37	2	24	6	5	34
Chongqing	43	3	33	7	0	25
Guangzhou	36	12	18	2	4	23
Shanghai	80	38	20	13	9	24
Wuhan	71	18	35	17	1	34
By sector						
Electronic equipment	46	13	25	5	3	21
Electronic components	47	22	17	5	3	30
Consumer products	19	5	9	3	2	2
Vehicles & vehicle parts	72	29	29	9	5	56
Garments & leather goods	43	2	20	16	5	13
General machinery	29	2	23	4	0	14
Textiles	10	0	7	3	0	4

Note: LLC, limited liability company; LLSC, limited liability shareholding company; SOE, state-owned enterprise.

Source: Authors' survey data.

share during the sample period. If an enterprise went through a restructuring, the manager was asked to describe any changes in their share distribution, and the firm was categorized as a reformed SOE. Non-SOE refers to a firm that was never an SOE but was included as a comparator.

As noted in chapter 3, the LLC is quite similar to a private company, with a board of directors providing oversight and day-to-day business conducted by a manager.[7] An LLSC raises capital through the sale of shares to the public (or state transfer) via an initial public offering and stock market listing (Zhang 2004b). It also has a governance structure similar to an LLC;

7. These firms also are required to have a supervisory board similar to the two-board system in Germany (rather than the unitary board system in the United States). The supervisory board can play one of four roles: honored guest, friendly adviser, censored watchdog, or independent watchdog. Only the fourth role has any real impact on the firm's operation. However, since the Corporate Law does not specify the precise function of a supervisory board, the board has no authority on the hiring and firing decisions of board members, unlike the German system. And with the continuing influence of the state, the roles played by supervisory boards in China have been confined to the first three roles, without much effect on corporate governance relative to the role played by the board of directors (Xiao, Dahya, and Lin 2004).

however, the board of directors for the LLSC has a stronger supervisory role than is the case for the LLC (Keister and Lu 2001). This difference in the role of the board of directors may be because shares for the LLSC can be actively traded in the stock exchange, whereas the shares for the LLC are not listed (see table 5.5 for differences between LLCs and LLSCs). The largest numbers of reformed SOEs in the sample are from Shanghai and Wuhan (80 and 71 firms, respectively), while there are 35 to 43 firms each from Beijing, Chongqing, and Guangzhou. The SOEs that not subject to reform are distributed more evenly across these five cities, ranging from 23 to 34 firms. In terms of sectoral distribution, the largest numbers of reformed SOEs are in the vehicles and vehicle parts industry, some 72 firms in all. The distribution of reformed SOEs is uneven across the other subsectors, with only 10 and 19 firms from textiles and consumer products, respectively.

Of the non-SOEs, 87 and 82 firms are from Chongqing and Guangzhou, respectively, followed by Beijing with 65 firms. Many non-SOEs are either joint ventures or collective firms with a residual in the "other" category. A significant number of private firms are drawn from Chongqing. Wholly owned foreign subsidiaries are from Beijing (4), Guangzhou (10), and Shanghai (8). Typically, non-SOEs are manufacturers of electronic components, electronic equipment, and vehicles and vehicle parts, reflecting recent flows of FDI to these cities (see table 5.6). There is one non-SOE firm in the textile sector, and four are in general machinery.

With respect to the average size of firms measured by the number of workers in 1996, firms in Chongqing tend to be larger, on average, while those in Guangzhou are among the smallest. All cities experienced a decline in average firm size from 1996 to 2001, with Chongqing

Table 5.5 Comparison of LLCs and LLSCs

Attribute	LLC	LLSC
Threshold for equity capital	0.1 million yuan	10 million yuan
Approving authority	Subprovincial	Provincial government or an authority designated by the State Council
Number of shareholders	2–49	5 or more
Shares traded[a]	No	Yes
Board of directors	Yes	Yes
Supervisory board	Yes	Yes

Note: LLC, limited liability company; LLSC, limited liability shareholding company.

a. To be listed in the stock market, firms need equity capital of over 50 million yuan.

Source: Xu, Zhu, and Lin (2001); Zhang (2004b); and Xiao, Dahya, and Lin (2004).

Table 5.6 Distribution of Non-SOEs by City and Sector, 1996–2001

Indicator	Subtotal	Joint venture	Private	Collective	WF	Others
Sample size (number)	330	94	39	56	22	119
By city						
Beijing	65	25	1	15	4	20
Chongqing	82	19	24	15	0	24
Guangzhou	87	25	8	9	10	35
Shanghai	46	12	2	12	8	12
Wuhan	50	13	4	5	0	28
By sector						
Electronic equipment	75	21	3	6	15	30
Electronic components	80	28	6	7	4	35
Consumer products	24	5	1	5	2	11
Vehicles & vehicle parts	115	27	21	34	0	33
Garments & leather goods	32	12	7	2	1	10
General machinery	4	1	0	2	0	1
Textiles	1	0	1	0	0	0

Note: SOE, state-owned enterprise; WF, wholly foreign-owned subsidiaries.

Source: Authors' survey data.

exhibiting the biggest drop. This is probably because more than half of the firms drawn from Chongqing are in some of the largest sectors (general machinery, textiles, and vehicles and vehicle parts), which witnessed a steep fall in the number of employees during this period. Comparing the average size of firms in 1996 to 2001, firms in all cities except for Guangzhou reduced their size by between 20 and 60 percent. Sampled firms in Guangzhou started out smaller, and these firms did not report a cut in their labor force.

The variation in size among sectors is fairly large. The consumer products sector is the smallest, with 618 employees, on average, per firm compared to more than 2,900 for textile firms in 1996 (see table 5.7). Firms in garments, general machinery, leather goods, and vehicles and vehicle parts are, on balance, larger than firms in consumer products, electronic components, and electronic equipment. As observed earlier, the size of firms in most sectors shrank, with the exception of the electronic equipment and components industries. Firms in electronic equipment saw their employment decline until 1998; thereafter, the size of these firms started to increase. Firms in electronic components increased in size until 2000, with a decline in 2001. As would be expected given China's history and stage of development, older firms tend to be in the textiles and general

Table 5.7 Average Size of Firms by City and Sector, 1996–2001
(number of employees)

Indicator	Age	2001	2000	1999	1998	1997	1996
Overall mean	18.6	935	980	1,012	1,083	1,152	1,199
By city							
Beijing	20.9	824	935	985	1,068	1,190	1,137
Chongqing	21.0	1,094	1,129	1,144	1,294	1,396	1,612
Guangzhou	18.9	814	856	820	837	854	848
Shanghai	14.8	1,091	1,108	1,148	1,170	1,311	1,383
Wuhan	17.6	842	867	956	1,043	1,036	1,037
By sector							
Electronic equipment	14.6	704	681	612	595	630	701
Electronic components	16.9	670	707	688	687	669	618
Consumer products	14.2	624	665	712	714	755	752
Vehicles & vehicle parts	18.0	1,186	1,251	1,338	1,465	1,560	1,681
Garments & leather goods	20.2	857	896	938	1,068	1,214	1,205
General machinery	33.2	1,190	1,349	1,515	1,691	1,751	1,813
Textiles	39.7	2,441	2,510	2,460	2,699	2,849	2,912

Source: Authors' survey data.

machinery sectors, while the more recently established firms are in consumer products. It is noteworthy that firms were able to reduce the number of workers during these periods, as the shedding of surplus workers was high on the restructuring agenda. In the sample, 43 percent of firms laid off workers as part of the restructuring effort, and much of this was done through early retirement (see table 5.8).

Measured by the value of fixed assets, firms in Shanghai are the largest, followed by Wuhan and Guangzhou (see table 5.9). Firms in all five of the cities studied increased their fixed assets over the sample period, suggesting that capital intensity (at least for the sampled firms) rose over this time period. Across the sectors, size distribution is fairly typical, taking account of relative factor intensity. At a glance, this does not suggest grossly inappropriate resource allocation across the sectors. However, the general machinery subsector is the exception—because firms in this industry do not possess much by way of fixed assets.

The data show a wide variation in average value added per worker among these five cities. In all three categories, firms in Shanghai outperform those from other cities, closely followed by firms in Guangzhou and Wuhan. This advantage in performance mirrors the differences among firms as measured by the size of fixed assets. The distribution of value added per worker among cities is also quite similar to that for fixed assets

Table 5.8 Dealing with Labor Surplus and Social Welfare Burden through Restructuring

Category/question	Percentage of reformed SOEs that answered Yes to the following questions	
	Number of observations	Yes (%)
Labor surplus		
Has the firm laid off workers since restructuring?	263	43.0
How they reallocated:		
through early retirement	137	70.7
through reemployment arranged by the government	137	4.4
through reemployment arranged by the firm	137	47.4
through local reemployment center	137	31.4
Other (unemployed, contract expiration, inner retirement, etc.)	137	12.4
Social welfare burden		
Did you dispose of hospitals/clinics?	220	12.3
Did you dispose of schools?	220	15.0
Did you dispose of housing for employees?	220	21.8
Did you dispose of others (most firms did not specify)?	220	37.9

Note: Number of observations indicates number of responses.
Source: Authors' survey data.

Table 5.9 Fixed Assets per Employee, by City and Sector, 1996–2001
(thousand yuan)

Indicator	2001	2000	1999	1998	1997	1996
Mean	116.5	107.3	102.0	94.7	91.3	93.9
By city						
Beijing	94.2	85.9	74.9	76.9	55.3	67.5
Chongqing	75.6	69.6	65.7	62.7	58.9	63.1
Guangzhou	107.6	115.2	110.1	100.3	114.7	74.9
Shanghai	174.3	157.6	128.5	128.4	132.5	156.1
Wuhan	125.6	108.6	109.0	103.1	95.9	97.0
By sector						
Electronic equipment	123.2	109.7	107.8	94.1	100.6	145.6
Electronic components	140.9	127.5	117.1	122.7	115.2	102.0
Consumer products	103.3	96.9	85.7	116.3	107.6	108.0
Vehicles & vehicle parts	128.5	120.3	115.4	99.1	96.6	91.3
Garments & leather goods	70.8	63.2	63.5	51.5	47.4	43.1
General machinery	77.5	81.9	75.9	71.7	64.7	75.0
Textiles	57.5	57.8	57.6	54.9	47.1	42.3

Source: Authors' survey data.

Table 5.10 Value Added per Employee, by City and Sector, 1996–2001
(thousand yuan)

Indicator	2001	2000	1999	1998	1997	1996
Mean	83.9	76.1	55.3	50.7	56.7	46.2
By city						
Beijing	74.7	87.5	58.1	36.3	62.2	80.1
Chongqing	37.6	27.6	18.5	22.2	24.9	19.2
Guangzhou	73.1	67.6	38.9	45.3	36.9	16.2
Shanghai	151.6	124.7	110.6	88.4	93.5	72.5
Wuhan	81.5	74.3	50.5	57.8	64.8	44.9
By sector						
Electronic equipment	181.5	129.7	97.3	94.9	133.9	126.9
Electronic components	53.6	57.7	46.2	37.6	41.0	32.1
Consumer products	91.1	85.1	66.7	54.5	54.6	46.2
Vehicles & vehicle parts	74.8	82.7	48.7	48.8	45.8	28.9
Garments & leather goods	39.9	35.3	32.9	29.3	28.4	23.4
General machinery	36.1	30.1	39.4	26.6	28.9	20.0
Textiles	11.9	12.3	10.2	6.1	6.4	6.1

Source: Authors' survey data.

(see table 5.10). In 1996, firms in Beijing had the highest value added per worker, followed closely by firms in Shanghai. By comparison, value added per worker was quite low in Chongqing and Guangzhou. By 2001, value added per worker in Shanghai had more than doubled—and was top-ranked among the cities studied (figure 5.1). Equally impressive was the jump in value added per worker achieved by firms in Guangzhou and Wuhan during the sample period; the increase brought them on par with the value added of firms in Beijing. Firms in Chongqing continued to lag behind, with less than half of the value added per worker of their counterparts in Beijing. Looking at the time-series data, however, all cities except for Beijing have raised value added per worker considerably. Quite strikingly, firms in Beijing experienced a sharp decline in value added per worker in the middle of the sample period, although they had recovered by the end of the period. In the group as a whole, Guangzhou achieved the biggest gains, albeit after starting out from a low base.

Differences in value added per worker by subsectors are as stark as those among cities. Value added per worker in electronic equipment manufacturing is large from the beginning of the sample period to the end, whereas it is the lowest in textiles. During the sample period, all sectors experienced rising value added per worker, especially vehicles and vehicle parts, but again starting from a low base initially. This mirrors the enormous strides made by China's auto industry since the mid-1990s.

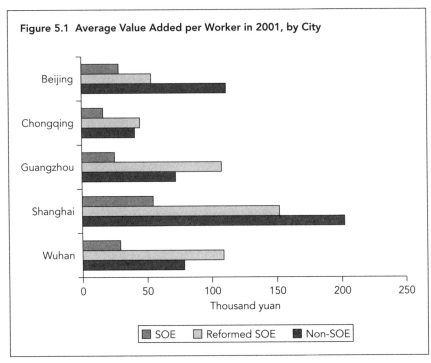

Figure 5.1 Average Value Added per Worker in 2001, by City

Thousand yuan

SOE   Reformed SOE   Non-SOE

Note: SOE, state-owned enterprise.
Source: Authors' survey data.

As mentioned earlier, SOEs in the sample tend most often to be restructured as LLCs and LLSCs. However, in cities such as Guangzhou, Shanghai, and Wuhan, a number of firms entered into joint venture partnerships with foreign firms (see table 5.11). The legal status of firms after restructuring (by sector) again indicates that LLCs and LLSCs are the favored choices—except in electronic components and vehicles and vehicle parts. In these sectors, joint ventures are more prevalent.

There is a wide variation in the years during which reform took place, in selected cities and in the sectors from which the data are drawn (see table 5.12). Although many SOEs underwent reform in 1998, a significant number of firms in Shanghai were reformed prior to 1996. Firms in Wuhan were reformed relatively early compared to firms in other cities. Many firms in subsectors producing electronic equipment, electronic components, and vehicles and vehicle parts were reformed prior to 1996.

As could be expected, the overview of performance in this survey indicates that the impact of reforms on firms varied across cities and

Table 5.11 Legal Status of Reformed SOEs, 1996–2001

Indicator	Total observations	Publicly listed[a]	Joint venture	LLCs	LLSCs	SOEs employee owned	Others	Cooperative/ collective
Sample size (number)	266	11	73	130	45	2	4	1
By city								
Beijing	37	1	2	24	6	1	3	0
Chongqing	43	0	3	33	7	0	0	0
Guangzhou	35	1	12	18	2	1	1	0
Shanghai	80	9	38	20	13	0	0	0
Wuhan	71	0	18	35	17	0	0	1
By sector								
Electronic equipment	46	2	13	25	5	0	1	0
Electronic components	47	2	22	17	5	1	0	0
Consumer products	19	2	5	9	3	0	0	0
Vehicles & vehicle parts	72	4	29	29	9	0	0	1
Garments & leather goods	43	1	2	20	16	1	3	0
General machinery	29	0	2	23	4	0	0	0
Textiles	10	0	0	7	3	0	0	0

Note: LLC, limited liability company; LLSC, limited liability shareholding company.

a. Listed on Shanghai or Shenzhen stock exchange.

Source: Authors' survey data.

Table 5.12 Number of Reforms Implemented, by City and Sector, 1996–2001

City and sector	Before 1996	1996	1997	1998	1999	2000	2001	2002
By city								
Beijing	2	1	2	4	5	7	8	8
Chongqing	3	5	9	7	5	5	5	4
Guangzhou	3	1	9	17	1	3	1	0
Shanghai	39	1	8	10	8	5	2	1
Wuhan	7	16	13	11	9	8	6	0
By sector								
Electronic equipment	15	3	7	8	3	5	5	0
Electronic components	20	1	6	6	6	5	2	1
Consumer products	5	0	4	3	1	1	0	0
Vehicles & vehicle parts	12	7	16	14	8	5	5	4
Garments & leather goods	2	4	5	11	7	6	4	4
General machinery	1	3	3	4	3	3	8	4
Textiles	0	6	0	3	0	0	0	1

Source: Authors' survey data.

subsectors. Reformed SOEs perform better in Guangzhou, Shanghai, and Wuhan, while firms in Beijing and Chongqing lag behind. Particularly notable is the growth in value added per worker of firms in Wuhan. In 1996, their value added per worker was comparable to that of firms in Beijing and Chongqing. By 2001, however, value added per worker of firms in Wuhan was twice as large as that of those in Beijing and Chongqing. Furthermore, reformed SOEs perform better than the average of all firms in Chongqing, Guangzhou, and Wuhan; they are on par with other firms in Shanghai and perform worse than other firms in Beijing (see tables 5.10 and 5.13). Sectoral averages show that firms in electronic equipment are the star performers, a finding that is both intuitively plausible and supported by the data on exports and FDI (see chapter 1). However, unlike the average for all firms by subsectors, reformed SOEs in vehicles and vehicle parts did better than those in electronic components and consumer products. Again, firms from the general machinery and textile subsectors rank at the bottom. Reformed SOEs in electronic equipment do not perform as well as the sector average. This may be because of the intense competition from a large number of non-SOEs in this sector, which one might assume would do better than the SOEs, including reformed SOEs. For the other subsectors, value added of reformed SOEs is comparable to the sector averages. Among the

Table 5.13 Average Value Added per Employee of Reformed SOEs, by City and Sector, 1996–2001
(thousand yuan)

Indicator	2001	2000	1999	1998	1997	1996
Mean	99.5	90.1	69.9	63.3	64.1	42.7
By city						
Beijing	53.3	42.3	33.3	26.5	25.6	24.9
Chongqing	44.6	41.2	35.6	31.2	28.7	23.5
Guangzhou	107.6	70.6	15.2	55.7	42.3	34.2
Shanghai	141.7	150.4	140.2	86.4	93.8	81.8
Wuhan	108.9	89.4	59.5	77.3	78.2	23.7
By sector						
Electronic equipment	150.9	126.7	81.2	104.6	121.3	51.1
Electronic components	101.9	115.9	90.2	68.6	50.2	39.6
Consumer products	105.5	65.2	46.9	−17.2	67.1	59.1
Vehicles & vehicle parts	138.3	126.6	102.0	94.2	80.2	60.9
Garment & leather goods	39.9	32.9	34.1	30.5	33.1	29.6
General machinery	34.2	27.2	27.2	26.3	27.3	16.4
Textiles	14.1	13.3	13.6	8.6	8.8	8.8

Source: Authors' survey data.

sectors, those that are top performers also had entered into a significant number of joint ventures when SOEs were restructured (electronic components, equipment, and vehicles and vehicle parts), which is what would be expected from the findings reported in chapter 4 of this volume. The exception is consumer products.

A closer look at the difference in performance across firms allows for a division of subsectors into two groups. In one group, the ranking of value added within the sector is SOEs, reformed SOEs, then non-SOEs, in ascending order. In the other group, the ranking is SOEs, non-SOEs, and then reformed SOEs (see figure 5.2). In either group, it is clear that value added of the SOEs was the lowest within the sector, which again reaffirms the findings reported in chapter 4 and earlier. This is as clear a picture as one can obtain in support of enterprise reform in China. It is broadly in line with the findings of Garnaut, Song, and Yao (2004), who state that "*gaizhi* (reformed) firms have performed much better than non-*gaizhi* firms in most respects. On average [their] profit rate was 50 percent higher [and] in 2001, a worker in a *gaizhi* firm produced three times as much

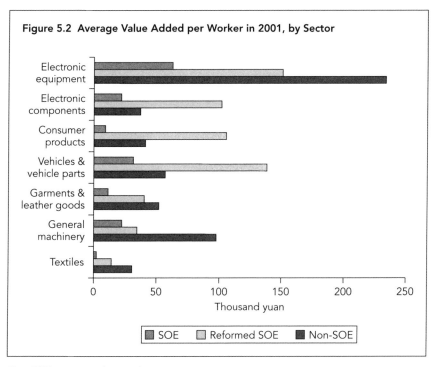

Figure 5.2 Average Value Added per Worker in 2001, by Sector

Thousand yuan

SOE   Reformed SOE   Non-SOE

Note: SOE, state-owned enterprise.
Source: Authors' survey data.

value added as a worker in a non-*gaizhi* firm" (pp. 24–25).[8] It is important to note, however, that non-SOEs are not always at the forefront with respect to performance. One should keep in mind that non-SOEs include a diverse collection of firms, ranging from nascent private firms to well-established multinationals.

Thus, from the data presented here, it appears that the restructuring efforts in China are bearing fruit. Firms in most cities have shed excess labor through early retirement and other means and have increased value added. Laid-off workers are being assisted (as described in chapter 3) by employment insurance and through reemployment centers set up by reformed SOEs or local governments.[9] The reform efforts have introduced different forms of ownership and of corporate governance associated with these ownership structures.

In the following section, the analysis attempts to untangle these different aspects of reform, in an effort to shed light on which aspects of the reform effort contributed the most to changes in performance.

EMPIRICAL METHODOLOGY

Most studies of SOE reform and privatization described in chapter 4 use a specification similar to equation (5.1) to examine how the performance of privatized enterprises compares with that of SOEs:

(5.1) $$Y = \alpha + \beta X + \gamma P + \varepsilon,$$

where Y is a measure of enterprise performance (either quantitative or qualitative), X consists of variables representing enterprise characteristics, and P comprises various policy measures associated with privatization. A wide range of variables can be included in Y, X, and P depending on the nature of the research questions.

The independent variable Y is often proxied quantitatively by output levels, value added, or growth rates of these variables. Qualitative measures for Y are also used extensively, especially in empirical studies for the former Soviet Union, where accounting data are sparse or unreliable.

---

8. Remember, though, that the results can be biased upward due to selection bias that affects these types of studies. The issue of selection bias is discussed in the following section.

9. There are many cases in which government agencies set up businesses to provide employment for workers who are laid off, but also to provide agencies with additional sources of funds (Duckett 2001). However, retraining of laid-off workers is a challenge. The evidence from Eastern Europe suggests that unskilled workers are disproportionately affected by privatization, and that the skill requirements following privatization are shifting upward (Commander 2004).

X can measure a wide range of enterprise characteristics, depending on the research question. Common characteristics include competition, capacity utilization, size of firm, access to finance, and year of privatization, as well as sectoral, regional, municipal, time, and firm dummies.

The main interest typically lies in the coefficient estimates associated with the vector of variables associated with policy measures. One common measure for P is the percentage of privately owned shares, or an ownership dummy capturing whether the private share exceeds certain threshold values. Other measures such as the existence of a soft budget constraint, manager turnover, and incentives for managers are often included as well.

As pointed out by Djankov and Murrell (2002, p. 746),

> the variety in the formulation of estimating equations is a reflection of two factors. First, there is the absence of a single compelling theory that models the process of change within an enterprise. Without such theory, specifications for estimating equations rely on ad hoc formulations. Second, the set of variables for which data are available varies greatly, with every study having deficiencies in some respect. Given these reasons for the variety of approaches, and none obviously superior to all others, it seems judicious to include a wide range of studies in drawing general conclusions.

In this study, value added is used as the main indicator of firm performance, in conjunction with the production function approach, since this is the prevailing model of privatization. As described later, rich data are available on the institutional and managerial characteristics of the reformed firms in China; and in this study, these data are used to test whether such institutional and corporate governance have any effect on the performance of reformed firms. Since the reform process in China proceeded rather slowly, there is a high likelihood that selection bias is present.[10] Selection bias is primarily parried by employing the fixed-effect in panels when such data are available.[11] Otherwise, the estimates can be biased—with the direction of bias depending on whether or not the better-performing firms are selected for reform. First, one must determine whether the firms were indeed selected for reform and determine what criteria were used for the selection. Then, panel estimation can be used in some specifications, to account for the selection bias. However, some data (mainly on institutional and managerial characteristics) are available only

---

10. Similar concerns are voiced by Garnaut, Song, and Yao (2004).

11. This approach is often used to measure the effect of privatization (by taking into account the firm-specific factors), since there is no agreed theory on modeling of the explicit selection of firms for privatization (Djankov and Murrell 2002).

for 2001, which prevents the use of panel estimation. Hence, the results of these estimations should be interpreted with appropriate caution.

Independent Variables

With regard to determining the relationship between enterprise performance and firm ownership, the first step involves isolating differences among firms with different ownership (Megginson and Netter 2001).

Firm Characteristics. Broadly speaking, based on the findings from the literature in Eastern Europe and the Commonwealth of Independent States (CIS), private ownership yields better performance than state ownership; foreign ownership seems to be associated with superior firm performance; and firms with a few large shareholders perform much better than those with diffused shareholding (Djankov and Murrell 2002). There are various ways of constructing this measure of ownership. One can use the share itself or create dummy variables if a particular type of share is larger than the threshold value.

The literature on enterprise restructuring in China suggests that enterprises with private or foreign ownership often perform better than those under state ownership, as one would expect.[12] However, there is little discussion on the relationship between enterprise performance and various degrees of diffused shareholding.

This survey provides detailed ownership information, especially information on changes in ownership structure and performance before and after SOE reforms in China. Among various measures of ownership and means of constructing this variable, firm ownership type and ownership shares were chosen to classify the types of firms in China.

The firms were first divided into three groups: SOE, reformed SOE, and non-SOE. SOEs are defined as those firms with 100 percent state ownership during the entire sample period. Reformed SOEs are defined as those former SOEs that were reformed to become LLCs, LLSCs, or joint ventures, with the state still retaining some portion of shares. Other types of firms that were never classified as SOEs in the past (such as joint ventures and wholly owned subsidiaries) are included in non-SOEs. Based on this classification, there are 266 reformed SOEs, 140 nonreformed

---

12. For example, see Lin and Zhu (2001), Liu (2005), Xu, Zhu, and Lin (2001), Wen, Li, and Lloyd (2002), Zhang and Zhang (2001), and Zhang (2004b). For listed firms, government ownership tends to depress the corporate values of these, although the relationship is not monotonic (Tian and Estrin 2005).

SOEs, and 330 non-SOEs in the sample. This balance among three categories facilitates comparison of enterprise performance across different ownership categories. However, there is considerable heterogeneity among the groupings of reformed SOEs and non-SOEs. Since there is detailed information on the ownership structure, the share of each type of ownership is included—to test whether the larger shares of one type of shareholder might be associated with better firm performance.

To account for the interindustry differences and intercity differences, dummy variables are included for the industrial subsectors and the city locations.

POLICY MEASURES

After reviewing 82 analyses appearing in 23 studies, Djankov and Murrell (2002) conclude that product market competition improves the productivity in transition economies as a whole.[13] If one further divides market competition into domestic and import competition, each is significant in explaining enterprise performance, although the most robust results are obtained when using the domestic competition variable.

Competition

When a ranking or lagged own-market share is employed as a proxy for domestic competitiveness, and when manager perception of import competition or the import penetration ratio is used as a proxy for import competition, a potential endogeneity problem arises. All four variables are problematic because the first two might be endogenous to enterprise performance and the latter two might be endogenous to domestic firm performance. Empirical studies try finding different ways to solve the endogeneity problem, such as using the Herfindahl index as a proxy for domestic competition (for example, Konings 1998), and changes in the statutory tariff rate to represent import competition (for example, Djankov and Hoekman 2000).

---

13. Individual studies report mixed results depending on the countries and variables used. Djankov and Murrell (2002) summarize studies on the relationship between productivity and competition. Productivity is proxied by TFP (55 analyses), labor productivity (19), sales growth (2), and others (6). As for competition, domestic competition is proxied by the Herfindahl index (25), percentage share of the firm with the largest sales (15), number of local competitors (12), and the firm's own market share (2). Import market share is proxied by the import penetration ratio (20) and industry tariff rate (8).

The survey presented in this chapter provides information on the degree of competition from both domestic and import sources. In addition, the survey obtained data on the number of new entrants in 2001. Hence, it was possible to use the number of local and overseas competitors to proxy for the domestic competition and import penetration in a cross-section regression, using the data for these two variables in 2001.

Soft Budget

The negative effect of soft budget constraints on enterprise productivity is highly significant in studies of Eastern European countries and generally significant in the CIS countries.[14] Studies based on Chinese data also find negative effects of soft budget constraints on firm performance. Zhang, Zhang, and Zhao (2002) argue that soft loans permit SOEs to employ excessive amounts of capital and lead to poor financial performance (return on assets) in China, based on a panel dataset of 1,838 firms in 26 industries during the period 1996–8. However, they do not have a good indicator for representing "soft loans," and simply claim that because SOEs have easier access to soft loans regardless of the expected returns, they should have a lower return on assets (ROA).

Using survey data on 681 enterprises in China for the period of 1980 to 1994, Li and Liang (1998) construct indicators of soft budget constraints based on the employment of nonproduction workers, investment with below-average rates of return, and the distribution of bonuses in excess of levels defined by the government. They find that nonproduction workers and excessive bonuses, respectively, contribute to 38 percent and 39 percent of the financial loss. And all enterprises in financial distress expect to be bailed out by the government.

A simultaneity problem exists in most empirical work on the soft budget constraint. Theoretically, "poorly-performing firms get bailed out, while good firms do not since they do not need to. Researchers want to examine whether soft budgets cause poor performance, yet the data may be overwhelmed by the relationship operating in the other direction. Researchers addressed this problem in various ways, but none is satisfactory" (Djankov and Murrell 2002, p. 53).

Thus, the soft budget should be measured as the expectation of managers on the likelihood of a government bailout when facing financial

---

14. Djankov and Murrell's (2002) result is based on the meta-analysis of 10 papers on this issue. All but one of the papers are on 25 transition economies and focus on Central and East European countries for the period 1992–9.

distress. Few empirical papers study the soft budget issue because of the difficulty in obtaining the data on expectations. An exception is the research of Anderson, Lee, and Murrell (2000), which uses survey data from Mongolia to test for the effect of soft budget constraints on firm performance. Because the design of the study and survey centered on the issue of the soft budget, they included questions regarding managers' expectations on state bailout where appropriate.

Following Anderson, Lee, and Murrell's approach, the survey presented here also included such questions regarding the expectation of a bailout rather than questions on the history of bailouts. Hence, endogeneity need not be a major concern. In addition, this survey gathered information on managers' expectations with regard to who would provide funds for such a bailout. This is potentially important in assessing whether a bailout by the state is more negatively associated with firm performance—or if it is just the possibility of a bailout by others that negatively affects firm performance. For instance, if firms expect banks to bail them out, would that expectation negatively affect the performance of these firms? If that is the case, then reform of the banks (in China's case, the privatization of four main banks) would not necessarily lead to better enterprise performance. Instead, the possibility of a bailout from any source should be excluded when firms and banks are faced with the threat of bankruptcy.

Another interesting question relates to the likelihood of a correlation between firm characteristics and the expectation of a bailout. The data collected for this study are used to investigate the effects of various ownership structures on the likelihood of receiving a bailout.

Incentives for Managers

Both incentives for managers and the dismissal of managers, together and individually, may exert enough positive effects on managers to improve firm performance (Megginson and Netter 2001). Most studies discuss the role of managers in China, and a few examine this issue in Central and Eastern Europe or the former Soviet Union. Lee (1990) uses two incentive dummies based on two survey questions: whether the enterprise has implemented all incentive reforms (such as a manager's bonus and performance contract), and any of the incentive reforms. The results show that the adoption of all incentive reforms increases productivity by 4 percent.

Research based on survey data of 769 SOEs over the years 1980–9 by Groves and others (1994) shows that bonuses for managers are positively associated with productivity in five manufacturing industries: building materials, chemicals, electronics, machinery, and textiles. Using the same dataset, Groves and others (1995) find that incentives for managers improve profitability by 7.3 percentage points.

Li (1997) estimated that a 1 percentage point increase in a manager's bonus raised total factor productivity (TFP) growth by 0.089 percentage point between 1980 and 1984, and 0.060 percentage points between 1985 and 1989. With the help of a panel dataset of 272 SOEs in China over the years of 1980–9, in contrast, Shirley and Xu (2001) find a negative but insignificant relation between a manager performance contract and TFP growth, using the same survey dataset as Groves and others (1994; 1995). In their study, Shirley and Xu (2001) use the presence of a performance contract as a proxy for manager incentives, although this cannot very well differentiate the degree of bonus incentives among firms. Utilizing a dataset of 680 SOEs in China from 1980 to 1994, Li and Wu (2002) test the relative effectiveness of ownership reform versus incentive mechanisms on productivity. While their results robustly support ownership reform—ownership diversification has an economically large and positive impact on the performance—they obtained mixed results on the impact of managerial autonomy and profit incentives. Claessens and Djankov (1999) use stock ownership as a proxy for manager incentives in Czech companies but fail to find any evidence of its effects on enterprise productivity.

From the literature, it appears that the best measure of incentives for managers should include data not only on managers' equity ownership and salaries but also on bonuses and stock options where these are obtainable. This study only collected information regarding the ownership share of managers. Hence this variable is used as an imprecise measure of incentives for managers.

Management Appointee and Turnover

Incentives work if and only if one believes that these managers have the knowledge and skills needed to efficiently operate a firm in a market environment. Where that is not the case, any incentive mechanism will be ineffective, and a change of managers is required. As an indicator of managerial competence, this study uses tertiary education as well as overseas training. Domestic education and foreign education are differentiated to see if a manager's education abroad has any positive effects on firm performance. Groves and others (1995) is the first study to examine the effect of management turnover in China. They find the turnover rate was very high during the sample period of 1980–9, which reflects the functioning of the market for managers. New managers bring about a 16 percent rise in labor productivity. With this dataset, Shirley and Xu (2001) also find that new managers bring an increase in TFP of about 4 percentage points. In line with the findings of cross-country research, Xu, Zhu, and Lin (2001) show, moreover, that there is a negative effect on ROA if the government appoints the chief executive officer and/or the same person serves as chief executive officer both before and after SOE restructuring.

Studies on manager turnover in Eastern Europe and CIS countries often suffer from an endogeneity problem. In many cases, new owners have appointed new managers; thus, separating the effects of changes in ownership from changes in managers is difficult, especially when the new owners take over the management. Among the studies on Eastern Europe, one by Claessens and Djankov (1999) provides evidence on manager turnover in the Czech Republic, utilizing the fact that managers were prevented from owning a significant share of the privatized firms. Claessens and Djankov (1999) find a high rate of management turnover in Czech companies in transition. Furthermore, the results show that labor productivity increased by 4.2 percent in privatized enterprise and by 3.5 percent in state-owned firms when there was a change in managers. But Frydman, Hessel, and Rapaczynski (2000b), employing data on the Czech Republic, Hungary, and Poland between 1991 and 1993, find that management turnover does not have a statistically significant effect on revenue growth in SOEs, but does have a sizable positive effect—an 18.5 percent increase—in privatized enterprises. Using data from Ukraine, Warzynski (2003) shows that manager turnover does not have any effect on productivity of SOEs but does have a small positive effect for privatized firms. This suggests that turnover itself may not be enough; but one must take a closer look both at how the turnover is affected and at other changes in managerial incentives and autonomy.

Data from the survey presented here include information on whether managers changed before and after the restructuring; and if so, who appointed these managers, along with some information on manager characteristics, such as education levels, their tenures at firms, and whether managers were promoted from within the firm.[15] From table 5.14 one can see that in close to half of the firms that became joint ventures or LLCs, new managers were appointed; but those that became LLSCs or remained

_____

15. There are four relevant questions in the survey: (1) Is the manager the same person before and after restructuring? (2) How many years did the manager serve the firm? (3) How was the manager appointed? (4) Was the manager promoted within the firm or brought in from outside?

Table 5.14 Appointment of Managers and Board of Directors by the State, by Enterprise Type, City, and Sector

Enterprise	JV	LLC	LLSC	SOE (Not reformed)
Number of observations	73	120	43	140
Different manager	47	57	15	0
Managers appointed by government	0	24	6	86
Has board of directors	72	115	43	13
Board of directors appointed by government	8	31	14	9

City	Beijing	Chongqing	Guangzhou	Shanghai	Wuhan
Number of observations	71	68	58	104	105
Different manager	9	19	12	47	42
Managers appointed by government[a]	29	24	18	18	36
Has board of directors	37	42	34	83	73
Board of directors appointed by government[a]	3	9	8	26	16

Sector	Electronic equipment	Electronic components	Consumer products	Vehicles & vehicle parts	Garments & leather goods	General machinery	Textiles
Number of observations	67	77	21	12	56	43	14
Different manager	19	2	13	35	17	11	5
Managers appointed by government[b]	17	28	2	95	15	15	9
Has board of directors	50	47	17	75	42	28	10
Board of directors appointed by government[b]	9	6	3	19	15	8	2

a. Managers/ board of directors appointed by subnational and/or national government.
b. Appointed by subnational and/or national government.
Source: Authors' survey data.

SOEs did not change their managers. In the case of LLCs and LLSCs, the government appointed less than half of the managers, while more than 60 percent of managers for SOEs were appointed by the government. The government did not appoint any managers for joint venture firms. In terms of the establishment of the board of directors, almost all reformed firms established the board of directors. For the board of directors, the government did not intervene as much as it did for the appointment of managers, although the government did so for eight joint venture firms.[16]

Manager Autonomy

Any effect on incentives is contingent upon the degree of autonomy that managers enjoy. After all, even if incentives were given, if these managers found their decisionmaking powers substantially constrained, one would not expect any incentive scheme to have much effect. Therefore, managers need both incentives and autonomy—and this calls for the inclusion of variables representing the degree of manager autonomy.

Lin and Zhu (2001) find a positive correlation between TFP growth and the managers' business decision autonomy, based on survey data of 40,238 industrial SOEs in 1998. Xu, Zhu, and Lin (2001) also use this dataset to find a positive correlation between ROA and managers' business and hiring/firing autonomy, but a negative impact on ROA if the CEO is appointed by the government and if the CEO remains after restructuring.

Bodmer (2002) studies the relationship between the manager's autonomy and productivity, using a survey of 769 SOEs during 1980–94 in China. He uses four dummy variables: manager's performance contract, the share of contract workers, manager's output autonomy, and manager's autonomy in hiring/firing workers. The empirical results show that the first three variables have significant and positive effects on productivity, although employment reform yields a negative but insignificant outcome, suggesting that this had little effect on productivity. McGoldrick and Walsh (2004), using a panel of 681 firms during 1980–94, find that labor and business decision autonomy has led to higher productivity of firms, even after accounting for selection bias.

In this survey, two questions were related to autonomy: whether managers could make business decisions independently and whether

---

16. The variable for government involvement in the establishment of the board of directors is constructed by combining the two questions regarding the appointment and approval of the board of directors in the questionnaire.

managers could make hiring/firing decisions independently. The first variable measures the overall autonomy enjoyed by the managers. Given the tendency for SOEs to hire more labor than necessary and the importance of labor-shedding after the restructuring, the estimates on the second variable can provide a clear sense for managerial discretion as well as guidelines for policy.

Decisionmaking Mechanism

As noted in chapters 2 and 4, a well-selected motivated board of directors can contribute significantly to the efficient and effective operation of a modern firm. And the composition of the board of directors and the distribution of voting rights reflect the effectiveness of the protection afforded to minority shareholders' interests.

The research by Lin and Zhu (2001) and by Xu, Zhu, and Lin (2001) finds a positive correlation between TFP/ROA and one-share-one-vote, using their survey data of 40,238 industrial SOEs in China in 1998.[17]

The survey instrument presented here included a question regarding the voting rights (asking whether the firms use one-share-one-vote or one-head-one-vote).[18] And based on the responses to this question, it is possible to test whether a mismatch between the financial stake and voting can affect firm performance.

SELECTION BIAS

In this type of study, especially on China, where the reforms were introduced gradually and in a piecemeal fashion, researchers cannot escape from the potential problems that arise from selection bias (compared to studies on mass privatization). It may be that reformed SOEs in China perform better than the SOEs that were not reformed, because these were better-performing firms to begin with. Unlike mass privatization in the Czech Republic and Russia, governments in China may have preferentially selected such enterprises in order to sustain the momentum for reform. For instance, Liu, Sun, and Woo (2005) find that sales and potential

---

17. In their dataset, only one-third of firms had one-share-one-vote.

18. This survey contains questions on whether or not a firm has a board of directors, the composition of the board, whether the general manager and the head of the board are the same person, and how the board is selected.

sales growth influence privatization decisions by the local authorities. Alternatively, policymakers in China may tend to divest their worst-performing firms in order to cut losses and hold on to the more profitable ones.[19]

As shown in table 5.4, there seems to be a systematic difference among SOEs and reformed SOEs before the restructuring. To test whether the Chinese government has handpicked SOEs to be reformed, a set of regressions was run with the status of reform as the dependent variable. For the independent variables, data from 1996 were used as the selection criteria since the data studied start from 1996. As mentioned earlier, the Chinese government can choose better-performing firms to be reformed, so that they can sustain the momentum of the reform effort. In this case, the higher the revenue (or profit), the higher the probability that this firm will be chosen to be reformed later. In addition, the government may choose to reform smaller firms first, as this will not generate less unemployment. In this specification, the coefficient estimate on the number of workers should be negative. The sample consists of 302 SOEs, of which 170 were reformed after 1996. Beijing and vehicles and vehicle parts producers were chosen as the basis for the dummy variables included in the estimation.

Table 5.15 shows the results from this estimation. As expected, the better the performance of firms (measured by revenue, profit, and value added), the more likely that these firms will be reformed. And the larger the firm, the less likely it will be reformed. However, the results on the number of workers depend on the inclusion of performance indicators (revenue, profit, or value added) to be significant. It may be that the decision was made jointly—based on both the performance and size of the firm.

The results on the dummies show large differences among locations and subsectors. Shanghai, Wuhan, and, to a lesser extent, Chongqing are municipalities that have adopted a more progressive attitude; and firms in these cities are more likely to be reformed than firms in Beijing. This result also reflects the composition of this sample (see table 5.4). These are the cities with the largest number of reformed SOEs in the sample. The results on cities are consistent with the authors' suspicion that firms are selected to be reformed and that one should be aware of the selection bias.

However, the differences among subsectors are counterintuitive. For instance, the results on consumer products and the garments industry are

---

19. Li and others (2001) make a similar argument.

Table 5.15 Selection Criteria

Variable	Model 1	Model 2	Model 3	Model 4	Model 5	Model 6	Model 7
Total revenue		0.361*	1.1733***				
		(0.213)	(0.408)				
Total profit				1.2695*	2.5149***		
				(0.677)	(0.934)		
Value added?						1.2186**	2.9924***
						(0.588)	(0.939)
Number of workers?	−0.0133		−0.1335***		−0.0697**		−0.1004**
	(0.027)		(0.047)		(0.035)		(0.041)
Chongqing	0.4536*	0.4231*	0.4865*	0.4211*	0.4456*	0.4262*	0.4675*
	(0.256)	(0.256)	(0.262)	(0.255)	(0.257)	(0.256)	(0.258)
Guangzhou	0.3456	0.3739	0.3404	0.3562	0.3180	0.3621	0.3153
	(0.255)	(0.256)	(0.258)	(0.256)	(0.257)	(0.256)	(0.257)
Shanghai	0.5897**	0.5525**	0.5178**	0.5457**	0.526**	0.5301**	0.4844*
	(0.247)	(0.248)	(0.255)	(0.248)	(0.251)	(0.248)	(0.252)
Wuhan	0.5457**	0.5745**	0.567**	0.5623**	0.5359**	0.5688***	0.5411**
	(0.229)	(0.231)	(0.231)	(0.23)	(0.231)	(0.231)	(0.231)

Electronic equipment	0.3032	0.3693	0.3341	0.3655	0.3369	0.3799	0.3600
	(0.243)	(0.241)	(0.245)	(0.243)	(0.247)	(0.243)	(0.248)
Electronic components	−0.1376	−0.0525	−0.1059	−0.0693	−0.1225	−0.0520	−0.1051
	(0.231)	(0.231)	(0.232)	(0.23)	(0.231)	(0.231)	(0.231)
Consumer products	1.2346***	1.285***	1.1863***	1.2988***	1.2524***	1.3153***	1.2765***
	(0.418)	(0.418)	(0.427)	(0.421)	(0.43)	(0.422)	(0.437)
Garments & leather goods	0.7725***	0.831***	0.8225***	0.8299***	0.8166***	0.8441***	0.8428***
	(0.246)	(0.246)	(0.249)	(0.247)	(0.248)	(0.248)	(0.25)
General machinery	0.4732*	0.5383**	0.6123**	0.5229**	0.5384***	0.5306**	0.5639**
	(0.248)	(0.25)	(0.255)	(0.25)	(0.251)	(0.25)	(0.251)
Textiles	0.0262	0.0931	0.2117	0.0970	0.1611	0.1043	0.2080
	(0.479)	(0.483)	(0.491)	(0.485)	(0.489)	(0.485)	(0.493)
Constant	−0.4684**	−0.5853***	−0.4734**	−0.5564***	−0.4531**	−0.5809***	−0.4676**
	(0.215)	(0.212)	(0.218)	(0.21)	(0.216)	(0.212)	(0.218)
Number of observations	302	302	302	302	302	302	302

Note: * significant at 10%, ** significant at 5%, and *** significant at 1%. Dummy variables for Beijing and for vehicles and vehicle parts are not included, to avoid multi-collinearity. Estimated using probit.

Source: Authors' computations.

somewhat perplexing. One should obtain negative coefficient estimates on consumer products and garments, since firms in these subsectors tend not to perform as well as firms in other sectors. However, the results obtained here are the opposite of what was expected after controlling for the size of the firm, location, and performance. These lagging firms are more likely to be reformed relative to firms in vehicles and vehicle parts, yet they tend to have lower value added and average profits than firms in vehicles and vehicle parts (see table 5.3 and figures 5.3 and 5.4). If, in fact, there is a positive selection bias, then these firms will not be selected to be reformed. However, in terms of the number of workers, firms in these sectors tend to be smaller than those in vehicles and vehicle parts. After controlling for the performance measure and the number of workers, one still obtains the result that firms in these two sectors are more likely to be reformed. This may be due to the industrial policies pursued by the Chinese government. Vehicles and vehicle parts has been designated as one of the pillar industries in China; hence, firms in this subsector are protected (or retain the SOE status) more than firms in other sectors.

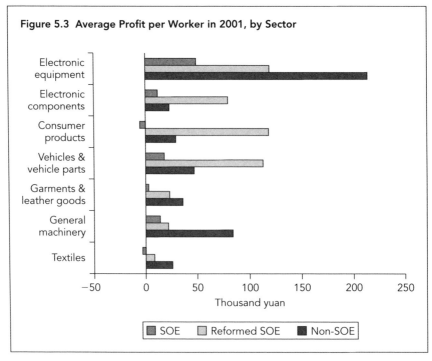

Figure 5.3 Average Profit per Worker in 2001, by Sector

Note: SOE, state-owned enterprise.
Source: Author's survey data.

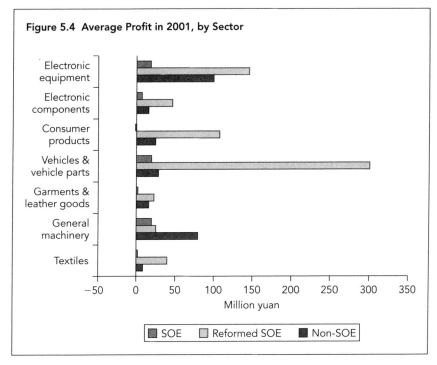

Figure 5.4 Average Profit in 2001, by Sector

Note: SOE, state-owned enterprise.
Source: Authors' survey data.

What these results suggest is that firms were deliberately selected to be reformed. The criteria used seem to be based on revenue (profit), number of workers, and the industry sectors. The results discussed later as empirical findings may derive from the inherent characteristics of the firm rather than stem from the reform efforts themselves. However, the direction of the bias is uncertain. On the one hand, the estimates will be biased upward if selection is purely based on performance. On the other hand, the bias could be reversed if the selection was also done by the subsector and the size of firms. Firms in strategic industries are less likely to be reformed, although their performance is better than those in other industries. In addition, larger firms are less likely to be reformed. Presumably, this is linked to the concerns over rising unemployment in the urban areas. With these criteria, the bias should be downward.[20]

_____

20. Although one can argue that since SOEs tend to employ more workers than necessary, the larger the SOEs, the more inefficient they are.

Thus, the selection criteria appear to be a rather complex combination of factors acting in opposite directions. Panel regressions will be used to account for the selection bias. The estimates obtained from the fixed-effect model should reveal the effect stemming from the reform itself. For testing the various institutional and managerial characteristics, selection bias will not apply, since the focus here is on specific firm characteristics rather than the status of reform.

EMPIRICAL TESTS AND FINDINGS

Starting with a baseline regression analysis, we present empirical results of SOE reform in China using the survey data.

Baseline Results

Before accounting for the possibility of selection bias, table 5.16 presents the results of the baseline regressions. The first column shows the outcomes when dummy variables are included only for the sector, city, and year (in addition to labor and capital). Again, Beijing and vehicles and vehicle parts are chosen as the basis of dummy variables. These variables indicate that firms in the electronic equipment industry turn in the best performance, with garment, machinery, and textiles subsectors the apparent laggards. Firms in Shanghai stand out as the star performers. These results do not change significantly when dummies are included for reformed SOEs and non-SOEs. In fact, the initial results confirm that the reformed SOEs perform much better than the SOEs.

To test whether various ownership types affect firm performance, the reformed SOE dummies are further disaggregated into joint ventures, LLCs, LLSCs, and others; and the non-SOE dummies, into joint ventures, private, collective, wholly owned foreign subsidiaries, and others. It turns out that reformed SOEs of various types still perform better than SOEs, with LLSCs leading the pack, followed by joint ventures. Reformed SOEs that chose the LLC route also show improvement, but less so than the gains made by the other types of reformed SOEs. The results for the non-SOEs are more varied. The better-performing non-SOEs are the joint ventures and others, while other types of non-SOEs perform poorly—although these estimates are not statistically significant at the conventional level.[21] Nonetheless, it is notable that collectives including township and

---

21. The imprecise estimates on disaggregated non-SOEs may be due to the small number of observations, especially once cities and sectors are controlled for.

Table 5.16 Basic Regression Results

Variable	Model 1	Model 2	Model 3
log (capital)	.2372***	.2415***	.2204***
	(.014)	(.014)	(.014)
log (labor)	.6853***	.6776***	.6734***
	(.019)	(.019)	(.019)
Ownership			
SOE reformed		.4079***	
		(.045)	
Joint venture			.5087***
			(.063)
LLC			.3512***
			(.056)
LLSC			.5674***
			(.083)
Others			.4181***
			(.104)
Non-SOE		.3599***	
		(.046)	
Joint venture			.5685***
			(.06)
Private			0.0792
			(.085)
Collective			0.0087
			(.058)
Wholly foreign owned			0.0989
			(.119)
Others			.3208***
			(.054)
Sector dummy			
Electronic equipment	.2452***	.2215***	.1924***
	(.058)	(.057)	(.057)
Electronic components	−0.0083	−0.0317	−.1084**
	(.047)	(.047)	(.048)
Consumer products	−0.0403	−0.1014	−.1176*
	(.069)	(.069)	(.069)
Garments & leather goods	−.2147***	−.2596***	−.2606***
	(.049)	(.049)	(.051)
General machinery	−.2031***	−.196***	−.1106*
	(.061)	(.063)	(.061)
Textiles	−.7301***	−.7511***	−.7539***
	(.096)	(.097)	(.098)

(Table continues on the following page.)

Table 5.16 continued

Variable	Model 1	Model 2	Model 3
Regional dummy			
Chongqing	0.0330	−0.0104	0.0045
	(.052)	(.052)	(.051)
Guangzhou	−0.0499	−0.0825	−.1096**
	(.055)	(.056)	(.055)
Shanghai	.2694***	.2243***	.2146***
	(.051)	(.051)	(.052)
Wuhan	0.0734	0.0401	0.0008
	(.057)	(.057)	(.056)
Constant	1.3780***	1.1463***	1.5447***
	(.132)	(.136)	(.138)
Observations	3602	3602	3602
R square	0.68	0.68	0.69

Note: * significant at 10%, ** significant at 5%, and *** significant at 1%. Dummy variables for Beijing and for vehicles and vehicle parts are not included, to avoid multicollinearity. The results on year dummies are not shown.

Source: Authors' computations.

village enterprises (TVEs), which were emblematic of Chinese industrial success in the recent past, are falling behind and may have exhausted their potential for increasing efficiency.

The performance of joint ventures is not surprising and is foreshadowed by the literature reviewed in chapter 4 of this volume. As expected, the infusion of foreign technology and management leads to more efficient operation. However, this line of argument is potentially undermined by the finding that wholly owned foreign subsidiaries do not do as well relative to SOEs in China. One would expect wholly owned subsidiaries to do better, because foreign owners would be more likely to transfer technology and better able to exert full managerial control. But this is not borne out, at least by the sample.

This raises questions as to whether SOEs entering into joint ventures were among the better-performing and better-endowed ones to begin with—and if this was what attracted foreign partners. To check this hypothesis, the value added per labor for non-SOE joint ventures was plotted against other firms, as was value added per labor of joint ventures with reformed SOEs (see figure 5.5). The latter was included to see if joint ventures in general targeted high-performing SOEs.[22] From this figure, it

---

22. See Huang (2003a) for a discussion of the relationship between reforms and FDI in China.

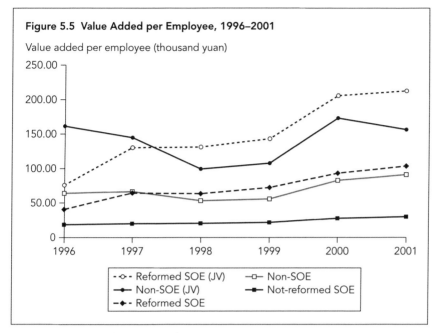

Figure 5.5 Value Added per Employee, 1996–2001

Note: JV, joint venture; SOE, state-owned enterprise.
Source: Authors' survey data.

is clear that joint venture firms are better-performing firms compared to others. Recall that former SOEs are classified as reformed joint venture SOEs for the entire time period if they entered into a joint venture following the restructuring effort. So, in 1996, all of these firms started as regular SOEs. Compared to those firms that were never reformed (and those that later became joint ventures), the value added per employee of joint ventures, even at the beginning of the period, is quite high; and joint ventures maintain this advantage throughout the time period. Thus, there is a possible selection bias with regard to this dimension as well. This question is revisited later in this chapter.

To further test the effect of the distribution of ownership, the data on shares owned by foreign and state entities are used, with each variable ranging from 0 (no ownership) to 100 (full ownership). Because the data for ownership shares are available only for 2001, it is assumed that the distribution of shares does not change over time, except for reformed SOEs—which were specifically asked about changes in ownership share. For reformed SOEs, ownership share data are available for the pre-reform period and for the period after the initiation of reform. The results are shown in table 5.17.[23] As expected, foreign ownership is associated with higher firm performance. These estimates are fairly large. A firm located in Shanghai that is wholly state owned does not benefit from being in Shanghai. Yet, if the firm is wholly foreign owned, being in Shanghai doubles its performance.

These results hold even when controlling for firm types (reformed SOEs and non-SOEs) (see table 5.17, column 2) and when the reformed SOEs are disaggregated into various types (see column 3). However, once both reformed SOEs and non-SOEs are disaggregated, the estimates on foreign shares are now negative and insignificant. The results for state ownership are still negative and significant but with larger coefficient magnitudes (see column 4).

So far, the time dimensions of the data have not been utilized, although year dummies were included to account for the yearly fluctuation in the general economic environment in China. All reformed firms are labeled as such if these firms have completed the reform process by the end of the sample period. The previous results suggest that those firms that underwent the reform process were better firms to begin with. To establish the causality, the available time-series information is utilized. By using data on the year in which the reform process was completed, one can test whether the reform had any real impact, and if so, how long it takes from the year in which the reform was completed for it to take effect. If, in fact, one finds that the reform has no effect in these regressions, then it is the case that Chinese officials chose better-performing firms to be reformed so as to minimize the social consequences (such as unemployment). However, if the reform had substantial effects, one should see a positive and significant coefficient on the reform dummy. To use panel specifications, especially fixed effects, one can use only reformed firms since the reform dummy will always be zero for nonreformed firms.

A "reformed" variable with the value of one was created for the years after the reform (and zero otherwise). The results are fairly similar to the results from the previous table, although the magnitudes of "reformed" variables are lower than anticipated (see table 5.18). One would expect that the magnitude of "reformed" should be close to the average of coefficients on the reformed SOE variables in table 5.16. However, the size of the coefficients on "reformed" are much smaller than estimates obtained on the

---

23. Firms producing electronic equipment again do well relative to others, while firms in the garment, machinery, and textile subsectors do worse. The performance of firms located in Shanghai and Wuhan leads that of firms located in the other three cities.

Table 5.17 Regression Results on Ownership

Variable	Model 1	Model 2	Model 3	Model 4
Dependent variable:				
log (value-added production)				
log (capital)	.2406***	.2377***	.2357***	.2235***
	(.014)	(.014)	(.014)	(.015)
log (labor)	.6889***	.678***	.6764***	.6749***
	(.019)	(.019)	(.019)	(.019)
Ownership				
Foreign share	.0023***	.0019***	.0021***	−0.0004
	(.001)	(.001)	(.001)	(.001)
State share	−.0019***	−.0014**	−.0021***	−.0018***
	(0)	(.001)	(0)	(.001)
SOE Reformed		.34***		
		(.047)		
Joint venture			.2292***	.4189***
			(.065)	(.079)
LLC			.272***	.3182***
			(.054)	(.057)
LLSC			.4294***	.4951***
			(.081)	(.086)
Others			.2785***	.3506***
			(.1)	(.108)
Non-SOE		.1886***		
		(.065)		
Joint venture				.4321***
				(.081)
Private				−0.1062
				(.105)
Collective				−0.1300
				(.08)
Wholly foreign owned				−0.0350
				(.143)
Others				.1833**
				(.074)
Observations	3,577	3,577	3,577	3,577
R square	0.68	0.69	0.69	0.69

Note: * significant at 10%, ** significant at 5%, and *** significant at 1%. The results on regional, sector, and year dummies are not shown. LLC, limited liability company; LLSC, limited liability shareholding company; SOE, state-owned enterprise.

Source: Authors' computations.

Table 5.18 Panel Regression Results

Variable	Model 1[a] (OLS)	Model 2 (fixed effect)
Dependent variable: log (value-added production)		
log (capital)	.2313***	.1459***
	(.014)	(.022)
log (labor)	.6798***	.7465***
	(.019)	(.022)
Reform status		
Reformed	.2469***	.075*
	(.039)	(.042)
Constant	1.5108***	1.8387***
	(.131)	(.231)
sigma_u		0.8716
sigma_e		0.5856
rho		0.6890
Observations	3,602	3,602
R square	0.68	0.68

Note: * significant at 10%, ** significant at 5%, and *** significant at 1%. OLS, ordinary least squares.
a. The results on regional, sector, and year dummies are not shown.
Source: Authors' computations.

previous specification. Recall that in the previous specification, firms are identified and coefficients are estimated for the entire period as reformed SOEs. If better-performing SOEs are selected to be reformed while poorer-performing SOEs are not, then one would find larger coefficient estimates on the specification in table 5.16 than those in table 5.18.

To account for firm-specific effects, panel regressions were used to test whether reform made a difference. Model 2 in table 5.18 shows the results from the fixed-effect model.[24] Since the fixed-effect model takes all the time-invariant, firm-specific characteristics, any time-invariant variables, such as cities and sectors, are not included in this specification. The result indicates that the reform had an impact, but a rather small one with marginal statistical significance at 10 percent.

Specifications were also run to test whether these reformed firms would do better over time after the reform effort of each firm was completed. One would expect that performance should improve as firms adjust to the changes introduced by reforms. Table 5.19 shows the results, including a variable "relative time." The "relative time" takes the value zero in the

---

24. The Hausman test rejects the random effect model.

Table 5.19 Panel Regression Results with Relative Times

Variable	Model 1[a]	Model 2	Model 3	Model 4[a]	Model 5	Model 6
		(Fixed effect)	(Random effect)		(Fixed effect)	(Random effect)
Dependent variable:						
log (value-added production)						
log (capital)	.2296***	.1456***	.1825***	.2296***	.1461***	.1822***
	(.014)	(.022)	(.016)	(.014)	(.022)	(.017)
log (labor)	.6731***	.7457***	.7262***	.6729***	.7457***	.7269***
	(.019)	(.022)	(.018)	(.019)	(.022)	(.018)
Reform period						
Period after reform (t)	.0585***	0.0074	.0385***	.049***	0.0267	.0474***
	(.008)	(.014)	(.01)	(.017)	(.02)	(.017)
Period after reform (t square)				0.0011	−0.0026	−0.0012
				(.002)	(.002)	(.002)
Constant	1.591***	1.8545***	1.6276***	1.592***	1.8466***	1.6243***
	(0.133)	(.23)	(.157)	(.133)	(.23)	(.157)
sigma_u		0.873	0.799		0.875	0.799
sigma_e		0.586	0.586		0.586	0.586
rho		0.689	0.651		0.691	0.651
Observations	3,602	3,602	3,602	3,602	3,602	3,602
R square	0.68	0.66	0.67	0.68	0.66	0.67

Note: * significant at 10%, ** significant at 5%, and *** significant at 1%.

a. The results on regional, sector, and year dummies are not shown.

Source: Authors' computations.

year of the reform completion and increases thereafter. The results from ordinary least squares (OLS) and from the random effects model show some small changes from the passage of time after the reform.[25] One would also expect to see such an adjustment period end eventually. Hence, columns 4 to 6 list the results from including a square term. It turns out that these square terms do not matter. This may be due to the lack of a long enough time series (the average duration after the reform in the data is two years), and the adjustment periods may be fairly long. Another way of interpreting the estimates on these coefficients is the productivity growth of these firms after the reform. If one takes such a view, then the reform was successful in introducing continuous improvement, which is the goal of the reform—although the magnitude of the growth in produc tivity is fairly small.

Provided that there was no bias in selecting the sample, these results suggest that more efficient SOEs were reformed and other less efficient ones remained under 100 percent state ownership. The literature on the Chinese reforms reviewed earlier suggests that there was a build-up of competitive pressures on SOEs through liberalization of the domestic market and trade. This pressure, in turn, forced some SOEs to become more efficient; and these were the firms eventually selected for ownership reform, with the less efficient SOEs following later. Various aspects of the changes in institutional and managerial characteristics brought by the reform process are now considered.

ROLE OF INSTITUTIONS AND MANAGEMENT

Previous studies indicate that reformed SOEs were relatively efficient at the inception of the reform process in 1996, and the firms have improved their productivity over time. Earlier results also indicate that firm-specific factors account for a large part of the difference in their performance. As discussed in detail in chapter 4, there are a number of factors that make firms more responsive to market forces and induce firms to pay more attention to efficiency. These factors are now explored. Because of the way this survey was structured, panel data cannot be used to test the effects stemming from institutional and managerial characteristics, since many of these firm-specific characteristics would be time-invariant. Instead, data from 2001 can be used to see if each specific factor significantly affects the level of efficiency. Table 5.20 (column 1) lists the results of using only the

---

25. The Hausman test accepts the random effect model.

Table 5.20 Regression Results on Various Institutional Factors

Variable	Model 1	Model 2	Model 3	Model 4	Model 5
Dependent variable:					
log (value-added production)					
log (capital)	.2395***	.2186***	.2373***	.2369***	.2442***
	(.037)	(.037)	(.037)	(.037)	(.037)
log (labor)	.6689***	.6829***	.6658***	.666***	.668***
	(.05)	(.049)	(.05)	(.05)	(.05)
Ownership					
SOE reformed					
Joint venture	.7506***	.7703***	.7518***	.7415***	.669***
	(.155)	(.158)	(.155)	(.166)	(.16)
LLC	.3297***	.3498***	.3295***	.3292***	.2726**
	(.123)	(.125)	(.123)	(.123)	(.125)
LLSC	.5663***	.536***	.5682***	.5564***	.4996***
	(.167)	(.17)	(.166)	(.166)	(.17)
Others	.4382***	.4355***	.4528***	.4548***	.3757**
	(.168)	(.169)	(.17)	(.171)	(.169)
Non-SOE					
Joint Venture	.5891***	.5781***	.5895***	.5797***	.5046***
	(.142)	(.142)	(.141)	(.147)	(.148)
Private	0.2199	0.2529	0.2387	0.2365	0.1393
	(.209)	(.213)	(.212)	(.213)	(.214)
Collective	0.1682	0.1152	0.1950	0.1942	0.1717
	(.15)	(.145)	(.153)	(.153)	(.15)

(Table continues on the following page.)

Table 5.20 continued

Variable	Model 1	Model 2	Model 3	Model 4	Model 5
Wholly foreign owned	0.4261	0.4995	0.4105	0.3937	0.3531
	(.308)	(.345)	(.308)	(.321)	(.309)
Others	.4066***	.4011***	.4142***	.4111***	.3353**
	(.138)	(.143)	(.139)	(.139)	(.143)
Other characteristics					
Number of domestic competitors		−.0002*			
		(0)			
Number of foreign competitors		0.0012			
		(.002)			
Number of new competitors		−.3958**			
		(.197)			
Manager has higher education			.2184*		
			(.114)		
Manager has higher education (home country)				.2156*	
				(.114)	
Manager has high education (abroad)				0.2405	
				(.179)	
Manager appointed by government					−.164*
					(.098)
Observations	638	611	638	638	638
R square	0.68	0.67	0.67	0.67	0.68

Note: * significant at 10%, ** significant at 5%, and *** significant at 1%. The results on regional, sector, and year dummies are not shown.

Source: Authors' computations.

data from 2001. The results are similar to the baseline results shown in table 5.16 (column 1).[26]

Competition

A number of studies have identified competitive pressure as a mechanism to boost the efficiency of firms. Column 2 of table 5.20 lists the results from including the number of competitors reported by firms, differentiated by foreign and domestic origin of competition. The results suggest that domestic competition has a significant and negative effect on the productivity. However, the magnitudes are small enough so that domestic competition has no real consequences for firm productivity, unless the firms regularly face more than 1,000 domestic competitors in their market. But the number of new entrants also has a negative and significant effect on productivity. This result may be linked to the growth in excess capacity and the reduction in the markups of the incumbent firms. If that is the case, then the estimates on domestic competition should capture this effect, unless new entrants are significantly more productive. Thus, after controlling for domestic competition, there should be no statistically significant result stemming from new entrants. This leads to the conclusion that it is not the number of competitors in a market per se that determines the productivity (and profitability), but the entry of new and more productive firms that has a negative effect on productivity (and profitability of SOEs).[27]

Quality of Managers

As hypothesized earlier, the education level of managers may have some effect on how well a firm is organized and run, especially when the education is received abroad. This is because the managers may be able to introduce management techniques that are widely used in industrialized countries (as described in chapter 1, similar to some of the benefits thought to derive from FDI). Column 3 of table 5.20 shows the results from including a higher education dummy in the base specification. The coefficient estimate on manager education is positive and significant at

---

26. However, none of the city dummies are significant in this specification.

27. This depends on the assumption that the nominal price did not change widely so as to mask the change in productivity due to competition.

the 10 percent level. In terms of the magnitude, this result is large enough to be economically important. When education is further disaggregated (as either domestic or obtained abroad), the results surprisingly suggest that domestic education is associated with better performance by firms than degrees earned abroad (see column 4). It may be that most of the foreign-educated managers are working at wholly owned subsidiaries. Or, it may be that education in domestic universities provides good networking opportunities that are advantageous to these managers, especially if *guanxi* exerts a significant influence on business operation.

The appointment of managers is also a critical issue. Even if SOEs are reformed, managers may still be appointed by the state. In a test for whether appointment by the state (including the requirement of approval of managers by the state) has any effect on firm performance, 20 percent of managers in this sample of reformed SOEs are appointed by the state (more than half of managers in SOEs are appointed by the state). Column 5 of table 5.20 lists the findings from this specification. The results clearly indicate that those firms with managers appointed by the state perform much worse than other firms. Given that estimates on other variables are stable, it is apparent that the appointment of managers by the state (or approval requirement) might not be made on the basis of business expertise, but is based instead on political and social criteria. If the goal is to make these reformed SOEs more efficient and more responsive to market forces, the appointment of managers might best be done by their new nonstate owners.

To gauge the strength of incentives for managers, data on the manager's share in the firm (including family members) are used. However, only 4 percent of the managers surveyed had any shares in these firms in 2001. Similar to the construction of ownership variable, the 2001 data are used for the entire time period, unless firms are reformed. In that case, managers' shares from both the pre- and the post-reform period can be used. The overall results from managers' shares in ownership indicate that this has little bearing on firm performance (see table 5.21). The only case in which managers' shares matter when firm types are - disaggregated (see column 4). Several specifications were also run in which managers' shares interacted with a dummy, indicating whether independent business/labor decisions are allowed. No statistically significant results were obtained on either manager shares or the interaction terms.

Table 5.21 Regression Results on Manager Incentives

Variable	Model 1	Model 2	Model 3	Model 4
Dependent variable: *log (value-added production)*				
log (capital)	.2373***	.2406***	.2301***	.221***
	(.014)	(.014)	(.014)	(.014)
log (labor)	.6858***	.6776***	.6726***	.6727***
	(.019)	(.019)	(.019)	(.019)
Ownership				
SOE reformed		.404***		
		(.045)		
Joint Venture			.3323***	.5046***
			(.059)	(.063)
LLC			.197***	.3473***
			(.053)	(.056)
LLSC			.4129***	.5605***
			(.082)	(.083)
Others			.247**	.4173***
			(.104)	(.104)
Non-SOE		.3435***		
		(.047)		
Joint venture				.5361***
				(.061)
Private				0.0091
				(.083)
Collective				0.0106
				(.058)
Wholly foreign owned				0.0988
				(.119)
Others				.3161***
				(.055)
Other characteristics				
Manager share	0.0011	0.0006	0.0013	0.0016
	(.001)	(.001)	(.001)	(.001)
Observations	3577	3577	3577	3577
R square	0.68	0.69	0.68	0.69

Note: * significant at 10%, ** significant at 5%, and *** significant at 1%. The results on regional, sector, and year dummies are not shown.

Source: Authors' computations.

Shareholder Meetings

Whether a firm holds a shareholder meeting can also influence firm performance. The shareholder meetings can mitigate agency problems and discipline the managers who fail to meet the expectations of shareholders. Table 5.22 lists the results of including the dummy variable that represents the use of shareholder meetings to strengthen governance. Interestingly, having a shareholder meeting has no effect on a firm's performance.

The question still remains as to what kind of voting structure a shareholder meeting should adopt. Essentially, there are two variants: one-share-one-vote and one-head-one-vote. The literature indicates that voting rights should be aligned with the financial stakes of the shareholders. Thus, the prior belief is that one-share-one-vote is a better voting mechanism than one-head-one-vote. The results presented in columns 2–4 of table 5.22 clearly indicate that this is valid. When a dummy variable representing one-share-one-vote is included along with a dummy for shareholder meeting, all the effects associated with a shareholder meeting are captured by the dummy on one-share-one-vote. When a dummy on one-share-one-vote is included in the specification by itself, it is positive and significant with a magnitude similar to the results of column 2. However, when a dummy representing one-head-one-vote is included, the estimates are not significant. Since dummies for one-share-one-vote and one-head-one-vote are conditional on having a shareholder meeting, these results indicate that merely having a shareholder meeting is not enough to ensure a good performance. In order to do so, a firm must adopt a one-share-one-vote procedure. Otherwise, a firm's performance is no different from that of a firm without a shareholder meeting.

Boards of Directors

Another characteristic of reformed and non-state-owned firms is the existence of a board of directors in non-SOE firms. The regression results from including a dummy variable representing the board of directors are shown in table 5.23. As expected, the estimate on the board of directors is positive and significant. Whether the board of directors is appointed or approved by the government does not seem to matter, although the estimates are negative and fairly large. The insignificance, especially for government appointment of boards of directors, may stem from the small number of observations. Recall that the results from manager appointment by the state indicate that government involvement was found to have negative

Table 5.22 Regression Results on Shareholder Meetings

Variable	Model 1	Model 2	Model 3	Model 4
Dependent variable:				
log (value-added production)				
log (capital)	.2399***	.2396***	.2395***	.2394***
	(.037)	(.037)	(.037)	(.037)
log (labor)	.6713***	.6715***	.6712***	.6691***
	(.05)	(.05)	(.05)	(.05)
Ownership				
SOE Reformed				
Joint venture	.7247***	.732***	.7357***	.7533***
	(.156)	(.156)	(.155)	(.155)
LLC	.2614**	.245*	.2528**	.3384***
	(.129)	(.13)	(.127)	(.125)
LLSC	.4494**	.4125**	.4254**	.5713***
	(.191)	(.189)	(.175)	(.166)
Others	.3281*	0.2627	0.2733	.4487***
	(.187)	(.185)	(.174)	(.169)
Non-SOE				
Joint venture	.5727***	.5723***	.5744***	.5908***
	(.142)	(.141)	(.142)	(.142)
Private	0.1756	0.1550	0.1596	0.2210
	(.208)	(.208)	(.207)	(.21)
Collective	0.1620	0.1612	0.1619	0.1682
	(.15)	(.149)	(.149)	(.15)
Wholly foreign owned	0.3920	0.4013	0.4061	0.4371
	(.311)	(.313)	(.311)	(.31)
Others	.3191**	.3092**	.3198**	.42***
	(.153)	(.153)	(.14)	(.142)
Other characteristics				
Having shareholder meeting	0.1295	0.0221		
	(.103)	(.118)		
One-share-one-vote		.2311*	.2431**	
		(.125)	(.109)	
One-head-one-vote				−0.0648
				(.107)
Observations	638	638	638	638
R square	0.67	0.68	0.68	0.67

Note: * significant at 10%, ** significant at 5%, and *** significant at 1%. The results on regional, sector, and year dummies are not shown.

Source: Authors' computations.

Table 5.23 Regression Results on Board of Directors

Variable	Model 1	Model 2	Model 3	Model 4
Dependent variable:				
log (value-added production)				
log (capital)	.237***	.2378***	.2372***	.2369***
	(.037)	(.037)	(.037)	(.037)
log (labor)	.6693***	.67***	.6692***	.6696***
	(.05)	(.05)	(.05)	(.05)
Ownership				
SOE reformed				
Joint venture	.5535***	.5462***	.5337***	.555***
	(.192)	(.192)	(.193)	(.192)
LLC	0.1345	0.1347	0.1413	0.1358
	(.164)	(.164)	(.163)	(.165)
LLSC	.3595*	.3571*	.3668*	.3608*
	(.202)	(.202)	(.202)	(.204)
Others	0.2724	0.2642	0.2421	0.2718
	(.186)	(.186)	(.186)	(.185)
Non-SOE				
Joint venture	.4035**	.397**	.4034**	.4043**
	(.169)	(.169)	(.169)	(.169)
Private	0.1068	0.1028	0.0966	0.1065
	(.216)	(.216)	(.215)	(.216)
Collective	0.1595	0.1578	0.1608	0.1580
	(.149)	(.149)	(.149)	(.15)
Wholly foreign owned	0.2424	0.2378	0.2148	0.2393
	(.318)	(.319)	(.318)	(.325)
Others	0.2254	0.2221	0.2072	0.2241
	(.174)	(.174)	(.175)	(.174)
Other characteristics				
Having board of director	.2468*	.2522*	.2709**	.2421*
	(.134)	(.134)	(.136)	(.143)
Board of directors appointed		−0.1783		
by government		(.285)		
Board of directors approved			−0.1360	
by government			(.139)	
CEO and chairman of board				0.0116
the same person				(.105)
Observations	638	638	638	638
R square	0.68	0.68	0.68	0.67

Note: * significant at 10%, ** significant at 5%, and *** significant at 1%. The results on regional, sector, and year dummies are not shown.

Source: Authors' computations.

consequences for the operation of a firm. Similar conjectures can apply for the appointment of a board of directors. Given the magnitudes of the estimate, further research in this area may be worthwhile.

Whether the manager is also a chairperson of the board of directors does not seem to influence the performance of a firm.

Thus, establishing a board of directors is advantageous for the owners of firms. However, it seems that the actual composition and appointment (or approval) of the members of the board do not influence the performance of firms, although this result may be due to the lack of variation in these data. Clearly, a larger study is needed to test whether the appointment of a board of directors has any effect on the performance of firms.

Manager Turnover, Manager Autonomy, and the Soft Budget Constraint

Finally, this analysis checks to see if various elements of SOE reform affecting managers, manager autonomy, and the soft budget constraint have any real effect on a firm's performance. Since these elements relate to only specific aspects of reform, only the 2001 data for reformed SOEs are used. Even if SOEs are reformed, where they retain the old managers, one would not expect firms to perform any better. Bringing in managers with better management skills may make firms more efficient. But where managers are still constrained in making business decisions by government, one would not expect them to perform well. The issue of soft budget always surfaces when reforming SOEs. Common belief, as noted in chapters 2 and 4, is that soft budgets are prominent among the reasons why SOEs do not perform efficiently. Therefore, it is critical to harden the budget constraints once these firms are reformed, if they are to operate more efficiently. These factors are examined separately in this section.

Table 5.24 reports the findings using only observations from reformed SOEs. Column 1 of this table shows the baseline specification similar to column 1 in table 5.20, with more restricted samples.[28] In a test to see if changes in management have any impact on firm performance, the results indicate that they do not (see table 5.24, column 2). Whether a reformed SOE retains its managers has no effect on firm performance, which is at

---

28. Besides capital and labor, the only other significant estimates are those on industry sectors, which are not shown in the table. Electronic components, garments, general machinery, and textiles all perform poorly compared to other sectors, even after controlling for the types of reformed SOEs.

Table 5.24 Regression Results Using Reformed SOEs Data Only

Variable	Model 1	Model 2	Model 3	Model 4	Model 5
Dependent variable: log (value-added production)					
log (capital)	.2803***	.2807***	.282***	.278***	.284***
	(.063)	(.063)	(.063)	(.063)	(.065)
log (labor)	.6676***	.6761***	.6656***	.6744***	.6666***
	(.088)	(.091)	(.089)	(.088)	(.091)
Ownership SOE Reformed					
Joint venture	0.2673	0.2932	0.2352	0.2286	0.2908
	(.242)	(.251)	(.246)	(.244)	(.246)
LLC	−0.0311	−0.0293	−0.0751	−0.0823	−0.0293
	(.202)	(.217)	(.205)	(.207)	(.21)
LLSC	0.1693	0.1407	0.1291	0.1284	0.1630
	(.235)	(.252)	(.239)	(.243)	(.245)
Others	−0.0962	−0.1547	−0.1201	−0.1588	−0.1122
	(.255)	(.272)	(.268)	(.263)	(.264)
Other characteristics					
Having different general manager after reform		−0.1458			
		(.125)			
General manager can make business decisions			0.2943		
			(.254)		
General manager can make labor decisions				0.1910	
				(.127)	
Having soft budget					0.0705
					(.144)
Observations	234	231	231	231	231
R square	0.75	0.76	0.76	0.76	0.76

Note: * significant at 10%, ** significant at 5%, and *** significant at 1%. The results on regional, sector, and year dummies are not shown. LLC, limited liability company; LLSC, limited liability shareholding company.

Source: Authors' computations.

variance with findings from other countries.[29] In these data, almost half of the firms have changed their managers, while the other half retained their pre-reform managers. So, the lack of data points should not pose a problem. Those firms that replaced their managers with new ones are supposedly mandated to operate firms in line with the market system. The question is whether firms that replaced managers found people with the needed

---

29. See, for instance, Fidrmuc and Fidrmuc (2004), using data from the Czech Republic. However, they find that only after three to four years does the poor performance of firms lead to a higher probability of the incumbent manager being dismissed.

Table 5.25 Turnover of Managers

Survey question	Yes (%)
Are the general manager of the post- and pre-restructuring firms the same person?	51
If not, where did the general manager end up?	
Retired	27.8
Moved to another SOE	27.8
Moved to other types of firms	19.5
Moved to a government position	0.8
Others	24.1

Source: Authors' survey data.

skills and familiarity with market imperatives. Given that the market for managers in China remains thin, it may be that new managers had experience and backgrounds similar to those of the managers they replaced, or limited experience. If this is the case, one would not expect to see much difference in their performance. Although information is not available on what positions the new managers held previously, information is available on what happened to the departing managers. Of the 49 percent of firms that changed managers following the restructuring, 28 percent of departing managers decided to retire. An equal share of departing managers became managers for other SOEs and 20 percent for other types of firms (see table 5.25). Thus, there seems to be a circulation of former SOE managers to both SOEs and other types of firms.

As alluded to earlier, even if a firm is reformed, it may still face significant constraints imposed by the government—especially concerning layoffs. It is often argued that SOEs (see chapters 1 and 2) do not optimize on the level of inputs, especially labor. This reflects the generally held belief that SOEs are fulfilling social objectives and providing a social safety net for a part of the urban workforce, leading to lower levels of efficiency compared to private firms.[30] The analysis in this study tests for whether

---

30. Dong and Putterman (2001) analyze labor utilization in SOEs using a firm-level panel dataset for 752 industrial SOEs in China for the period of 1980–94. They first estimate the labor coefficient in the Cobb-Douglas production function using the sample data, and then construct a variable for the labor redundancy rate by dividing the difference between the actual labor force and the estimated labor force by the actual labor force. They find that 30–40 percent of workers in SOEs are redundant, and the share of SOEs in their samples with redundant labor increased from 65 percent in 1991 to 73 percent in 1994. Excess labor and other social burdens placed on SOEs are closely linked to the soft budget constraints discussed in chapter 2. Lin (1999) has argued that a hardening of the budget constraint could follow once SOEs are relieved from the policy-induced burdens and allowed to adjust their production lines to utilize their comparative advantage.

the lack of autonomy in managers' decisionmaking has affected the performance of reformed SOEs. Autonomy was measured by asking firms if they consult with their board of directors or municipal authorities before making business decisions. The results are presented in table 5.24, columns 3 and 4. Column 3 shows the results using autonomy on business decisions, whereas column 4 shows the results using autonomy on labor-related decisions. Both sets of results indicate that lack of autonomy did not adversely affect these firms.

Finally, this chapter investigates whether firms facing a soft budget perform poorly relative to those faced with a hard budget. Contrary to what might be expected, the results in table 5.24, column 5, indicate that the expectation of a soft budget does not appear to influence firm performance. Using alternative specifications for the source of such assistance is further disaggregated (the state, banks, investors, and member firms), with similar results.[31] This is a surprising finding since there is a strongly held view that SOEs perform poorly because of the existence of a soft budget constraint. Unlike other studies that use the past history of bailout as a measure of soft budget, in this analysis firms were explicitly asked about their *expectation*, regardless of whether they received financial assistance in the past.[32] Therefore, this measure of soft budget does not suffer from the endogeneity problem found in other studies. Even with a reasonable measure of the soft budget, no statistically significant results are found. Again, the same sectors perform much worse than others. The only explanation might be that there are city- and sector-specific factors which are highly correlated with the existence of a soft budget. Indeed, there is a wide variation in the numbers of firms reporting the existence of soft budgets across cities and sectors. More firms in Chongqing and Wuhan expect to receive some form of assistance from the state if they face financial difficulty, while the firms in Beijing least expect help to be forthcoming (see table 5.26). Similarly, firms in the machinery and textiles sectors expect to receive assistance more so than firms in other sectors. Among the different types of reformed firms, joint ventures do not expect much help from either

---

31. This study also tested whether assistance from either the state or banks has any effect on the productivity. The results were insignificant.

32. It may be that the budget constraint was loosened significantly during the reform period, so that the expectation on the assistance was low. Three developments suggest that this may be the case. The first is the expansion of the stock market, which allowed SOEs and LLSCs to access additional capital through listing. In addition, the debt-equity swap in the late 1990s loosened budget constraints. Finally, during this period, the banking sector remained relatively unaffected by the reform process and subject to strong political pressure to assist SOEs (Zhang 2004b).

Table 5.26 Source of Expected Assistance, by City, Sector, and Type of Reformed SOE
(percent)

Type of assistance	Beijing	Chongqing	Guangzhou	Shanghai	Wuhan
State help	4	15	3	9	13
Bank help	4	13	10	4	11
State and bank help	8	25	10	13	23

	Electronic equipment	Electronic components	Consumer products	Vehicles & vehicle parts	Garments & leather goods	General machinery	Textiles
State help	12	4	5	9	5	16	29
Bank help	10	8	10	6	9	7	21
State and bank help	18	12	14	15	13	21	50

	Joint venture	LLC	LLSC
State help	8	17	18
Bank help	8	9	29
State and bank help	16	25	38

Note: LLC, limited liability company; LLSC, limited liability shareholding company.

Source: Authors' survey data.

the state or banks. But firms that were reformed as LLSCs expect assistance from both the state and banks. By contrast, LLC firms expect the helping hand of the state, but not many expect similar assistance from banks.

A test is also run to see if the current levels of revenue and profits or the number of employees have any effect on the expectation that they will receive assistance from other entities. The results on the soft budget constraint itself do not suggest that any of these three variables affect their expectations (see table 5.27). However, when the soft budget is restricted to mean assistance from either the state or banks, the firms with the larger

Table 5.27 Estimation on Soft Budget

Variable	Model 1	Model 2	Model 3	Model 4	Model 5
Total profit	0.1449			0.1589	
	(0.123)			(0.13)	
Total revenue		0.0210			0.0233
		(0.03)			(0.034)
Worker			0.0071	−0.0087	−0.0051
			(0.043)	(0.047)	(0.049)
Chongqing	0.3185	0.3181	0.3158	0.3162	0.3170
	(0.315)	(0.315)	(0.314)	(0.314)	(0.314)
Guangzhou	0.3740	0.3793	0.3866	0.3671	0.3754
	(0.303)	(0.303)	(0.303)	(0.304)	(0.304)
Shanghai	0.3901	0.3984	0.4195	0.3871	0.3960
	(0.264)	(0.264)	(0.262)	(0.264)	(0.265)
Wuhan	0.9281***	0.9311***	0.9302***	0.922***	0.9281***
	(0.282)	(0.282)	(0.282)	(0.282)	(0.282)
Electronic equipment	−0.4096	−0.416*	−0.4209*	−0.4155	−0.4192*
	(0.251)	(0.251)	(0.254)	(0.254)	(0.254)
Electronic components	−0.509*	−0.5192*	−0.5369**	−0.5163*	−0.5226*
	(0.266)	(0.267)	(0.268)	(0.269)	(0.27)
Consumer products	0.2082	0.2004	0.1876	0.1986	0.1956
	(0.371)	(0.372)	(0.375)	(0.374)	(0.375)
Garments & leather goods	0.0492	0.0365	0.0109	0.0446	0.0348
	(0.303)	(0.305)	(0.301)	(0.305)	(0.306)
General machinery	−0.6723**	−0.6802**	−0.6958**	−0.6743**	−0.6807**
	(0.306)	(0.307)	(0.306)	(0.307)	(0.308)
Textiles	−0.0341	−0.0393	−0.0647	−0.0179	−0.0293
	(0.541)	(0.54)	(0.528)	(0.527)	(0.526)
Constant	0.2198	0.2265	0.2350	0.2363	0.2352
	(0.272)	(0.274)	(0.287)	(0.287)	(0.287)
Observations	263	263	263	263	263

Note: * significant at 10%, ** significant at 5%, and *** significant at 1%. Dummy variables for Beijing and for vehicles and vehicle parts are not included, to avoid multicollinearity. Estimated using probit.
Source: Authors' computations.

numbers of employees were more likely to expect that help would be forthcoming, controlling for their performance (table 5.28). In addition, firms in Chongqing and Wuhan also tend to expect assistance from the state and banks.

When controlling for the types of reformed firms, the results show that firms which are converted to joint ventures and LLCs are less likely to expect any assistance from the state and from banks (table 5.29), while larger firms (in terms of number of employees) and firms in Chongqing and Wuhan still expect the support if they face trouble in the future. Controlling for the types of firms, sectoral differences do not arise. These results suggest

Table 5.28 Estimation on State and Bank Assistance

Variable	Model 1	Model 2	Model 3	Model 4	Model 5
Total profit	0.2506**			0.0287	
	(0.11)			(0.114)	
Total revenue		0.0855**			0.0103
		(0.037)			(0.033)
Workers			0.1822***	0.1781***	0.1757***
			(0.044)	(0.048)	(0.05)
Chongqing	0.5934*	0.6054*	0.668**	0.6675**	0.6675**
	(0.325)	(0.323)	(0.331)	(0.33)	(0.33)
Guangzhou	0.0224	0.0272	0.2058	0.2003	0.1987
	(0.355)	(0.355)	(0.365)	(0.367)	(0.367)
Shanghai	−0.0311	−0.0581	0.0627	0.0550	0.0502
	(0.315)	(0.316)	(0.32)	(0.326)	(0.328)
Wuhan	0.4848*	0.5093*	0.6477**	0.6452**	0.6457**
	(0.294)	(0.292)	(0.302)	(0.302)	(0.302)
Electronic equipment	0.1334	0.1464	0.2483	0.2498	0.2495
	(0.264)	(0.264)	(0.27)	(0.271)	(0.271)
Electronic components	0.0150	0.0569	0.1648	0.1690	0.1718
	(0.284)	(0.285)	(0.29)	(0.292)	(0.292)
Consumer products	−0.1635	−0.1317	0.0243	0.0262	0.0274
	(0.391)	(0.392)	(0.392)	(0.393)	(0.393)
Garments & leather goods	0.0170	0.0675	0.1136	0.1210	0.1253
	(0.317)	(0.318)	(0.32)	(0.326)	(0.327)
General machinery	0.1795	0.2105	0.2185	0.2232	0.2260
	(0.294)	(0.295)	(0.291)	(0.293)	(0.293)
Textiles	1.0224**	1.0441**	0.7306	0.7414	0.7475
	(0.454)	(0.455)	(0.501)	(0.502)	(0.502)
Constant	−1.0465***	−1.0947***	−1.4359***	−1.4338***	−1.4339***
	(0.301)	(0.297)	(0.321)	(0.321)	(0.321)
Observations	266	266	266	266	266

Note: * significant at 10%, ** significant at 5%, and *** significant at 1%. Dummy variables for Beijing and for vehicles and vehicle parts are not included, to avoid multicollinearity. Estimated using probit.
Source: Authors' computations.

Table 5.29 Expectation of Assistance from State and Bank, by Firm Type

Variable	Model 1	Model 2	Model 3	Model 4	Model 5
Total profit	0.2629**			0.0434	
	(0.106)			(0.119)	
Total revenue		0.0852***			0.0125
		(0.032)			(0.034)
Workers			0.1807***	0.1741***	0.1724***
			(0.043)	(0.046)	(0.049)
Joint venture	−0.8703***	−0.867***	−0.7364**	−0.7472**	−0.7472**
	(0.334)	(0.334)	(0.336)	(0.339)	(0.339)
LLC	−0.7499**	−0.7386**	−0.7508**	−0.7508**	−0.7497**
	(0.302)	(0.303)	(0.309)	(0.308)	(0.308)
LLSC	−0.3035	−0.3011	−0.2659	−0.2699	−0.2698
	(0.321)	(0.321)	(0.328)	(0.327)	(0.327)
Chongqing	0.7803**	0.7885**	0.8265**	0.827**	0.827**
	(0.348)	(0.347)	(0.357)	(0.356)	(0.356)
Guangzhou	0.2732	0.2778	0.3892	0.3848	0.3846
	(0.382)	(0.382)	(0.392)	(0.392)	(0.392)
Shanghai	0.1728	0.1468	0.1720	0.1659	0.1625
	(0.345)	(0.346)	(0.35)	(0.353)	(0.355)
Wuhan	0.7041**	0.7253**	0.8076**	0.8072**	0.8084**
	(0.327)	(0.326)	(0.335)	(0.334)	(0.334)
Electronic equipment	0.1987	0.2065	0.3151	0.3170	0.3157
	(0.271)	(0.271)	(0.283)	(0.283)	(0.283)
Electronic components	0.0944	0.1316	0.2387	0.2452	0.2471
	(0.288)	(0.29)	(0.295)	(0.298)	(0.298)
Consumer products	−0.2044	−0.1797	0.0046	0.0046	0.0050
	(0.412)	(0.413)	(0.415)	(0.416)	(0.416)
Garments & leather goods	−0.1329	−0.0876	0.0093	0.0170	0.0198
	(0.337)	(0.339)	(0.346)	(0.349)	(0.35)
General machinery	0.1679	0.1937	0.2221	0.2273	0.2291
	(0.3)	(0.3)	(0.297)	(0.298)	(0.298)
Textiles	0.9735**	0.9908**	0.6983	0.7133	0.7173
	(0.444)	(0.445)	(0.481)	(0.48)	(0.481)
Constant	−0.6234*	−0.6713**	−1.0034***	−0.9986***	−0.9996***
	(0.335)	(0.331)	(0.356)	(0.356)	(0.356)
Observations	266	266	266	266	266

Note: * significant at 10%, ** significant at 5%, and *** significant at 1%. Dummy variables for Beijing and for vehicles and vehicle parts are not included, to avoid multicollinearity. Estimated using probit.
Source: Authors' computations.

that the budget constraint has become harder for former SOEs that became joint ventures and LLCs located outside of Chongqing and Wuhan. Recall that smaller SOEs tended to be reformed to become LLCs, whereas the larger ones became LLSCs. Therefore, it seems that larger former SOEs (which became LLSCs) still have softer budget constraints, especially if they are large and located in either Chongqing or Wuhan.

Table 5.30 Effects of Different Variables on Productivity

Variable	Typical finding	Authors' result
Reform of ownership (including privatization)	+	+
Foreign-ownership share	+	+
State share	−	−
Competition	+	−
Quality of manager (education)	+	+[a]
Government appointment of managers	−	−
Incentives for manager	+	0
Shareholder meeting	+	+[b]
Existence of board of directors	+	+
Government appointment of board of directors	−	0
Manager turnover	+	0
Manager autonomy	+	0
Soft budget constraint	−	0
Selection bias	yes	yes

Note: + (or −) means that positive (or negative) coefficient estimates are expected; 0 means no statistically significant estimates.
a. Only for domestic education.
b. Only if one-share-one-vote is adopted.
Source: Authors' computations.

SUMMARY AND CONCLUSIONS

The empirical evidence obtained from this study is broadly consistent with findings in the literature (see table 5.30). Various factors found to be important determinants of firm performance in transitional economies are found to be statistically significant and economically important in China as well, although there are some differences.

State ownership is consistently associated with inefficiency compared to privately owned firms. In these results, 100 percent of the state-owned firms that had not been restructured by 2001 were found to be the least efficient firms in the sample.[33] While restructured firms are more efficient than nonreformed SOEs, non-SOEs are the most efficient firms in the sample. This result is largely driven by the existence of joint ventures (both in non-SOE and reformed SOE categories), however. Furthermore, the restructuring effort itself did not seem to improve the efficiency of

33. In 2000, 36 percent of SOEs made losses, whereas the average for all industrial firms of various ownerships was 23.4 percent. The corresponding figure for LLSCs was 19 percent (Zhang 2004b).

firms per se, but more efficient firms were restructured first. Since these firms were well run to begin with, they were more attractive for foreign partners. Combining these two results, it seems that the state has strategically chosen which firms to restructure, so as to minimize the potential political risk arising from massive unemployment and to win support for ownership reform.

More puzzling are the results on private and wholly owned foreign subsidiaries. The prior belief was that these firms should be the most efficient types. These results, however, indicate just the opposite.[34] There are two possible explanations. One is that these burgeoning private firms may lack the supporting institutions needed to realize their full potential. There is some evidence that even though banks were encouraged to lend to these firms in recent years, in the past, private firms had difficulty obtaining loans from banks.[35] In addition, the performance outcomes might be influenced by differential treatment in terms of taxes and fees collected by the various levels of government from SOEs and from private firms. For foreign firms, it may be that a Chinese partner is needed in order to navigate the Chinese market, due to the complexities of regulation and bureaucracy and the mediating role of *guanxi*. In the future, when market institutions develop, these firms may perform better than they currently do. Second, it may be that some of these "wholly owned foreign" firms may be domestically owned enterprises with foreign capital that derives from "round-tripping" (see chapter 3). In this case, one would not expect these firms to perform above the level of private firms, since these are domestic firms in disguise and none of the additional advantages typically associated with FDI are present. This calls for a closer look at the firms in the sample.

Among the reformed SOEs, there are differences in performance. As already mentioned, joint ventures are the most efficient firms, followed by LLSCs, and LLCs. The differences seem to arise from management and corporate governance, as hypothesized in chapter 1.[36] The establishment of a board of directors is found to be conducive to the improved efficiency of firms, along with the establishment of shareholder meetings. However, the shareholder meetings have to be such that the financial stakes and

---

34. In Wen, Li, and Lloyd's (2002) study, wholly owned foreign subsidiaries do not perform as well as joint ventures.

35. Dong, Putterman, and Unel (2004) also find that firms with a private share of more than 50 percent do not necessarily perform better than SOEs.

36. The performance difference between LLCs and LLSCs may also be due to the smaller firm size and lower capital intensity of LLCs relative to LLSCs (Zhang 2004b).

control of the firm are well aligned: Firms with one-head-one-vote do not perform as well as those with one-share-one-vote.

Even though government involvement in appointing the board of directors does not seem to have much bearing on the firm's performance, its appointment of managers was found to be detrimental to a firm's performance. The counterintuitive results on boards of directors, given the results for managers and the findings reported in the literature, may be because of an insufficient number of observations in this sample.

Thus, the actual impact of restructuring efforts so far seems to be quite limited. As noted in the literature, efficiency gains of firms may be trace-able, in part, to selection bias—especially when firms are gradually restructured, as is the case in China. Governments tend to reform the most efficient firms first and gradually extend reforms to other firms so that they can maintain the momentum of the reform and make the changes more politically palatable. The results reported here indicate that this is the case in China.[37]

This does not mean that the reform efforts have not been fruitful. On the contrary, they have introduced a number of efficiency-enhancing elements into the Chinese economy—and reformed firms are actively upgrading their production technologies and processes. As these results indicate, establishing shareholder meetings and boards of directors leads to efficiency gains. And less involvement by the state—especially with regard to reducing ownership stakes and allowing firms to choose their managers—leads to more efficient firms when compared to those with a higher involvement by the state.

In terms of upgrading efforts following restructuring, two-thirds of reformed SOEs in the sample introduced new production technologies— 40 percent through licensing and 48 percent by in-house development— indicating that these firms possess the requisite absorptive capacity.[38] This is again consistent with the finding that the more efficient firms are typi-cally chosen for reform. With continuous accumulation of internal capa-bilities, coupled with collaboration with others, these firms are beginning to behave more like the dynamic firms found in industrial countries.

But in order to truly transform the Chinese economy so that it operates at full efficiency—and to enable more Chinese firms to improve their process and product technologies—the restructuring efforts in China need

---

37. Dong, Putterman, and Unel find that, in the case of Nanjing, poorer-performing SOEs were restructured first (Dong, Putterman, and Unel 2004).

38. See Nabeshima (2004) for a detailed discussion on the different modes of technology trans-fer in East Asia and their implied requirements.

to proceed further: The state needs to tackle many hurdles that have until now been sidestepped. One such issue is the question of excess labor in large SOEs.

Firms in this sample were able to reduce the number of workers when undergoing restructuring, and many of those who were laid off were sent to reemployment centers provided by the firm or the municipal government. However, among the SOEs that have not yet been reformed, their inability to shed excess labor (and social burden) stands out as the major constraint to restructuring, along with the difficulties associated with the restructuring of their debt (see tables 5.31 and 5.32).[39] Even some of the reformed firms have not been able to relinquish their social burdens.[40] But the challenges of excess burden and debt restructuring are not unique to certain subsectors or to particular cities; these are encountered in all five cities and across all sectors in the sample. If further reform of ownership is to proceed rapidly, the state must correct these problems before it can embark upon either the full restructuring of its industries—or, as a potential future—full privatization.

---

39. Guo and Yao (2005) also find that worker redundancy and excessive debt obligation are two factors hindering the further reform efforts.

40. Lin and Zhu (2001) also find that 76 percent of restructured firms still carry social welfare obligations from the pre-restructuring era.

Table 5.31 Reasons for Not Restructuring SOEs, by City

Type of reason	Observations	Percentage of firms that answered Yes to the questions in column 1						
		Average	Beijing	Chongqing	Guangzhou	Shanghai	Wuhan
The business is in good shape, so there is no need to restructure.	131	9.2	5.9	0	0	29.2	11.5
The firm cannot solve the problem of surplus labor and social burden.	131	38.9	32.4	48.0	31.8	50.0	34.6
Employees are reluctant to change their state-employed status.	131	4.6	5.9	4.0	0	12.5	0
The firm cannot solve the debt problem.	131	34.3	29.4	52.0	31.8	20.8	38.5
The restructuring cost (asset evaluation fee, for example) is too high.	131	14.5	2.9	16.0	9.1	16.7	30.8
Employees are reluctant to buy stocks.	131	3.1	5.9	4.0	4.5	0	0
The local government has no incentives.	131	1.5	2.9	4.0	0	0	0
The firm is identified as a special industry, unsuitable for restructuring.	131	6.9	11.8	0	9.1	0	11.5
The manufacturing equipment and technologies are out-of-date, and products are not competitive.	131	7.6	5.9	8.0	4.5	12.5	7.7
Other reasons	131	20.6	32.3	28.0	27.3	8.3	3.8

Note: "Other reasons" include the following: no suitable restructuring schemes available, not ready, waiting for confirmation from the government or the group supervisor, and so forth.

Source: Authors' survey data.

Table 5.32 Reasons for Not Restructuring SOEs, by Sector

Type of reason	Observations	Average	Electronic equipment	Electronic components	Consumer products	Vehicles & vehicle parts	Garments & leather goods	General machinery	Textiles
			Percentage of firms that answered Yes to questions in column 1						
The business is in good shape, so there is no need to restructure.	131	9.2	17.6	3.8	0	14.5	0	0	0
The firm cannot solve the problem of surplus labor and social burden.	131	38.9	35.3	42.3	50.0	36.4	53.8	35.7	25.0
Employees are reluctant to change their state-employed status.	131	4.6	0	15.4	0	1.8	7.7	0	0
The firm cannot solve the debt problem.	131	34.3	11.8	42.3	0	29.1	53.8	42.9	75.0
The restructuring cost (asset evaluation fee, for example) is too high.	131	14.5	0	23.1	50.0	14.5	7.7	21.4	0
Employees are reluctant to buy stocks.	131	3.1	0	7.7	0	1.8	0	7.1	0
The local government has no incentives.	131	1.5	5.9	0.0	0	1.8	0	0	0
The firm is identified as a special industry, unsuitable for restructuring.	131	6.9	11.7	11.5	50	5.4	0	0	0
The manufacturing equipment and technologies are out-of-date, and products are not competitive.	131	7.6	5.9	15.4	7.2	0	7.1	0	2.1
Other reasons	131	20.6	23.5	15.4	0	21.8	15.4	35.7	0

Note: "Other reasons" include the following: no suitable restructuring schemes available, not ready, waiting for confirmation from the government or the group supervisor, and so forth.

Source: Authors' survey data.

CHAPTER 6

MAKING PRIVATIZATION WORK

Governments across the world have tended to shy away from privatizing the state's industrial assets. When they have done so, it is because they are influenced by a combination of factors. In some instances there is a rightward shift in the government's political orientation. Easing fiscal pressures through the sale of public assets is another motive, as is a growing dissatisfaction with the performance of state sector corporations. A lesser but occasional reason can be the attempt to deepen financial markets that would help stimulate and funnel private savings into more effective use.[1]

In parts of Eastern Europe and the former Soviet Union, a radical change in the political regime provided the opening for systemic reforms before those with strong vested interests in maintaining state ownership could mobilize political opposition. Selective privatization in Western Europe and in many of the developing countries more often reflects fiscal concerns,[2] a change in thinking with regard to the relative advantages of private over public provision, and a desire to enlarge political support by transferring the ownership of public assets to the voting public. An initial round of privatizations in Europe during the 1980s snowballed into a worldwide movement that has led to a scaling back of the public sector

---

1. Opper (2004) shows empirically how political factors influence privatization in transition economies. She finds that high unemployment and a high proportion of urban residents tend to slow the push for privatization, especially for the larger state-owned enterprises, while a more developed private sector stimulates the drive for further privatization.

2. A study by Brune, Garrett, and Kogut (2004) proposes another reason why developing countries pursued the privatization of public assets during 1985–99. The conclusions of this study are based on cross-country regressions drawing on data from 96 countries. Brune, Garrett, and Kogut show that the scale of a country's obligations to the International Monetary Fund (IMF) influenced the extent of its divestiture of public assets. Moreover, IMF conditionality with respect to privatization affected sales in the 1990s.

share of GDP in most countries. How privatization might evolve in China is the question addressed in this volume. Much depends on the assessment of recent experience with the various forms and gradations of ownership reform. Can a country such as China better realize its industrial objectives by privatizing? If so, what is the best path to follow, and how can future decisions be informed by research on experience in China and other countries?

Worldwide privatization has been most extensive in the manufacturing industry; but governments have also transferred the ownership of many networked industries (some that can be classified as natural monopolies) into private hands. The public sector's profile is now lower in most countries, although direct and indirect state ownership are still widespread. The rush to privatize has largely abated, however, and earlier enthusiasm has been tempered by a nuanced, and even skeptical, appreciation of how privatization affects factor productivity, profitability, quality of service, investment, technological change, wealth distribution, voter sentiment, and other performance indicators. In most of the OECD countries that spearheaded ownership reforms, the state retains a sizable stake in numerous industrial corporations. State bodies continue to exercise substantial influence over corporate governance in key subsectors of the economy (Bortolotti and Siniscalco 2004). Moreover, where the state has relinquished ownership it has, at least with respect to the networked industries, maintained extensive regulatory oversight. In sum, privatization has made deep inroads into the public sector—most notably in the area of manufacturing, and least of all in the networked industries and natural monopolies. The extreme privatization predictions of the 1980s and early 1990s have not been realized anywhere: Public ownership of utilities, industries, and other types of productive assets has not been erased, although it has declined, often steeply. Expectations of major gains in productivity and profitability have been modulated by sober experience. Gains have been realized in most cases, but not consistently, and only when sales of public entities were complemented by other policies and by the building of missing or embryonic market institutions.[3] Broadly speaking, privatization has led to improvements, but not consistently. Sometimes increases in profitability have not been sustained,

---

3. Tornell (1999) maintains that transferring ownership from the state must be followed by true privatization, which entails establishing the property rights of the new owners, hardening budget constraints, and strengthening the judiciary and bankruptcy laws. In the absence of such institutional development, there is a risk that private mafias will displace government bureaucrats.

and spurts in productivity that immediately precede privatization and continue during the first few years following the change in ownership have tended to subside.[4] Some evidence also suggests that partial privatization, where the state retains a portion of the control rights, produces more favorable results.

TAKING STOCK OF CHINA'S PRIVATIZATION

Against this backdrop, how should one view China's attempts at ownership reform? There can be no doubt that the tempo of ownership reform quickened after the mid-1990s. As a consequence, the composition of industrial ownership is being radically transformed, starting with the privatization of the small SOEs. Whether the newly privatized entities now have an arm's-length relationship with the state is a separate matter: Undoubtedly, many firms maintain formal or informal links, as in Russia. Nevertheless, the fact remains that the state has been willing to dispose of industrial assets, and this privatization process will continue. It should be remembered, however, that the industrial sector is only one important part of the total economy—and the majority of nonindustrial assets remain in the public domain. Some observers are of the view that the pace of ownership reform in China has been about right: Anything faster could have precipitated problems similar to those experienced by the Commonwealth of Independent States (CIS) countries that opted for "big bang" reforms. These observers maintain that China has had to tread a fine line in order to accommodate a host of constraints and has, by and large, struck the appropriate trade-off between efficiency and stability without apparently sacrificing much growth. This line of reasoning has assigned primacy to the costs of privatization in a socialist economy, where social security for public sector employees was provided (via tacit arrangement) by their employers, not directly by the state. Were privatization to lead to large-scale redundancies, the current state of the social security system in China is such that many workers would have neither unemployment insurance nor adequate pensions to fall back on; and many would lose housing, schooling, and medical benefits as well as a range of minor

---

4. Green and Haskel (2004) find gains in productivity in the course of the restructuring that precedes the privatization of U.K. publicly owned companies, but little improvement thereafter. They also find that the quality of services depends upon the tightness of regulation.

subsidized amenities provided by their *danwei*.[5,6] Thus, widespread layoffs would cause hardship and could trigger social unrest. In fact, hardship is already evident in the rust belt cities of the northeast and central regions of China.

The case against rapid privatization in the earlier stages of transition has two additional strands: First, in the context of a socialist economy with few large private pools of liquid capital, a sale of public assets favors those with good connections and access to (generally public) financing, enabling them to annex the lion's share of the assets that are privatized. The upshot of this can be a sudden widening of wealth and income disparities, another possible source of instability in a society where memories of an egalitarian distribution of both income and wealth are still fresh.

Second, when foreigners with deeper pockets than local investors are permitted to bid for state-owned firms, governments are reluctant to lose control of strategic industries that have typically been established through a considerable outlay of public funds. Strategic industries are generally those that are technology-intensive and with above average value added. For industrializing economies, these industries are perceived as an avenue for diversifying away from "commodified" consumer manufactures with falling entry barriers that generate meager returns. Foreign ownership can lead to an infusion of capital, management skills, and new technology that can fulfill strategic objectives; but in the hands of the new owners, the industry's objectives can diverge from national objectives. In Latin America, for example, foreign ownership of automobile assembly may explain the absence of a significant deepening of local expertise and technological advances.

Each of these considerations appears to have influenced Chinese decisionmakers throughout the 1990s, inducing them to act with the utmost caution. But as China has moved into a mature stage of transition, the costs of such gradualism have steadily mounted. In spite of extensive tinkering with enterprise autonomy and managerial incentives, the losses of state-owned enterprises (SOEs) mounted steadily through the 1980s, burdening the state-owned banks with nonperforming loans and storing

---

5. *Danwei* refers to the basic social unit that provided (and to a lesser degree still provides) an axis for an individual's existence in urban areas. See Bray (2005) for a discussion of its genesis.

6. Some of the theoretical work on the optimum speed of transition reviewed by Campos and Coricelli (2002) argues for a pace commensurate with the private sector's ability to absorb laid-off SOE workers. This literature also suggests that the contraction of the SOE sector be coordinated by the capacity to expand the social safety net.

up enormous contingent liabilities. In some instances, asset-stripping by employees and managers hollowed out SOEs and transferred equipment to daughter enterprises, collectives, and privately owned firms. This may have been less pervasive in the case of China, although it is difficult to know in the absence of careful study. What did become apparent in the 1990s was the lack of dynamism, managerial expertise, and technological capability among even the leading SOEs. These firms remained relatively sheltered from competition and, in addition, enjoyed preferential access to bank financing that softened their budget constraints. Throughout this period, SOEs absorbed two-thirds or more of all bank lending; and for this reason, financial resources were disproportionaly channeled to provinces with a heavy concentration of SOEs, a trend that contributed to the widening of regional disparities.

The start of the Ninth Five-Year Plan in 1996 provided firms an opportunity to adopt the more aggressive enterprise reform strategy described in chapters 1 and 3 of this volume. By "grasping the big and letting go of the small," the Chinese government attempted to reap many of the gains from privatization while minimizing the costs. It sought to divest the large number of small and medium-size state-owned enterprises (SMSOEs), so as to cut state sector losses and reduce the flow of bank financing to inefficient SOEs, while minimizing the level of redundancies. It was also far easier to dispose of, liquidate, or merge smaller enterprises than it was to find buyers for the larger ones. In addition, by retaining control over the bigger SOEs, the state was better able to pursue industrial strategies of its choosing.

Nearly a decade after ownership reform has shifted to higher gear, it is now possible to take stock and assess the effectiveness of privatizing the small firms and corporatizing only a fraction of the larger enterprises. Undoubtedly, this process has further reduced the state's share of the industrial GDP to less than 20 percent. The proportion of loss-making enterprises also fell in 2004, and average profitability, while notoriously unstable, has inched upward. Well over 1,200 SOEs are now listed on China's two stock exchanges, and the formation of limited liability companies (LLCs) and limited liability shareholding companies (LLSCs) has begun to change the nature of corporate governance in China. There is an ongoing effort to tighten managerial accountability, to improve the quality of management through the hiring of foreign managers for the largest firms starting in 2005, and an attempt to strengthen minority shareholder rights.

Perhaps most significant are the gains in the performance of reformed SOEs, as reflected in a few selected indicators. As mentioned earlier,

LLSCs have done better than LLCs, and both have edged ahead of the unreformed SOEs. This is a considerable achievement and suggests that the adopted strategy is working. But what about the costs of reform? Would it have been possible to do better by following an alternative approach? Should the strategy be modified, and if so, in what manner? These are some of the questions that are explored in this concluding chapter.

ASSESSING GRADUALISM

Slow reform perpetuates distortions and inefficiencies—and the misallocation of resources always incurs costs. By further entrenching vested interests, a gradual approach can create vicious circles that act as a brake on the reform efforts. Former CIS and Soviet countries that opted for more far-reaching reforms were, on balance, doing better 10 years later with regard to growth, income distribution, and governance; although, as noted, some important research in the 1990s argued for gradual reform that matched the capacity of the private sector to absorb laid-off workers. Has China been able to avoid some of these costs? The answer is not obvious, and the high rate of GDP growth should not obscure the cost to China of maintaining a large and relatively inefficient state enterprise sector. Compared to Korea, which attained comparable growth rates in the 1960s and 1970s, China's incremental capital-output ratios are substantially higher—and worse, have risen over the past decade—suggesting that the efficiency with which capital is used has declined. Stated differently, because of resource misallocation, China's net national product may be growing more slowly than its GDP. Although the SOE sector certainly is not the only source of inefficiency, it is a major culprit—especially because it continues to absorb such a large portion of the financial capital of the economy. This has the added disadvantage of starving other firms and sectors of capital (such as the smaller privately or collectively owned industrial enterprises in urban and rural areas that are generating much of the increase in employment).

Piecemeal ownership reform and intensifying competition have forced SOEs to raise their productivity, but much more improvement is needed. This will require further large cuts of the workforce—adding to the millions already laid off. The problems confronting unemployed former SOE workers would have been far less severe if the time gained through the sequencing of ownership reform had been used to deploy more effective active labor market policies and to construct an adequate social safety net. But the slow pace of ownership reform has had a knock-on effect on other reforms as well. Social security reforms, for example, were initiated more than 15 years ago, and the beginnings of a system are in place. But the (provincially and municipally) fractionated structure that has emerged is far from adequate given the current needs and may be perpetuating interprovincial inequality.[7] Thus, the costly postponement of privatization has not resulted in a more streamlined and competitive state enterprise sector. Arguably, it has not significantly lessened the pain of adjustment, by minimizing layoffs by the affected enterprises, or by ameliorating hardship through the provision of a well-funded, nationwide safety net.[8]

CONGLOMERATE GROUP FORMATION AS AN INTERIM STRATEGY

There have been other consequences of deferring full privatization and pursuing alternative ways of reforming SOEs. Throughout much of the 1990s and into the present, the authorities have attempted to import East Asian models of industrial organization and imbue them with Chinese characteristics, in the hope that these would revive the state sector and sidestep the need for privatizing industrial entities and create world class firms that enter the ranks of the Fortune 500. The two interlinked approaches adopted were industrial consolidation through mergers and the setting up of enterprise groups modeled on Japanese and Korean industrial conglomerates—especially in the state-designated "pillar industries" that are viewed as the drivers of growth. These approaches were central to the government's industrial policy over the past decade and have been aggressively implemented by both national and subnational industrial bureaus.

The effort to salvage or revive ailing state enterprises by merging them with profitable ones can avoid problems associated with layoffs or in rarer cases, the loss of productive capacity. But it saddles healthy firms with unwanted and frequently expensive responsibilities.[9] A merger of firms, each with its own organizational idiosyncrasies and cultural attributes, is a

---

7. By the end of 2002, pension accounts had accumulated 100 billion yuan as against the targeted 480 billion yuan. Moreover, only six to seven provincial governments (out of 31) were not making losses on their pension accounts ("Time Bomb" 2004).

8. Were such a centralized system to be put in place, it would concentrate vast resources in the hands of a central agency. Such an outcome also has its downside, as is becoming evident from the recent experience of mature industrialized countries.

9. According to a report quoted by Meyer and Lu (2005), 2,000 loss-making SOEs were rescued through mergers between 1994 and 1997.

complicated process that can fail even under favorable circumstances.[10] A forced marriage of two unwilling partners, one of which is incurring losses, is doubly problematic and incurs the risk of compromising the performance of the successful partner. Although this practice has been widely used for some time, no comprehensive attempt has been made to analyze the consequences and relative costs of restructuring through mergers as an alternative to outright divestiture or closure of failing enterprises. The state sector has tended to internalize the costs of such policies even when they have the potential to weaken the most dynamic SOEs financially and divert managerial resources to the often futile effort of integrating disparate firms. Since ownership reform has moved into higher gear, forced mergers have presumably become less common. But it is hard to tell what is happening from the number of bankruptcies announced and the data released on state enterprises. Because the classification of firms has changed from time to time, there is a lack of consistent data on SOEs from 1995 to the present and insufficient information on the details of ownership reform.

Forming enterprise groups is the complementary approach, modeled loosely on Japanese *keiretsu*, to create vertically integrated industrial structures and provide weaker firms with a support system. In some instances, these groups came "ready made," because they comprise the enterprises supervised by an industrial bureau that could be transformed from a government agency into a holding company.[11] This stratagem had the apparent advantage of shrinking the state bureaucracy while providing the newly formed enterprise group with an organizational armature and preserving any preexisting production relationships among firms.

Just as it is difficult to assess how mergers have affected enterprise performance, there is no empirical evidence on whether the Chinese-style groups have strengthened the competitiveness of their constituent firms, especially in the "pillar industries." There are broad and fluctuating indicators of returns on assets, some data on the number of enterprises operating at a loss, instances of reformed SOEs that have made remarkable

---

10. The experience with restructuring large, relatively healthy corporations in capitalist economies (such as Siemens in Germany) underlines the great difficulty of modifying accumulated culture and practices and charting a new course (Stewart and O'Brien 2005).

11. Under the Group Company System introduced in 1992, a parent enterprise provided overall managerial guidance, and was responsible for personnel policy and for safeguarding state assets. Affiliated daughter enterprises retained their legal identity and entered into contracting or leasing arrangements with the parent company (Meyer and Lu 2005).

strides in developing manufacturing capability, and a great deal of evidence on the international competitiveness of Chinese producers that have steadily enlarged their market share at the expense of competitors throughout East Asia and Central America.[12] Observers also now have a far better appreciation for the strengths and weaknesses of conglomerates, corporate groupings, and "pillar industries" in other East Asian countries and in the West. The apparent international competitiveness of some Chinese SOEs notwithstanding, the verdict on these entities, whether from the United States, the United Kingdom, or from Japan or Korea, is at best mixed—and often negative.[13] This is not to deny that in the automobile sector, for example, close networking between assemblers and component suppliers operating under competitive conditions can be fruitful. What the evidence does suggest, however, is that diversified conglomerates generally do less well than more focused companies. And one can infer from the literature that conglomerates assembled at the instigation of government agencies principally to meet nonmarket objectives will be at a disadvantage and will do their utmost to keep budget constraints as soft as possible. Similarly, the jury is out on the feasibility of building a vertically integrated pillar industry, given the increasing fuzziness of industrial boundaries. As Steinfeld (2004b, p. 184) points out, "From a product architecture perspective, it may be impossible to determine the exact boundaries of a given industry. Yet Chinese industrial policy, by selecting 'pillar' industries does precisely this. . . . For a country to be strong in autos, aerospace, or telecom, what fundamentally does it need? Software companies? Semiconductor design houses? Handset manufacturers? Steel firms? Marketing firms?"

The key policy initiatives adopted by the Chinese authorities to build a profitable and competitive state-owned manufacturing sector— management (or performance) contracting, mergers, the formation of enterprise groups, foreign acquisitions, and corporatization with the state retaining a controlling share—have not demonstrated their efficacy in the face of an increasingly open and competitive economic milieu.[14] Whether

---

12. As of July 2004, there were 14 Chinese firms mainly drawn from the engineering and telecommunications subsectors in the Fortune 500 ("China: SOE Reforms" 2005).

13. A study of the largest 250 nonfinancial firms in the United Kingdom and Germany found that firms prefer to grow through mergers and acquisitions rather than through an organic, internally driven process. Furthermore, managers tended to consistently overestimate the gains from mergers and acquisitions, in spite of long experience to the contrary. Their priorities are seemingly not influenced by outcomes (Kirchmaier 2003).

14. See Steinfeld (2004a) and Zhang (2004b). Some scattered evidence based on the performance of leading Chinese reformed firms that are active in international markets points to the

or not these approaches were once adequate or even superior alternatives to privatization, it is difficult to argue today that they are a more attractive means of meeting the overarching objectives of growth, building technological capability, creating globally competitive corporate entities, and generating employment commensurate with China's needs. Chinese and cross-country evidence fairly consistently underscore the relative advantages of privately owned firms, joint ventures, and semi-public firms over the wholly state-owned enterprises. The literature on privatization and on industrial development more broadly stresses the mediating role of institutions in achieving successful outcomes. Few now claim that privatization should be the centerpiece of industrial reform after tallying the collateral damage from poorly executed privatizations. But on balance, the privatization of the manufacturing sector would be significantly superior to continuing with the status quo for the reformed firms themselves. It would diminish the costs SOEs impose on banks, and it could stimulate other market, institutional, and social security reforms that have proceeded slowly.

MEDIUM-TERM POLICY OBJECTIVES

The remainder of this chapter examines the objectives, procedures, and institutional reforms that should engage China's policymakers over the medium term.

There is always the risk that current corporate models might not prove to be durable and that current convictions about the sources of industrial dynamism will need to be revised. Indeed, the business literature is replete with warnings of the short shelf-life of business models. Keeping these concerns very much at the forefront, it appears that a technologically dynamic and globally competitive corporate sector has certain attributes that may be of relevance for China over the medium and long terms. These include:

1. Privately owned companies operating in an open and competitive market environment for products and for corporate control, through mergers and takeovers

---

teething difficulties being encountered. Haier, for instance, made a net profit of $44 million in 2004 (the same as in 2003) on revenues of a little less than $2 billion ("Haier's Net Profit" 2005). Sichuan Changhong Electric made losses in 2004, mainly because of problems with operations in the United States. And TCL's profits in 2004 were halved following its merger with Thomson of France ("Changhong Hit" 2005; "TCL Spree" 2005).

2. A mix of large firms with global reach, and many SMEs with the stock of these business entities refreshed through entry, exit, and the growth of firms

3. Corporate governance institutions that encourage managerial initiative while strengthening accountability and the rights of minority shareholders

4. A competition policy backed by the requisite legal and regulatory apparatus that defines and enforces rules, so as to create a market environment that supports items 1 and 2

5. A national innovation system that stimulates corporate innovation through fiscal incentives, the supply of skills, the enforcement of intellectual property rights, budgetary support for research and demand for technologically advanced products, the harnessing of information technology, and institutions that encourage networking among and between corporations, universities, and research institutes.

MARKET ENVIRONMENT AND THE ROLE OF THE STATE

The success of firms as an outcome of interplay between firms and the market environment was mentioned in chapter 1. On the side of the firm, management, strategy, and organization are key. There is no single combination that works best in all situations, and the sheer diversity of success stories—and of failures—argues for caution. However, the quality of management is vital in family-owned and public LLCs alike. It is management that takes the lead in crafting strategy and then shaping and leading an organization to implement the strategy and respond to outcomes.[15] Certain forms of ownership, institution, and market conditions are more likely to bring out the best in management than others. Here it has been argued, based on the evidence presented in this volume, that private ownership more strongly motivates management, leads to greater strategic agility, and gives management much more latitude to adapt organizations to changing market exigencies.

However, private ownership is only one important piece of the puzzle: Market functioning and market rules are two closely related pieces. One might go so far as to say that dynamic management and competitive markets are two sides of the coin. Integrated national markets that are

---

15. For example, a study of the electronics components industry in Korea highlights the critical role of management in devising strategy and providing leadership (Kim and Lee 2002).

open to external competition demand more from firms—and in both theory and practice—deliver better results. Markets with fewer regulatory barriers to entry are more contestable and do not allow firms an easy life. Likewise, low barriers to exit help weed out the weak performers.

One arena of competition comprises products that firms sell. Another is the financial market for corporate ownership, which tracks the performance of firms via share price and exposes weak companies (and their management) to the threat of takeover. The financial market also presents avenues for the merger of firms that see advantages in combining forces. Where the shares of firms are actively traded, there is ample financing for takeovers. And if the investment banking and legal infrastructure are in place, the market for corporate control can force managers and firms to pay continuous—sometimes excessive—attention to efficiency and profitability, generally to the advantage of minority shareholders, not to mention the economy as a whole.

Competitive product markets depend on financial institutions to mediate the funding that can lower entry barriers to new firms, allow profitable firms with good opportunities to grow, and finance (in whole or in part) mergers and takeovers. In other words, competitive product markets are almost inseparable from deep and competitive financial markets.

How does China fare with respect to each of these? The short answer is that the situation is improving, but the road ahead could be a long one. First and foremost, the transfer of ownership from state to private hands has commenced. Changes are beginning to become evident, but the partially privatized state enterprises essentially remain in the grip of the state. The management in many cases has not been replaced or the organizational structures modified, and even where new managers have been appointed, they have been drawn from a small, fairly homogeneous pool vetted by the Communist Party.[16] Control rights of these firms still generally reside with the state, and since only a fraction of their shares are publicly traded, "reformed" SOEs listed on the stock markets are not subject to the threat of takeover. And in most cases, it is not apparent that budget constraints have been tightened to levels equivalent to those of a free market economy.

Second, China is rapidly lowering trade barriers, and the degree of openness is certainly on the rise. Moreover, national market integration is increasing but has many gaps. County officials continue to favor local

---

16. However, see the earlier reference to the plan to hire foreign managers and thereby diversify the pool of managerial talent.

suppliers, most notably in the auto sector, and strive to protect their tax base; they pull strings to provide local firms with preferential bank funding, discriminate against producers from other parts of China, discourage takeovers of local firms by enterprises from other provinces, and tolerate a legal environment that makes it difficult for firms to enforce contracts.[17] This, of course, particularly discourages long-distance trading. The transport and logistics infrastructure is improving but still suffers from many deficiencies arising from physical constraints and high transaction costs that impose additional barriers to competition. Road tolls are high—and account for up to 20 percent of the cost of truck-borne freight (Woetzel 2003, p. 79).

Entry barriers for firms that can compete with current and former SOEs have also declined, but there remains much variance among cities. Shanghai and coastal cities such as Dalian, Guangzhou, Shenzhen, and Wenzhou have taken an aggressive approach to deregulation and created an attractive investment climate. However, many of the cities in the interior, such as Benxi, Guiyong, Lanzhou, and Xian, lag behind (Dollar and others 2003).

The model that Chinese policymakers currently view as more appropriate for China attaches greater significance to the competitive potential and innovative capacity of the large corporations and the enterprise groups. In Japan and Korea, such corporate entities have played a leading role; and around the world, the dominance of the giant mulitnational corporations is, if anything, rising, not diminishing. Currently, China has no firms with the industrial heft, brand name, and technological resources comparable to those of the industrialized countries (Nolan 2001).[18] But China sees some urgency in the need to grow such firms, so as to establish a presence in the global marketplace.

Large Chinese multinationals could emerge by way of market-determined mergers and acquisitions orchestrated by the more dynamic industrial firms. In principle, privatizing the major SOEs could initiate this process. However, there remains the risk that foreign firms would buy into the best of these—and that others lack the managerial capacity and the human resources to become world-class corporations. A few Chinese firms such as Lenovo and TCL have become giants on the national scale,

---

17. This is motivated by the desire to protect both local sources of fiscal revenue and avenues for exercising patronage.

18. Firms like Haier and TCL are still only 10 percent the size of major multinationals such as Sony and Philips (Woetzel 2003). Also, large SOEs are spending little more than 1 percent of their operating income on research and development, compared with 5 percent for foreign multinationals ("China: SOE Reforms" 2005).

but they are just starting to acquire a global profile with a few overseas acquisitions.[19]

Clearly, the Chinese authorities have little faith in the ability of their SOEs to mount the global stage unaided by the government after they have been privatized. This may reflect risk aversion or the unwillingness of state bureaucracies to let go of valuable assets and watch their fiefdoms shrink. Or it could simply reflect the government's assessment of the quality of managerial and technical skills or the resilience of industrial organizations. Whatever the mix of reasons behind these decisions, both national and subnational governments have revealed a preference to privatize in slow steps, while pouring money into these entities in an effort to transform them into world-class players. China wants its own companies with profiles that rival Samsung, Hyundai, Hon Hai Precision, Matsushita, Canon, and Toyota. Policymakers appear to believe that ample supplies of capital, technology transfer, and a patient imitation of East Asian corporate models provide the makings of a more potent recipe than privatization alone, which leaves firms accustomed to a sheltered life at the mercy of the market. Since 1997, a select group of the most promising SOEs have been receiving special support from the government (Smyth 2000). These include the firms Haier, Baoshan Steel, Sichuan Changhong Electric, Shanghai Tianyuan Shipbuilding, and SMIC. Such funding no doubt supplements and supports the internal resources of these firms.[20]

From the East Asian perspective, this strategy certainly is not without merit. East Asian governments frequently assisted, sometimes substantially, the development of what eventually became world-class corporations. However, in the vast majority of cases, they were nurturing private companies. There are instances (Korea's POSCO and a few Singaporean government-linked corporations [GLCs] among the exceptions) of publicly owned manufacturing firms that entered the ranks of the leading multinationals. But East Asian governments have generally focused on a small number of promising firms, and the more enlightened have been prepared to eventually acknowledge failure and cut their losses.

---

19. The purchase by Lenovo of IBM's PC division makes it the third-ranked producer of personal computers after Dell and Hewlett-Packard. Other smaller companies such as Geely and Chery, producers of small cars, are also planning to enter foreign markets and set up overseas production facilities ("Deal On" 2005).

20. Woetzel (2003, p. 51) maintains, "Historically, Chinese manufacturing capacity has not earned its cost of capital." And Zhang (2005) adds that China's three top breweries, with more than a third of the domestic market, registered total profits of $100 million in 2004, equal to one-seventh of Heineken's.

In the case of China, there are still hundreds of large SOEs and reformed SOEs, and the volume of resources they soak up is enormous. But even with its vast savings, China might consider the merits of holding on to so many of the large at such cost. It may be far better to be selective in the attempt to grow firms, innovative in efforts to tailor strategy, realistic in admitting failure, and more optimistic with regard to the prospects of privately owned world-class firms created through mergers and acquisitions and directed by the market system.

INDUSTRIAL CONSOLIDATION

The tempo of competition in product markets has not yet been matched by competition in the market for corporate control. While the drafting of rules for mergers and acquisitions in China was initiated in 1999, the guidelines were issued at the end of 2002—and it is too early to know if they will intensify competition, sharpen the incentives for managers, and promote the restructuring of SOEs. Thus far, the state has been unwilling to surrender its control rights over publicly listed reformed SOEs. In turn, the market treats the sale of shares in these companies by state holding companies (as was done in mid-2005) not as a diminution of state control but as a dilution in the stake of other shareholders. It appears, therefore, that even with the mergers and acquisitions rules in place, market participants are keenly aware of the wariness of public agencies toward allowing financial markets to operate in a manner that would loosen the state's grip on the former SOEs.[21]

A process of consolidation mediated by the market and led by autonomous enterprise managers is more likely to result in competitive firms. Reformed SOEs such as Lenovo, TCL, CIMC, the Shougang Group, and Changhong Electronics are all emerging as apparently viable and internationally competitive businesses—because management was given more latitude.[22] Comprising a number of geographically dispersed enterprises, CIMC, for example, is the largest manufacturer of shipping containers in the world. It was founded in 1980, and after some ups and downs in the 1980s embarked on an expansionary strategy modeled on that

---

21. On the progress made in facilitating mergers and acquisitions, and on the many remaining hurdles, see Norton and Chao (2001) and "Merger and Acquisition Rules to Entice Investors" (2002).

22. Sull and Wang (2005) describe the strategies being deployed by such firms to win market share. However, on Shougang's somewhat checkered performance and conglomerate diversification, see Movshuk (2004).

of Mitsubishi Heavy Industry (and Cisco Systems) in the early 1990s. CIMC's efforts to grow through consolidation involved acquiring container manufacturing enterprises scattered along China's east coast, from Dalian to Xinhui in the Pearl River Delta. The company now has 38 percent of the world market and two-thirds of the domestic market for shipping containers and is among China's more remarkable success stories (Meyer and Lu 2005).

Two factors account for the emergence of CIMC as an industrial leader. First is the autonomy it has enjoyed from interference by the central government, because containers were not viewed as a strategic industry. Moreover, the organization of the Shenzhen Party Committee (to which the company reports) has also allowed CIMC a large measure of operational latitude.[23] Huawei, also registered in Shenzhen, shares similar advantages.

Second, possibly because of its autonomy, CIMC has been fortunate with respect to the quality of its management. This management has been able to integrate CIMC's several acquisitions and steadily expand its market share. It has also spurred diversification into airport ramps and power generating equipment (Meyer and Lu 2005).

Other reformed state firms have also joined the ranks of market leaders in China and have become major OEMs (original equipment manufacturers). The best-known examples are Lenovo,[24] Changhong Electric, Shougang Steel, and Konka.[25] In each case, these companies were able to break loose from the pack because management effectively sought and exploited their relative independence. Management had the vision to build production capacity through consolidation and to acquire the technological capability that is vital to competitiveness.

Some of the firms listed in table 6.1, could, in time, become world-class multinational corporations. But as the experiences of CIMC, Lenovo, TCL, Huawei, and Changhong Electric show, success may require a level of autonomy from the state, pressure of market competition on the management, and strengthening of managerial skills that only a more far-reaching privatization is likely to deliver.

---

23. CIMC is registered with the municipality of Shenzhen.

24. Liu Chuanzhi, the CEO of Lenovo, observed that although his firm was an SOE, it was "structured as a private firm" (Woetzel 2003, p. 41).

25. Shenkar (2005) recounts the way Changhong Electric has acquired a large slice of the low-end TV market in the United States through its close association with Wal-Mart, which for special promotions, buys huge numbers of its TVs that are sold under the Apex Digital brand. Nolan and Yeung (2001) describe how the Shougang Group used the autonomy gained through management contracting and other reforms to restructure the companies and enhance performance.

COMPETITION POLICY

As the reach of the market expands and more SOEs are privatized, sustaining market contestability will require stronger institutions, including an effective competition policy. The enforcement of competition or antitrust policies rules principally to regulate market power by controlling collusive price-fixing and other competition-reducing agreements; actions by firms with significant market share to enlarge or further secure their market position; mergers between firms that have the potential for excessively concentrating market power; and vertical restraints and price-fixing arrangements.[26]

Competition policies have been most vigorously applied in North America and, increasingly, in the European Union. So far, only three East Asian economies have introduced competition policies with sufficiently broad coverage, the requisite laws, the independent regulatory body, and a judiciary empowered to enforce the rules. The three are Japan, Korea, and Taiwan (China). However, the consequences for market functioning and economic performance in these economies have not been systematically evaluated. Nonetheless, the consensus view from the industrialized countries where mergers and acquisitions activity is intense and firms are quick to exercise market power is that competition policy is important to protect consumers and safeguard productivity and innovation. Competitive pricing reinforces the effects of entry and exit. It raises consumer welfare and reduces business costs. With globalization and the intensification of efforts by major firms to dominate key markets throughout the world, competition policies have taken on greater significance—as evidenced by debates swirling around mergers and acquisitions in Europe. This raises the question as to whether such policies should be introduced in China, along with ownership reforms.

There are at least three reasons why an appropriately designed competition policy should be deployed in China—but only if it can be implemented by a regulatory agency that enjoys a substantial measure of autonomy and the judicial apparatus is suitably equipped to enforce the laws. Given the current state of China's judicial system and the limited autonomy enjoyed by most regulators, this is a tall order. However, as with the Securities and Exchange Commission in the United States, the Chinese authorities have shown that they can rise to the challenge when

---

26. For example, see Ross (2004), who reviews competition policy in Canada.

Table 6.1 Top 30 Selected Major Manufacturing Companies in China, 2002–3

Rank 2003	Rank 2002	Company	Major products	Revenues	Profits	Profits (% revenue)	Market value	Profits (% market value)	Controlling ownership[a]
6	5	Baoshan Iron & Steel	Iron and steel	$4,092.70	$516.10	12.61	$6,227.70	8.29	State[b]
13	6	Lenovo Group	Computers	$2,593.30	$133.80	5.16	$2,490.90	5.37	State
21	22	TCL International Holdings	Home appliances	$1,562.40	$78.00	4.99	$806.60	9.67	State
22	24	Sichuan Changhong Electric	Home appliances	$1,520.40	$21.30	1.40	$1,759.60	1.21	State
23	18	Beijing Shougang	Iron and steel	$1,519.90	$82.50	5.43	$1,593.50	5.18	State
27	20	Qingdao Haier Holdings	Home appliances	$1,395.80	$48.00	3.44	$895.20	5.36	Collective
30	21	Guangdong Midea Holding	Home appliances	$1,312.90	$18.70	1.42	$402.40	4.65	State
31	25	Angang New Steel	Metal fabrication and hardware	$1,301.30	$71.80	5.52	$910.90	7.88	State
33	36	Chongqing Changan Automobile	Auto manufacturing	$1,194.10	$100.90	8.45	$1,013.00	9.96	State
37	43	China International Marine Containers	Packaging and containers	$1,096.80	$56.20	5.12	$5,304.80	1.06	State
39	28	Jinzhou Petrochemical	Chemicals	$1,091.10	$1.50	0.14	$479.50	0.31	State
40	57	Great Wall Technology	Computers	$1,056.20	$8.40	0.80	$47.70	17.61	Foreign
41	—	TCL Communications Equipment	Home appliances	$1,053.80	$33.40	3.17	$318.40	10.49	State
47	44	Konka Group	Home appliances	$971.50	$4.30	0.44	$428.50	1.00	Private
55	79	Beiqi Futian Vehicle	Auto manufacturing	$915.70	$15.30	1.67	$316.50	4.83	State
57	53	Brilliance China Automotive Holdings	Auto manufacturing	$884.30	$91.70	10.37	$628.90	14.58	State

62	46	Gree Electric Appliances of Zhuhai	Home appliances	$849.30	$35.90	4.23	$541.00	6.64	Collective
64	75	Dongfeng Automobile	Auto parts and equipment	$845.70	$74.50	8.81	$1,824.20	4.08	State
65	63	Tsingtao Brewery	Beverages	$838.00	$27.90	3.33	$784.50	3.56	State
66	51	Wuhan Steel Processing	Iron and steel	$816.50	$7.80	0.96	$506.00	1.54	State
72	—	Ningbo Bird	Diversified holdings	$769.30	$26.10	3.39	$391.80	6.66	Joint venture[c]
73	85	Shenzhen Kaifa Technology	Computers	$746.50	$7.30	0.98	$897.00	0.81	Joint venture
77	88	Hisense Electric	Home appliances	$679.40	$4.20	0.62	$385.40	1.09	State
80	69	Tsinghua Tongfang	Computers	$657.20	$22.20	3.38	$758.20	2.93	State
86	73	Guangdong Kelon Electrical Holdings	Home appliances	$589.30	$12.20	2.07	$5,518.70	0.22	Collective
89	92	Shanghai Automotive	Auto parts and equipment	$576.20	$129.30	22.44	$2,085.40	6.20	State
91	97	FAW Car	Auto manufacturing	$574.50	$29.90	5.20	$1,166.00	2.56	State
93	80	SVA Electron	Electronics	$562.50	$12.60	2.24	$2,054.40	0.61	Joint venture
96	93	Shanghai Founder Yanzhong Sci.	Computers	$545.20	$15.60	2.86	$364.80	4.28	State
97	—	Amoisonic Electronics	Electronics	$542.00	$73.30	13.52	$584.20	12.55	Joint venture

— Not available.

a. Controlling ownership is based on a phone inquiry into China Enterprises Conferderation and online research.

b. State-owned enterprises include enterprises with controlling shares hold by the state.

c. Joint-venture enterprises may also include enterprises with shares by state or collective or private.

Source: The statistics are derived from "China's 100 Largest Companies" (2003).

the stakes are high. Strengthening the courts and the rule of law are separate matters altogether.

Why should competition policy complement the reform of SOEs? First, an explicit competition policy can help to guide the timing and nature of privatization and, where regulation is involved, can provide yardsticks for the regulators. Second, the level of industrial concentration in China is low relative to other East Asian economies; and there are far too many single plant enterprises in each industry. Thus, there is both a plentiful scope for the combining of firms and a strong trend toward consolidation—motivated in part by the creation of enterprise groups. Although desirable, such consolidation should be achieved by market forces that are subject to rules laid down by competition policy designed both to ensure an orderly change in industrial organization and to reduce barriers to the entry of new firms. Such entry is the best safeguard there is of a competitive market environment and is an important conduit for innovation.

Third, a competition policy is needed to dismantle the numerous barriers erected by provincial and county governments to limit and deflect mergers and the exit of firms in an effort to help rationalize China's fragmented industrial structure. Over time, local governments in China have exploited decentralization to pursue industrial policies that generate local employment and expand their fiscal base.[27] These policies have included the use of directed credit from banks and protection for local producers from both competition and takeovers. As noted earlier, many of the formal barriers to reform have been removed, but the informal impediments that remain need to be challenged by powerful regulators who can credibly enforce rules through judicial channels.

A final reason why a competition policy is needed arises from China's progressive integration with the global economy. One critical manifestation of such deepening integration is the volume of FDI that pours into China from its neighbors and the western industrialized countries. Increasingly, China is also investing abroad—and is already the fifth largest source of FDI. These flows, which are likely to grow as Chinese firms invest in overseas manufacturing facilities and resource-based industries, will have far-reaching consequences for the structure of Chinese

---

27. Two variants of provincial-level industrial policies under China's decentralized system are described by Thun (2004). His paper focuses on the development of the auto industry by Shanghai and Guangdong. Following WTO accession, the environment is changing for the more fragmented and provincially protected industries in China. There are likely to be some exits and consolidation of firms—but also new entry by firms such as Chery and Geely.

industry by way of mergers and the rationalization of production, a process that has already begun. A move to accelerate the privatization of the SOEs would most likely stimulate FDI and create the potential for a concentration of market power in China—but also affect the global market power of multinational corporations. The ramifications of cross-border mergers and acquisitions, highlighted by tensions between the United States and the European Union, suggest that a coordination or more ambitiously, an eventual harmonization of China's competition policy with those of its major trading partners may well be desirable. Deeper integration will demand an elaboration and strengthening of both regulatory and legal institutions in line with accelerated privatization.

China has a number of laws to control certain types of anticompetitive behavior of SOEs and government agencies; and the government has designated the Administration of Industry and Commerce of China to serve as a regulator of this legislation.[28] But these laws fall well short of an effective competition policy that could bolster the process of privatization; see, for example, Williams (2003). Four kinds of policy initiatives are needed.

First, competition law needs to be defined with an emphasis on enhancing economic efficiency. This would entail specifying the quantitative markers and standards for market participants and fully accounting for the impact of the laws on incentives for market participants (Owen, Sun, and Zheng 2004). Second, such law, as Lloyd, Vautier, and Crampton (2004) state, should adhere to the concept of neutrality with respect to SOEs. "That is, neutrality of market access and treatment between government-owned enterprises and privately owned enterprises" (p. 230). Third, the independence of regulatory agencies is an important attribute, especially where privatization of SOEs and industrial consolidation are part of the mix. Moreover, independence must be accompanied by adequate budget, staffing, and authority for the regulatory agency to conduct in-depth assessments and implement policy decisions. Fourth, and finally, the quality of the judiciary is vital to the framing and enforcement of competition policies. Without an impartial judiciary to weigh and rule on the evidence and build case law, the institutional infrastructure will remain weak, even if the other components are put in place.[29]

---

28. These include a law for Countering Unfair Competition (introduced in 1993) and the Commercial Banking Law (legislated in 1995).

29. On issues relating to the rule of law in East Asian economies, see Perkins (2004).

CORPORATE GOVERNANCE

Although competitive markets can induce privatized SOEs to raise their level of performance, effective corporate governance provides not only additional incentives for management to improve performance but also greater protection for minority shareholders.[30] The authors' survey findings indicate that monitoring by a board of directors has had a positive effect on SOE productivity in recent years (see chapter 5). The role of governance has been further underscored by a spate of scandals in industrialized and transition economies, even those with strong and tested institutions. These scandals have shown how the management of private corporations can evade market discipline and subvert or mislead regulators unless market institutions are bolstered by strictly enforced fiduciary rules and effective boards of directors that scrutinize corporate strategy and accounts and hold management to task. The unpalatable truth is that corporate entities in market economies are prone to lapses that can be costly for shareholders. Similarly, the numerous cases of asset-stripping and tunneling in transition economies also show that market forces alone cannot always safeguard the interests of shareholders. Especially vulnerable are the interests of minority shareholders. The difference between state-owned and privately owned companies regulated by robust market institutions is that the latter cannot normally incur and conceal large losses almost indefinitely. So long as they continue to enjoy political support, SOEs with soft budget constraints can remain in the red year after year—often without the management incurring any penalty.

While the literature on corporate governance is especially rich, defining rules that are appropriate for China's circumstances and consonant with China's legal and accounting institutions is far more difficult. The rules must allow for cultural nuances that can undermine the efficacy of rules devised for Western capitalist economies.

Strengthening corporate governance of reformed SOEs in China and making the boards of directors serve as agents of the minority shareholders is subject to a major constraint. The constraint derives from the unwillingness of the state to relinquish dominant ownership and effective control of LLCs and LLSCs. This involves selecting the top management and influencing (if not determining) the composition of the board of directors. It means that wealth maximization for shareholders is only one company objective. State control is also used to retain leadership

---

30. For a useful and comprehensive survey, see Becht, Bolton, and Roell (2002).

over strategic industries, to minimize urban job losses from industrial restructuring, and to benefit from potential patronage. These objectives, according to Clarke, "set up a conflict of interest between the state as a controlling shareholder and other shareholders. In using its control for purposes other than value maximization, the state exploits minority share-holders who have no other way to benefit from their investment" (Clarke 2003, p. 2). The effort to improve governance by forging a relationship between reformed enterprises and a "main bank" encounters the same difficulty. Until the bank is privately owned and autonomous, it is unlikely that it will play an independent role, counterbalance the influence of insiders, and deflect government pressures (Tam 1999).[31]

In market economies where minority shareholders' rights can be sup-ported by the courts, the board of directors is under additional pressure to perform its duties by the threat of shareholder litigation. This also is not practicable in China because "the courts are not politically powerful and are hence reluctant to take cases involving large sums of money and pow-erful defendants" (Clarke 2003, p. 15). Thus, the duties of independent directors—of good faith and diligence—are not "meaningful" in the view of the shortcomings of the legal system and the limited capacity of regula-tors such as the China Securities Regulatory Commission (CSRC) to enforce the duties of directors.[32]

In short, so long as the Chinese state insists on preserving the "domi-nance of socialist public ownership" (Tam 1999, p. 96) when it reforms SOEs, the capacity of the boards of directors to serve investors' interests is definitely limited. This partially vitiates one of the gains from ownership reforms, which is to drive firms to maximize shareholder value and, by assuring the accountability of management, to broader participation in financial markets. It is when the state acquiesces to full privatization, which would involve relinquishing control rights over most privatized companies, that regulators could usefully address the separation of board leadership from management leadership (MacAvoy and Millstein 2003);

---

31. A study of corporate governance in Germany by Jeremy and Nibler (2000) found that German banks with substantial stakes in large firms exert almost no influence on governance, although other dominant shareholders can play a significant role.

32. "In Praise of Rules" (2001, p. 15) stated this as follows: "The crux of the problem is that governance can't improve faster than legislation but legislation can't move faster than social practice. So even if tomorrow morning every one of China's chief executives woke up as a passionate believer in good corporate governance, it might still prove elusive. This is because best practice in companies depends upon best practice outside companies, above all in the legal system. And China has one of the worst in the world."

the composition of the board of directors; the incentives given to outside directors; the duties of the audit committee; the attention given by board members to the firm's strategy; and so forth. There is no dearth of recommendations on how to make a board of directors more effective. But the state must first commit itself to genuine privatization. The authors' analysis, and that of Yao (2004), shows that initial steps toward privatization have been fruitful and suggests that further gains could be realized from stronger governance, but only if private investors are placed in the driver's seat.

INNOVATION POLICY

As noted in chapter 1, in a globalizing world cost competitiveness, product quality, and timely delivery must increasingly be complemented by the capability to introduce process or product innovations and effectively use information technology. In particular, Chinese corporations that seek to challenge the large multinational corporations in global markets will need to match the technological prowess of their competitors.[33] But few of the SOEs currently possess much in the way of innovation capability and privatization. And sharpening incentives will not, by itself, persuade management to strive for greater innovation. For this to happen in the more dynamic SOEs, a push is needed from technology policies and institutions, some of which have been introduced in China only in the past decade.

China has begun constructing a national innovation system and is actively creating the university-level capacity to produce the skills needed by an innovative economy. The government is also requiring research institutes to cover some or all of their costs by working with businesses to develop and commercialize technology. Similar signals have been sent to the leading universities, pressing them to cover a portion of their costs through knowledge transfers to the business sector. Additional incentives are being provided through the intellectual property regime—especially by way of actions to enforce rights. Will these strategies be enough to make privatized SOEs pursue strategies calculated to enhance competitiveness through innovation? The experience in China and other countries does not suggest that many former SOEs, even under new

---

33. As Woetzel (2003, p. 33) observes, "There are a few examples of winning based purely on low costs." Global leadership requires firms to develop leading edge technologies.

management, are likely to aggressively pursue technological advances. Hence, the authorities might need to broaden the national innovation strategy to include greater financial incentives for firms to conduct research. Incentives might also be needed to induce firms to more actively assimilate technology from other sources and to enter into alliances with firms, universities, and research centers so as to gain access to and to derive leverage from the kind of research that could result in technologies with commercial potential. National innovative policies in Japan, Korea, the United States, and European countries provide useful pointers on how such policies work. However, the mixed results of the policies in these countries indicate that while governments can propose change, it is the firm's actions that are decisive. Ultimately, it is the firm's management, its strategy, and the market environment that are likely to make the biggest difference.

Privatized SOEs are more likely to rise to the challenge and embrace a strategy based on innovation and the assimilation of information technology. This sector is now so intrinsic to marketing, fulfillment, supply chain management, and customer relations that few firms can afford not to tap its potential (see OECD 2004). And this is especially true for firms with broad regional or global ambitions. If they do not exploit information technology, their competitors will, and they will, in turn, use the extra leverage to enlarge their own market share. But as information technology diffuses and becomes commoditized, firms cannot expect to enhance profitability by adopting new tools that everyone else is using, too. To gain an edge demands—as Nicholas Carr has correctly observed—creativity in utilizing information technology (IT) and rigorous efforts at controlling investment outlay on equipment and software, and operating costs.[34] Some of China's most aggressively competitive reformed SOEs (such as Lenovo) are showing that they can be the equal of Dell in their home market. Many more SOEs need to follow in Lenovo's footsteps through changes in ownership and organizational culture.

CONCLUSION

For more than two decades, China has been moving away from a planned central government and toward an open market economy, and with accession to the WTO, this process is likely to accelerate. Some of the

---

34. See "Does IT Matter?" (2004) and "The IT Advantage Thrown into Question" (2004).

institutions of a market economy are in place, while others are being developed. Under such circumstances, further ownership reform seems inevitable; but the alternative models of enterprise ownership and governance are few in number.

There is the partial privatization of the large and medium-size enterprises (LMEs), with the state retaining the majority share and the control rights. This is the approach currently being followed with modest gains in productivity, profitability, managerial capability, and technological advances. An alternative is for the state to reduce its share in the reformed SOEs and surrender part or all of its control rights. One might call this the European model. In a robustly competitive free-market environment, and in conjunction with sound corporate governance, this model can yield good results. There is also the Japanese-Korean model in which firms form networked groups around either a lead corporation or a main bank (that is a source of patient capital) within a framework of private ownership. The outcome has been a form of stakeholder capitalism that was conducive to development of manufacturing capability in the 1970s through the mid-1990s. Last, but not least, is the shareholder-oriented free market model, which in its purest form is exemplified by the U.S. economy.

China has been experimenting with each of these models by accommodating private ownership, creating *keiretsu*-style enterprise groups and partially privatizing some of the larger SOEs, while retaining full ownership of the most strategic SOEs. The findings presented here, and those of other researchers, suggest that in the current Chinese context, joint ventures that have combined foreign management and technology with the local expertise and production capacity of Chinese SOEs have performed better than other types of firms. The pure SOEs have done the least well. But in the current environment, all types of firms are subject to the pervasive influence of the state.

If China is committed to perfecting a dynamic market economy—even one with a substantial public sector—then Chinese and cross-country experiences argue for a smaller economic role for the state, a privatization of most industrial SOEs, and more of an arm's-length relationship between the state and business firms.[35] The restructuring of industry through new entry, consolidation, and exit could most efficiently be

---

35. No doubt, the direct relationships between large firms and industrial or regulatory bureaus will not soon attenuate; and lobbying by firms and industrial associations, commonplace in market economies, will intensify (Kennedy 2005).

accomplished with the mediation of market forces—not by industrial policy that entails the participation of the state-owned banks. After 2003, the state clearly widened its efforts to privatize. This will undoubtedly push the restructuring of industry one stage further. But the full economic benefits of privatizing the state's industrial assets will not be realized until the state cedes control rights and perceives its role to be that of managing the market, not directing it.

REFERENCES

Agarwal, Rajshree, and Michael Gort. 2001. "First-Mover Advantage and the Speed of Competitive Entry." *Journal of Law and Economics* 44 (1): 161–77.

American Rural Small Scale Industry Delegation to China. 1977. *Rural Small Scale Industry in the People's Republic of China*. Berkeley, CA: University of California Press.

Amsden, Alice H., and Wan-Wen Chu. 2003. *Beyond Late Development: Taiwan's Upgrading Policies*. Cambridge, MA: MIT Press.

Anderson, James H., Young Lee, and Peter Murrell. 2000. "Competition and Privatization Amidst Weak Institutions: Evidence from Mongolia." *Economic Inquiry* 38 (4): 527–49.

Aslund, Anders. 2002. *Building Capitalism: The Transformation of the Former Soviet Bloc*. New York: Cambridge University Press.

———. 2004. "Misguided Blame Game." *The Transition* 14/15 (10 & 1): 25–26.

Aussenegg, Wolfgang, and Ranko Jelic. 2002. "Operating Performance of Privatized Companies in Transition Economies: The Case of Poland, Hungary, and the Czech Republic." Paper presented at FEMA 2003 Helsinki Meeting, Helsinki, Finland, November.

Baer, Werner, and James T. Bang. 2002. "Privatization and Equity in Brazil and Russia." *Kyklos* 55 (4): 495–522.

Bai, Cong-En, David D. Li, Zhigang Tao, and Yijiang Wang. 2000. "A Multitask Theory of State Enterprise Reform." *Journal of Comparative Economics* 28 (4): 716–38.

Baily, Martin Neil. 2002. "The New Economy: Post Mortem or Second Wind." Paper prepared for the Distinguished Lecture on Economics in Government, ASSA Meeting Atlanta, Georgia, January 4–6.

Balcerowicz, Leszek. 2003. "Post-Communist Transition in a Comparative Perspective." Paper presented at Practitioners of Development Seminar Series, World Bank, Washington, DC, November 18.

Baltowski, Maciej, and Tomasz Mickiewicz. 2000. "Privatisation in Poland: Ten Years After." *Post-Communist Economies* 12 (4): 425–43.

Barnett, Steven. 2000. "Evidence on the Fiscal and Macroeconomic Impact of Privatization." IMF Working Paper WP/00/130, International Monetary Fund, Washington, DC.

Baumol, William J. 2002. *The Free Market Innovation Machine.* Princeton, NJ: Princeton University Press.

Becht, Marco, Patrick Bolton, and Ailsa Roell. 2002. "Corporate Governance and Control." ECGI-Finance Working Paper 2/2002, European Corporate Governance Institute, Brussels.

Becker, Jasper. 1996. *Hungry Ghosts.* New York: The Free Press.

———. 2000. *The Chinese.* Oxford: Oxford University Press.

Beijing Statistics Bureau. 2004. *Beijing Statistical Yearbook.* Beijing: Beijing Statistics Bureau.

"Beijing Tightens Foreign Banks' Funding." 2004. *Financial Times,* August 4.

Belka, Marek, Saul Estrin, Mark E. Schaffer, and I. Singh. 1995. "Enterprise Adjustment in Poland: Evidence from a Survey of 200 Private, Privatized, and State-Owned Firms." CEPR Discussion Paper 233, Centre for Economic Policy Research, London.

Berger, Suzanne, and Richard K. Lester. 1997. *Made by Hong Kong.* New York: Oxford University Press.

Berglof, Erik, Andrei Kunov, Julia Shvets, and Ksenia Yudaeva. 2003. *The New Political Economy of Russia.* Cambridge, MA: MIT Press.

Best, Michael H. 1997. "New Competitive Dynamics and Industrial Modernization Programs: Lessons from America and Asia." Paper presented at conference, "International Competitiveness: Institutional Strategies for Transitional Economies," Lake Bled, Slovenia, April 17–18.

Bhattasali, Deepak, Shantong Li, and Will Martin. 2004. *China and the WTO: Accession, Policy Reform, and Poverty Reduction Strategies.* Washington, DC: World Bank and Oxford University Press.

Bhaumik, Sumon, and Saul Estrin. 2003. "Why Transition Paths Differ: Russian and Chinese Enterprise Performance Compared." William Davidson Institute Working Paper 525, William Davidson Institute, Ann Arbor, MI.

Bian, Morris L. 2005. *The Making of the State Enterprise System in Modern China.* Cambridge, MA: Harvard University Press.

Bieshaar, Hans, Jeremy Knight, and Alexander Van Wassenaer. 2001. "Deals That Create Value." *McKinsey Quarterly* (1): 64–73.

"Big Names Join China Stock Market Reform." 2005. *Financial Times,* June 20.

Blanchard, Olivier, and Michael Kremer. 1997. "Disorganization." *Quarterly Journal of Economics* 112 (4): 1091–126.

Blanchard, Olivier, and Andrei Shleifer. 2000. "Federalism with and without Political Centralization: China versus Russia." NBER Working Paper 7616, National Bureau of Economic Research, Cambridge, MA.

Blaszczyk, Barbara, Iraj Hoshi, Evzen Kocenda, and Richard Woodward. 2003. "Ownership and Performance in Transition Economies: An Overview." In Barbara Blaszczyk, Iraj Hoshi, and Richard Woodward, eds. *Secondary Privatisation in Transition Economies.* Basingstoke, Hampshire, U.K.: Palgrave MacMillan, 1–21.

Boardman, Anthony E., and Aidan R. Vining. 1989. "Ownership and Performance in Competitive Environments: A Comparison of the Performance of Private, Mixed, and State-Owned Enterprises." *Journal of Law and Economics* 32 (1): 1–33.

Bodmer, Frank. 2002. "The Effect of Reforms on Employment Flexibility in Chinese SOEs, 1980–94." *The Economics of Transition* 10 (3): 637–58.

Bornstein, Morris. 1999. "Framework Issues in the Privatisation Strategies of the Czech Republic, Hungary, and Poland." *Post-Communist Economies* 11 (1): 47–78.

Bortolotti, Bernardo, and Mara Faccio. 2004. "Reluctant Privatization." ECGI-Finance Working Paper 40/2004, European Corporate Governance Institute, Brussels.

Bortolotti, Bernardo, Marcella Fantini, and Domenico Siniscalco. 2003. "Privatisation around the World: Evidence from Panel Data." *Journal of Public Economics* 88 (1): 305–32.

Bortolotti, Bernardo, and Paolo Pinotti. 2003. "The Political Economy of Privatization." Working Paper 45.2003, Fondazione Eni Enrico Mattei, Milan, Italy.

Bortolotti, Bernardo, and Domenico Siniscalco. 2004. *The Challenges of Privatization: An International Perspective*. New York: Oxford University Press.

Bottelier, Pieter. 2002. "Financial Sector Reform across Asia." Cambridge, MA: John F. Kennedy School of Government, Harvard University. Processed.

Boubakri, Narjess, and Jean-Claude Cosset. 1998. "The Financial and Operating Performance of Newly Privatized Firms: Evidence from Developing Countries." *Journal of Finance* 53 (3): 1081–110.

Boutellier, Roman, Oliver Gassmann, and Maximilian Zedtwitz. 2000. *Managing Global Innovation*. Berlin: Springer Verlag.

Boycko, Maxim, Andrei Shleifer, and Robert Vishny. 1995. *Privatizing Russia*. Cambridge, MA: MIT Press.

Brada, Josef C. 1996. "Privatization Is Transition—Or Is It?" *Journal of Economic Perspectives* 10 (2): 67–86.

Brandt, Lorent, Hongbin Li, and Joanne Roberts. 2001. "Why Do Governments Privatize?" Toronto, Ontario: University of Toronto. Processed.

Bray, David. 2005. *Social Space and Governance in Urban China*. Stanford, CA: Stanford University Press.

Broadman, Harry G. 2001. "The Business(es) of the Chinese State." *The World Economy* 24 (7): 849–75.

———, ed. 2002. *Unleashing Russia's Business Potential: Lessons from the Regions for Building Market Institutions*. Washington, DC: World Bank.

Brown, David J., and John S. Earle. 2000. "Competition and Firm Performance: Lessons from Russia." Working Paper 296, Stockholm Institute of Transition Economics, Stockholm, Sweden.

Brune, Nancy, Geoffery Garrett, and Bruce Kogut. 2004. "The IMF and the Global Spread of Privatization." *IMF Staff Papers* 51 (2): 195–219.

"Built on What?" 2005. *Business China*, March 14.

Burkart, Mike, Fausto Panunzi, and Andrei Shleifer. 2002. "Family Firms." NBER Working Paper 8776, National Bureau of Economic Research, Cambridge, MA.

"Busted." 2003. *Business China*, July 7.

Byrd, William A. 1991. *The Market Mechanism and Economic Reform in China*. Armonk, NY: M.E. Sharpe.

Byrd, William A., and Qingsong Lin, eds. 1990. *China's Rural Industry: Structure, Development, and Reform*. New York: Oxford University Press.

Cai, Youngshun. 2002. "The Resistance of Chinese Laid-Off Workers in the Reform Period." *The China Quarterly* (170): 327–44.

Caloghirou, Yannis, Stavros Ioannides, and Nicholas S. Vonortas. 2003. "Research Joint Ventures." *Journal of Economic Surveys* 17 (4): 541–70.

Campos, Nauro F., and Fabrizio Coricelli. 2002. "Growth in Transition: What We Know, What We Don't, and What We Should." *Journal of Economic Literature* 40 (3): 793–836.

Carlaw, Kenneth I., and Richard G. Lipsey. 2003. "Productivity, Technology, and Economic Growth: What Is the Relationship?" *Journal of Economic Surveys* 17 (3): 457–95.

Carlin, Wendy, Steven Fries, Mark Schaffer, and Paul Seabright. 2001. "Competition and Enterprise Performance in Transition Economies: Evidence from a Cross-Country Survey." William Davidson Institute Working Paper 376, William Davidson Institute, Ann Arbor, MI.

Carlin, Wendy, Mark E. Shaffer, and Paul Seabright. 2004. "A Minimum of Rivalry: Evidence from Transition Economies on the Importance of Competition for Innovation and Growth." *Contributions to Economic Analysis & Policy* 3 (1): http://www.bepress.com/bejeap/contributions/vol3/iss1/art17

Carter, Colin A., Funing Zhong, and Fang Cai. 1996. *China's Ongoing Agricultural Reform.* Burlingame, CA: The 1990 Institute.

"A Cauldron of Free Enterprise." 2003. *Far Eastern Economic Review,* July 3.

Chai, Joseph. 1997. *China: Transition to a Market Economy.* Oxford: Oxford University Press.

Chang, Eric C., and Sonia M. L. Wong. 2004. "Political Control and Performance in China's Listed Firms." *Journal of Comparative Economics* 32 (4): 617–36.

"Changhong Hit by U.S. Problems." 2005. *Financial Times,* April 19.

Charan, Ram, and Jerry Useem. 2002. "Why Companies Fail." *Fortune,* May 27: 50–62.

Che, Jiahua, and Yingyi Qian. 1998. "Institutional Environment, Community Government, and Corporate Governance: Understanding China's Township-Village Enterprises." *Journal of Law, Economics, and Organization* 14 (1): 1–23.

"Checking China's Vital Signs." 2004. *The McKinsey Quarterly* (Special Edition: "China Today").

Chen, Aimin. 1998. "Inertia in Reforming China's State-Owned Enterprises: The Case of Chongqing." *World Development* 26 (3): 479–95.

Chen, Hongyi. 2000. *The Institutional Transition of China's Township and Village Enterprises: Market Liberalization, Contractual Form Innovation, and Privatization.* Aldershot, U.K.: Ashgate.

Chen, Yun. 1986. "Planning and the Market." *Beijing Review* 29 (29): 14–15.

Cheng, Leonard K., and Changqi Wu. 2001. "Determinants of the Performance of Foreign Invested Enterprises in China." *Journal of Comparative Economics* 29 (2): 347–65.

Cheng, Yuk-shing, and Dic Lo. 2002. "Explaining the Financial Performance of China's Industrial Enterprises: Beyond the Competition-Ownership Controversy." *The China Quarterly* (170): 413–40.

Chesbrough, Henry W. 2003a. "The Era of Open Innovation." *MIT Sloan Management Review* 44 (3): 35–41.

———. 2003b. *Open Innovation: The New Imperative for Creating and Profiting from Technology.* Boston, MA: Harvard Business Review Press.

Cheung, Kui-yin, and Ping Lin. 2004. "Spillover Effects of FDI on Innovation in China: Evidence from the Provincial Data." *China Economic Review* 15 (1): 25–44.

"China: Banks Extend New Welcome to Small Businesses." 2002. *Oxford Analytica*, August 26.

"China: Beijing Looks to Parts Exports for Auto Growth." 2004. *Oxford Analytica*, May 21.

"China: Burdened Banks." 2003. *Oxford Analytica*, July 17.

"China Buys Respite from Protectionists." 2004. *Financial Times*, December 14.

"China: Circulating Capital." 2003. *Oxford Analytica*, July 29.

"China Closes Foreign Investment Gap." 2003. *Financial Times*, August 25.

"China: Foreign Entrants to Aid Semiconductor Industry." 2003. *Oxford Analytica*, July 2.

"China: Government Restructuring Will Benefit Investors." 2003. *Oxford Analytica*, March 24.

"China Lays Out Plans for Reform of Business." 2003. *Financial Times*, May 23.

"China: Local-Level Protests Pose Problems for Beijing." 2003. *Oxford Analytica*, August 28.

"China: Merger and Acquisition Rules to Entice Investors." 2002. *Oxford Analytica*, October 31.

"China: On the Right Tracks." 2004. *Business China*, June 7.

"China Overtakes Japan as Third Largest Exporter." 2005. *Financial Times*, April 15.

"China: Round-Tripping Inflates FDI Inflows." 2003. *Oxford Analytica*, July 29.

"China: SOE Reforms to Create National Champions." 2005. *Oxford Analytica*, March 15.

"China: State Pension Fund." 2002. *Oxford Analytica*, December 3.

"China: Stock Market Foreign Investment Limit Raised." 2005. *Oxford Analytica*, July 12.

"China Struggles to Untie Its Hands." 2002. *Financial Times*, May 27.

"China's 100 Largest Companies." 2003. *Fortune*, August 25.

"China's Banks Smarten Up as They Switch from State Control to Commercial Lending." 2005. *Financial Times*, June 20.

"China's Corporate Cost Advantage Is a Myth." 2005. *Financial Times*, April 29.

"China's Unwelcome Growth: Joblessness." 2003. *Straits Times*, August 21.

"Chinese Manufacturers Continue to Reduce Prices." 2005. *Financial Times*, June 3.

Chong, Alberto, and Florencio López-de-Silanes. 2005. "The Truth about Privatization in Latin America." In Alberto Chong and Florencio López-de-Silanes, eds. *Privatization in Latin America: Myths and Reality.* Washington, DC: Stanford University Press and World Bank.

Chongqing Statistics Bureau. 2004. *Chongqing Statistical Yearbook.* Chongqing: Chongqing Statistics Bureau.

"Chongqing Takes Great Leap Forward to Match Shanghai." 2003. *Financial Times*, August 23.

Claessens, Stijin, and Simeon Djankov. 1999. "Enterprise Performance and Management Turnover in the Czech Republic." *European Economic Review* 43 (4–6): 1115–24.

Claessens, Stijin, Simeon Djankov, and Gerhard Pohl. 1997. "Ownership and Corporate Governance: Evidence from the Czech Republic." World Bank Policy Research Paper 1737, World Bank, Washington, DC.

Claessens, Stijn, Simeon Djankov, and Larry H. P. Lang. 2000. "The Separation of Ownership and Control in East Asian Corporations." *Journal of Financial Economics* 58 (1–2): 81–112.

Clarke, Donald C. 2003. "Corporate Governance in China: An Overview." Seattle, Washington: University of Washington School of Law. Processed.

———. 1996. "The Creation of a Legal Structure for Market Institutions in China." In John McMillan and Barry Naughton, eds. *Reforming Asian Socialism: The Growth of Market Institutions*. Ann Arbor, MI: University of Michigan Press.

Commander, Simon. 2004. "The Changing Demand for Skills: Evidence from the Transition." IZA Discussion Paper 1073. Bonn, Germany: Institute for the Study of Labor.

"Corporatizing China." 2002. *Business China*, July 22.

Cragg, Michael I., and I. J. Alexander Dyck. 2003. "Privatization and Management Incentives: Evidence from the United Kingdom." *The Journal Law, Economics & Organization* 19 (1): 176–217.

"Crash: Slowing Sales in China's Automotive Sector Signal Trouble Ahead." 2004. *Business China*, October 11.

Cull, Robert, Jana Matesova, and Mary M. Shirley. 2002. "Ownership and the Temptation to Loot: Evidence from Privatized Firms in the Czech Republic." *Journal of Comparative Economics* 30 (1): 1–24.

Cull, Robert, and Lixin Colin Xu. 2000. "Bureaucrats, State Banks, and the Efficiency of Credit Allocation: The Experience of Chinese State-Owned Enterprises." *Journal of Comparative Economics* 28 (1): 1–31.

Daily, Catherine M., Dan R. Dalton, and Albert A. Cannella Jr. 2003. "Corporate Governance: Decades of Dialogue and Data." *Academy of Management Review* 28 (3): 371–82.

"Deal On." 2005. *Business China*, March 14.

"Decision of the Central Committee of the Communist Party of China on Reform of the Economic Structure (Adopted by the 12th Central Committee of the Communist Party of China at Its Third Plenary Session on October 20, 1984." 1984. *China Review*, October 29.

Dewenter, Kathryn. 2003. "The Risk-Sharing Role of Japanese Keiretsu Business Groups: Evidence from Restructuring in the 1990s." *Japan and the World Economy* 15 (3): 261–74.

Dewenter, Kathryn, and Paul H. Malatesta. 1997. "Public Offerings of State-Owned and Privately-Owned Enterprises: An International Comparison." *Journal of Finance* 52 (4): 1659–79.

Dickson, Bruce J. 2003. *Red Capitalists in China: The Party, Private Entrepreneurs, and Prospects for Political Change*. New York: Cambridge University Press.

DiMaggio, Paul. 2001. *The Twenty-First Century Firm*. Princeton, NJ: Princeton University Press.

Ding, D. Z., L. Ge, and M. Warner. 2002. "Beyond the State Sector: A Study of HRM in Southern China." Research Papers in Management Studies Working Paper 21/2002. The Judge Institute of Management, Cambridge, U.K.

Disney, Richard, Jonathan Haskel, and Ylva Heden. 2003. "Restructuring and Productivity Growth in U.K. Manufacturing." *Economic Journal* 113 (489): 666–94.

Djankov, Simeon. 1999. "Ownership Structure and Enterprise Restructuring in the Commonwealth of Independent States." World Bank Policy Research Paper 2047, World Bank, Washington, DC.

Djankov, Simeon, and Bernard Hoekman. 2000. "Market Discipline and Corporate Efficiency: Evidence from Bulgaria." *Canadian Journal of Economics* 33 (1): 190–212.

Djankov, Simeon, and Peter Murrell. 2002. "Enterprise Restructuring in Transition: A Quantitative Survey." *Journal of Economic Literature* 40 (3): 739–92.

Djankov, Simeon, and Gerhard Pohl. 1998. "The Restructuring of Large Firms in the Slovak Republic." *Economics of Transition* 6 (1): 67–85.

Dlouhy, Vladimir, and Jan Mladek. 1994. "Privatization and Corporate Control in the Czech Republic." *Economic Policy* 19 (supplement): 155–70.

"Does IT Matter?" 2004. *The Economist*, April 3.

Dollar, David, Anqing Shi, Shuilin Wang, and Colin Xu. 2003. *Improving City Competitiveness through the Investment Climate: Ranking 23 Chinese Cities.* Washington, DC: World Bank.

Dong, Xiao-yuan, and Louis Putterman. 2001. "On the Emergence of Labour Redundancy in China's State Industry: Findings from a 1980–1994 Data Panel." *Comparative Economic Studies* 43 (2): 111–28.

Dong, Xiao-yuan, Louis Putterman, and Bulent Unel. 2004. "Enterprise Restructuring and Firm Performance: A Comparison of Rural and Urban Enterprises in Jaingsu Province." William Davidson Institute Working Paper 668, William Davidson Institute, Ann Arbor, MI.

Donnithorne, Audrey. 1967. *China's Economic System*. New York: Praeger.

"A Dragon Out of Puff." 2002. *The Economist*, June 15.

Duckett, Jane. 1998. *The Entrepreneurial State in China*. New York: Routledge.

———. 2001. "Bureaucrats in Business, Chinese-Style: The Lessons of Market Reform and State Entrepreneurialism in the People's Republic of China." *World Development* 29 (1): 23–37.

Dyck, I. J. Alexander. 1997. "Privatization in Eastern Germany: Management Selection and Economic Transition." *American Economic Review* 87 (4): 565–97.

Dyck, I. J. Alexander, and Luigi Zingales. 2002. "The Corporate Governance Role of the Media." NBER Working Paper 9309, National Bureau of Economic Research, Cambridge, MA.

Earle, John S., and Saul Estrin. 1997. "After Voucher Privatization: The Structure of Corporate Ownership in Russian Manufacturing Industry." CEPR Discussion Paper 1736, Centre for Economic Policy Research, London.

Earle, John S., Saul Estrin, and Larisa Leshchenko. 1996. "Ownership Structures, Matters of Control, and Enterprise Behavior in Russia." In Simon Commander, Qimiao Fan, and Mark E. Schaffer, eds. *Enterprise Restructuring and Economic Policy in Russia*. Washington, DC: World Bank.

Earle, John S., and Almos Telegdy. 2002. "Privatization Methods and Productivity Effects in Romanian Industrial Enterprises." *Journal of Comparative Economics* 30 (4): 657–82.

East Asia Unit. 2003. *East Asia Update, April 2003*. Washington, DC: World Bank.

Ellerman, David. 2001. "Lessons from Eastern Europe's Voucher Privatization." *Challenge* 44 (4): 14–37.

Ewing, Richard D. 2003. "Hu Jintao: The Making of a Chinese General Secretary." *The China Quarterly* (173): 17–34.

Feldstein, Martin. 2003. "Why Is Productivity Growing Faster?" NBER Working Paper 9530, National Bureau of Economic Research, Cambridge, MA.

Fewsmith, Joseph. 2002. "Generational Transition in China." *The Washington Quarterly* 25 (4): 23–45.

Fidrmuc, Jana P., and Jan Fidrmuc. 2004. "Fire the Manager to Improve Performance? Managerial Turnover and Incentives after Privatization in the Czech Republic." CEPR Discussion Paper 4351, Centre for Economic Policy Research, London.

Fine, Charles H. 1998. *Clockspeed: Winning Industry Control in the Age of Temporary Advantage*. New York: Perseus Publishing.

"The Flows Reformulate." 2005. *Business China*, March 14.

Friedman, John. 2005. *China's Urban Transition*. Minneapolis, MN: University of Minnesota Press.

Frydman, Roman, Cheryl Gray, Marek Hessel, and Andrzej Rapaczynski. 1999. "When Does Privatization Work? The Impact of Private Ownership on Corporate Performance in the Transition Economies." *Quarterly Journal of Economics* 114 (4): 1153–91.

Frydman, Roman, Marek Hessel, and Andrzej Rapaczynski. 2000a. "The Limits of Discipline: Ownership and Hard Budget Constraints in the Transition Economies." C.V. Starr Center for Applied Economics Working Papers RR# 00–02, New York University, New York.

———. 2000b. "Why Ownership Matters? Entrepreneurship and the Restructuring of Enterprises in Central Europe." C.V. Starr Center for Applied Economics Working Papers RR# 00–03, New York University, New York.

Galal, Ahmed, Leroy Jones, Pankaj Tandoon, and Ingo Vogelsang. 1994. *Welfare Consequences of Selling Public Enterprises: An Empirical Analysis*. Washington, DC: World Bank.

Gang, Fan. 2002. "Progress in Ownership Changes and Hidden Risks in China's Transition." *Transition Newsletter* 13 (3): 1–5.

Gao, Qiang. 1995. "Problems in Chinese Intragovernmental Fiscal Relations, Tax-Sharing System, and Future Reform." In Ehtisham Ahmad, Gao Qiang, and Vito Tanzi, eds. *Reforming China's Public Finances*. Washington, DC: International Monetary Fund, 15–24.

Garnaut, Ross, and Ligang Song. 2000. "Private Enterprise in China: Development, Constraints, and Policy Implications." Paper presented at Australian National University conference, "China: Growth and Sustainability in the 21st Century," Canberra, Australia, September.

Garnaut, Ross, Ligang Song, Stoyan Tenev, and Yang Yao. 2005. *China Restructures: Letting the Small Go in China's State Enterprises Sector*. Washington, DC: World Bank and International Finance Corporation.

Garnaut, Ross, Ligang Song, and Yang Yao. 2004. "SOE Restructuring in China." Canberra, Australia: Australian National University. Processed.

Garrett, Banning. 2001. "China Faces, Debates, the Contradictions of Globalization." *Asian Survey* 41 (3): 409–27.

Gehlbach, Scott. 2003. "Taxability and Low Productivity Trap." CEFIR Academic Paper 31, Center for Economic and Financial Research, Moscow.

Geppert, Linda. 2005. "Silicon Gold Rush." *IEEE Spectrum* 42 (6): 62–6.

Gilmore, Fiona, and Serge Dumont. 2003. *Brand Warriors China: Creating Sustainable Brand Capital*. London: Profile Books.

Gold, Thomas, Doug Guthrie, and David Wank, eds. 2002. *Social Connections in China: Institutions, Culture, and the Changing Nature of Guanxi*. Cambridge, UK: Cambridge University Press.

Goldman, Marshall. 1997. "The Pitfalls of Russian Privatization." *Challenge* 40 (3): 35–49.

———. 2003. *The Privatization of Russia*. London: Routledge.

Gompers, Paul, Josh Lerner, and David Scharfstein. 2003. "Entrepreneurial Spawning: Public Corporations and the Genesis of New Ventures, 1986–99." NBER Working Paper 9816, National Bureau of Economic Research, Cambridge, MA.

Gordon, M. J. 2003. "Is China's Financial System Threatened by Its Policy Loans Debt?" *Journal of Asian Economics* 14 (2): 181–8.

Gore, Lance L.P. 1998. *Market Communism: The Institutional Foundation of China's Post-Mao Hyper-Growth*. Oxford: Oxford University Press.

Graham, Edward M. 2003. *Reforming Korea's Industrial Conglomerates*. Washington, DC: Institute of International Economics.

Green, Richard, and Jonathan Haskel. 2004. "Seeking a Premier League Economy: The Role of Privatisation." In David Carol, Richard Blumdell, and Richard B. Freeman, eds. *Seeking a Premier League Economy: The Economic Effect of British Economic Reforms, 1980–2000*. Chicago: University of Chicago Press.

Green, Stephen. 2003. *China's Stock Market: A Guide to Its Progress, Players, and Prospects*. London: Profile Books, Ltd.

———. 2005. "Privatization in the Former Soviet Bloc: Has China Learned the Lessons?" In Stephen Green and Guy S. Liu, eds. *Exit the Dragon? Privatization and State Control in China*. Malden, MA: Blackwell Publishing.

———. 2005. "The Privatization Two-Step at China's Listed Firms." In Stephen Green and Guy S. Liu, eds. *Exit the Dragon? Privatization and State Control in China*. Malden, MA: Blackwell Publishing.

Green, Stephen, and He Ming. 2005. "China's Privatization Ministry? The State-Owned Assets Supervision and Administration Commission." In Stephen Green and Guy S. Liu, eds. *Exit the Dragon? Privatization and State Control in China*. Malden, MA: Blackwell Publishing.

Green, Stephen, and Guy S. Liu. 2005. "China's Industrial Reform Strategy: Retreat and Retain." In Stephen Green and Guy S. Liu, eds. *Exit the Dragon? Privatization and State Control in China*. Malden, MA: Blackwell Publishing.

Grosfeld, Irena, and Iraj Hashi. 2003. "Mass Privatisation, Corporate Governance, and Endogenous Ownership Structure." William Davidson Institute Working Paper 596, William Davidson Institute, Ann Arbor, MI.

Grossman, Sanford J., and Oliver D. Hart. 1986. "The Costs and Benefits of Ownership: A Theory of Vertical and Lateral Integration." *Journal of Political Economy* 94 (4): 691–719.

Groves, Theodore, Yongmiao Hong, John McMillan, and Barry Naughton. 1994. "Autonomy and Incentives in Chinese State Enterprises." *Quarterly Journal of Economics* 109 (1): 183–209.

———. 1995. "China's Evolving Managerial Labor Market." *Journal of Political Economy* 103 (4): 873–92.

Guangzhou City Statistics Bureau. 2004. *Guangzhou City Statistical Yearbook*. Guangzhou: Guangzhou City Statistics Bureau.

Guo, Kai, and Yang Yao. 2005. "Causes of Privatization in China: Testing Several Hypotheses." *Economics of Transition* 13 (2): 211–38.

Gupta, Nandini, John C. Ham, and Jan Svejnar. 2001. "Priorities and Sequencing in Privatization: Theory and Evidence from the Czech Republic." William Davidson Institute Working Paper 323a, William Davidson Institute, Ann Arbor, MI.

Guthrie, Doug. 1999. *Dragon in a Three Piece Suit*. Princeton, NJ: Princeton University Press.

"Haier's Net Profit Is Flat Despite Revenue Surge." 2005. *Asian Wall Street Journal*, April 8–10.

Hammer, Michael. 2004. "Deep Change: How Operational Innovation Can Transform Your Company." *Harvard Business Review* 82 (4): 84–93.

Han, Sun Sheng, and Xiang Wu. 2004. "City Profile: Wuhan." *Cities* 21 (4): 349–62.

Han, Sun Sheng, and Yong Wang. 2001. "City Profile: Chongqing." *Cities* 18 (2): 115–25.

Hanousek, Jan, Evzen Kocenda, and Jan Svejnar. 2004. "Ownership, Control, and Corporate Performance after Large-Scale Privatization." William Davidson Institute Working Paper 652, The William Davidson Institute, Ann Arbor, MI.

Harper, Joel. 2000. "The Performance of Privatized Firms in the Czech Republic." Working Paper, Florida Atlantic University, Boca Raton, FL.

Hart, Oliver D. 1983. "The Market Mechanism as an Incentive Scheme." *Bell Journal of Economics* 14 (2): 366–82.

Hart, Oliver D., and John Moore. 1990. "Property Rights and the Nature of the Firm." *Journal of Political Economy* 98 (6): 1119–58.

Hashi, Iraj, and Lindita Xhillari. 1999. "Privatization and Transition in Albania." *Post-Communist Economies* 11 (1): 99–125.

Havrylyshyn, Oleh. 2004. "Avoid Hubris but Acknowledge Successes: Lessons from the Postcommunist Transition." *Finance and Development* 41 (3): 38–41.

Havrylyshyn, Oleh, and Donal McGettigan. 2000. "Privatization in Transition Countries." *Post-Soviet Affairs* 16 (3): 257–86.

Hayes, Robert H., and Gary P. Pisano. 1994. "Beyond World-Class: The New Manufacturing Strategy." *Harvard Business Review* 72 (1): 77–86.

Healy, Paul M., Krishna G. Palepu, and Richard. S. Ruback. 1992. "Does Corporate Performance Improve after Mergers?" *Journal of Financial Economics* 31 (2): 135–75.

Heytens, Paul, and Cem Karacadag. 2003. "The Finances of China's Enterprise Sector." In Wanda Tseng and Markus Rodlauer, eds. *China: Competing in the Global Economy*. Washington, DC: International Monetary Fund.

Heytens, Paul, and Harm Zebregs. 2003. "How Fast Can China Grow?" In Wanda Tseng and Markus Rodlauer, eds. *China: Competing in the Global Economy*. Washington, DC: International Monetary Fund.

Ho, Samuel P. S. 1994. *Rural China in Transition: Non-Agricultural Development in Rural Jiangsu, 1978–1990*. Oxford: Clarendon Press.

Holz, Carsten A. 2000. "The Impact of Competition and Labor Remuneration on Profitability in China's Industrial State-Owned Enterprises." Hong Kong: Hong Kong University of Science and Technology. Processed.

———. 2002. "Long Live China's State-Owned Enterprises: Deflating the Myth of Poor Performance." *Journal of Asian Economics* 13 (4): 493–529.

Hout, Thomas M. 1999. "Are Managers Obsolete?" *Harvard Business Review* 77 (2): 161–68.

Howell, Jude. 1993. *China Opens Its Doors*. Denver, CO: Lynne Rienner Publisher's, Inc.

Hsu, Robert C. 1991. *Economic Theories in China, 1979–1988*. Cambridge, UK: Cambridge University Press.

Hu, Albert G. Z. 2001. "Ownership, Government R&D, and Productivity in Chinese Industry." *Journal of Comparative Economics* 29 (1): 136–57.

Hu, Albert Guangzhou, and Gary H. Jefferson. 2004. "Returns to Research and Development in Chinese Industry: Evidence from State-Owned Enterprises in Beijing." *China Economic Review* 15 (1): 86–107.

Hu, Xiaobo. 2000. "The State, Enterprises, and Society in Post-Deng China." *Asian Survey* 40 (4): 641–57.

Hua, Sheng, Xuejun Zhang, and Xiaopeng Luo. 1993. *China: From Revolution to Reform*. London: Macmillan Press.

Huang, Yasheng. 2003a. *Selling China: Foreign Direct Investment during the Reform Era*. New York: Cambridge University Press.

———. 2003b. "The Institutional Foundation of Foreign-Invested Enterprises (FIEs) in China." Cambridge, MA: Harvard University. Processed.

———. 2004. "Why More May Be Actually Less: Financing Bias and Labor-Intensive FDI in China." In Yasheng Huang, Anthony Saich, and Edward Steinfeld, eds. *Financial Sector Reform in China*. Cambridge, MA: Harvard East Asian Press.

"The Human Tide Surveys into Cities." 2003. *Far Eastern Economic Review*, January 9.

"In Praise of Rules." 2001. *The Economist*, April 7.

Industry and Transport Department of the National Bureau of Statistics. 2000. *Zhongguo Gongye Jiaotong Nengyuan 50 Nian Tongji Culiao Huibian (A Compilation of 50 Years of Statistical Materials on Chinese Industry, Transport, and Energy)*. Beijing: China Statistics Press.

"Industry Profits Jump 57%." 2003. *China Daily*, July 25.

"Is the Wakening Giant a Monster?" 2003. *The Economist*, February 13.

Islam, Nazrul. 2003. "Productivity Dynamics in a Large Sample of Countries: A Panel Study." *Review of Income and Wealth* 49 (2): 247–72.

"The IT Advantage Thrown into Question." 2004. *Financial Times*, August 16.

Jefferson, Gary, Albert G. Z. Hu, Xiaojing Guan, and Xiaoyun Yu. 2003. "Ownership, Performance, and Innovation in China's Large- and Medium-Size Industrial Enterprise Sector." *China Economic Review* 14 (1): 89–113.

Jefferson, Gary, Thomas G. Rawski, Li Wang, and Yuxin Zheng. 2000. "Ownership, Productivity Change, and Financial Performance in Chinese Industry." *Journal of Comparative Economics* 28 (4): 786–813.

Jefferson, Gary, Thomas G. Rawski, and Yuxin Zheng. 1992. "Growth, Efficiency and Convergence in China's State and Collective Industry." *Economic Development and Cultural Change* 40 (2): 239–86.

Jefferson, Gary, Inderjit Singh, Junling Xing, and Shouqing Zhang. 1999. "China's Industrial Performance: A Review of Recent Findings." In Gary Jefferson and Inderjit Singh, eds. *Enterprise Reform in China: Ownership, Transition, and Performance*. Oxford, U.K.: Oxford University Press.

Jefferson, Gary, and Jian Su. 2002. "China's Economic Growth: An Investigation into the Process of Endogenous Growth at the Firm Level." Paper prepared in cooperation with the National Bureau of Statistics of China for the World Bank, Washington, DC.

Jefferson, Gary H., and Zhong Kaifeng. 2004. "An Investigation of Firm-Level R&D Capabilities in East Asia." In Shahid Yusuf, Anjum Altaf, and Kaoru Nabeshima, eds. *Global Production Networking and Technological Change in East Asia*. New York: Oxford University Press.

Jeremy, Edwards, and Marcus Nibler. 2000. "Corporate Governance in Germany: The Role of Banks and Ownership." *Economic Policy* 15 (31): 237–67.

Ji, You. 1998. *China's Enterprise Reform*. New York: Routledge Press.

Jiandong, Jin. 1989. "China's Stock and Bond Market." *Beijing Review* 32 (44): 24–7.

Jiang, Zemin. 1989. "Speech at the Meeting in Celebration of the 40th Anniversary of the Founding of the People's Republic of China." *Beijing Review* 32 (41): 11–24.

Johnson, D. Gale. 1998. "China's Great Famine: Introductory Remarks." *China Economic Review* 9 (2): 103–9.

Johnson, Simon, Florencio López-de-Silanes, and Andrei Shleifer. 2000. "Tunnelling." NBER Working Paper 7523, National Bureau of Economic Research, Cambridge, MA.

Johnson, Simon, and Andrei Shleifer. 1999. "Coase v. the Coasians." NBER Working Paper 7447, National Bureau of Economic Research, Cambridge, MA.

Jones, Leroy, Yahya Jammal, and Nilgun Gokur. 1999. "Impact of Privatization in Côte d'Ivoire." Working Paper, Boston Institute for Developing Economies, Washington, DC. Processed.

Jovanovic, Boyan, and Peter L. Rousseau. 2002. "Mergers as Reallocation." NBER Working Paper 9279, National Bureau of Economic Research, Cambridge, MA.

Kalirajan, K. P., and Cao Yong. 1993. "Can Chinese State Enterprises Perform Like Market Entities: Productive Efficiency in the Chinese Iron and Steel Industry." *Applied Economics* 25 (8): 1071–80.

Kalyuzhnova, Yelena, and Wladimir Andreff. 2003. *Privatisation and Structural Change in Transition Economies*. Basingstoke, Hampshire, U.K.: Palgrave MacMillan.

Kay, John. 2003. *Twenty Years of Privatisation (Prospect)*. http://www.johnkay.com/political/249.

Keister, Lisa A. 2000. *Chinese Business Groups: The Structure and Impact of Interfirm Relations during Economic Development*. Oxford: Oxford University Press.

Keister, Lisa A., and Jin Lu. 2001. "The Transformation Countries: The Status of Chinese State-Owned Enterprises at the Start of Millennium." *NBR Analysis* 12 (3): 5–31.

Kennedy, Scott. 2005. *The Business of Lobbying in China*. Cambridge, MA: Harvard University Press.

Khanna, Tarun, and Krishna Palepu. 2002. "Emerging Giants: Building World-Class Companies in Emerging Markets." Harvard Business Case 703–431.

Kikeri, Sunita, and John Nellis. 2002. "Privatization in Competitive Sectors: The Record to Date." World Bank Policy Research Paper 2860, World Bank, Washington, DC.

Kim, Jong-Il, and Lawrence J. Lau. 1994. "The Sources of Economic Growth of the East Asian Newly Industrialized Countries." *Journal of the Japanese and International Economies* 8 (3): 235–71.

Kim, Linsu 1997. *Imitation to Innovation: The Dynamics of Korea's Technological Learning*. Boston, MA: Harvard Business School Press.

———. 2003. "Crisis, Reform, and National Innovation in South Korea." In William Keller and Richard J. Samuels, eds. *Crisis and Innovation in Asian Technology*. Cambridge, U.K.: Cambridge University Press.

Kim, Youngbae, and Byungheon Lee. 2002. "Patterns of Technological Learning among the Strategic Groups in the Korean Electronic Parts Industry." *Research Policy* 31 (4): 543–67.

Kirchmaier, Thomas. 2003. "Corporate Restructuring of British and German Non-Financial Firms in the Late 1990s." *European Management Journal* 21 (4): 409–20.

Kleinberg, Robert. 1990. *China's Opening to the Outside World*. Boulder, CO: Westview Press.

Kocenda, Evzen. 2002. "Development of Ownership Structure and Its Effect on Performance: Czech Firms from Mass Privatization." CEPR Discussion Paper 3139, Centre for Economic Policy and Research, London.

Kocenda, Evzen, and Jan Svejnar. 2003. "Ownership and Firm Performance after Large-Scale Privatization." William Davidson Institute Working Paper 417a, William Davidson Institute, Ann Arbor, MI.

Konings, Jozef. 1998. "Firm Performance in Bulgaria and Estonia: The Effects of Competitive Pressure, Financial Pressure, and Disorganization." William Davidson Institute Working Paper 185, William Davidson Institute, Ann Arbor, MI.

Kornai, Janos. 1992. *The Socialist System: The Political Economy of Communism*. Princeton, NJ: Princeton University Press.

———. 2003. "Ten Years after 'The Road to a Free Economy': The Author's Self-Evaluation of Privatisation." In Yelena Kalyuzhnova and Wladimir Andreff, eds. *Privatisation and Structural Change in Transition Economies*. Basingstoke, Hampshire, U.K.: Palgrave MacMillan.

Kornai, Janos, Eric Maskin, and Gerard Roland. 2003. "Understanding the Soft Budget Constraint." *Journal of Economic Literature* 41 (4): 1095–136.

Kumar, Krishna B, Raghuram G. Rajan, and Luigi Zingales. 1999. "What Determines Firm Size?" NBER Working Paper 7208, National Bureau of Economic Research, Cambridge, MA.

La Porta, Rafael, and Florencio Lopez-de-Silanes. 1997. "The Benefits of Privatization: Evidence from Mexico." NBER Working Paper 6215, National Bureau of Economic Research, Cambridge, MA.

———. 2000. "Government Ownership of Banks." NBER Working Paper 7620, National Bureau of Economic Research, Cambridge, MA.

La Porta, Rafael, Florencio Lopez-de-Silanes, and Andrei Shleifer. 2003. "What Works in Securities Laws?" NBER Working Paper 9882, National Bureau of Economic Research, Cambridge, MA.

La Porta, Rafael, Florencio Lopez-de-Silanes, Andrei Shleifer, and Robert W Vishny. 1998. "Law and Finance." *Journal of Political Economy* 106 (6): 1113–55.

Lall, Sanjaya, and Manuel Albaladejo. 2003. "China's Export Manufactured Export Surge: The Competitive Implications to East Asia." Paper prepared for the East Asia PREM Unit, World Bank.

Lam, Willy Wo-Lap. 1999. *The Era of Jiang Zemin*. New York: Prentice Hall.

Langlois, John D. 2004. "Party and Government and China's Financial System." In Yasheng Huang, Anthony Saich, and Edward Steinfeld, eds. *Financial Sector Reform in China*. Cambridge, MA: Harvard East Asian Press.

Lardy, Nicholas R. 1992. *Foreign Trade and Economic Reform in 1978–1990*. Cambridge, U.K.: Cambridge University Press.

———. 1998. *China's Unfinished Economic Revolution*. Washington, DC: Brookings Institution.

———. 2002. *Integrating China into the Global Economy*. Washington, DC: Brookings Institution.

Lardy, Nicholas R., and Kenneth Lieberthal, eds. 1983. *Chen Yun's Strategy for China's Development: A Non-Maoist Alternative*. Armonk, NY: M.E. Sharpe.

Lee, Keum. 1990. "The Chinese Model of the Socialist Enterprise: An Assessment of Its Organization and Performance." *Journal of Comparative Economics* 14 (3): 384–400.

"Lenovo Buys IBM's PC Unit for $1.75bn." 2004. *Financial Times*, December 9.

Leung, Hiu-Kwong, and Y. Y. Kueh. 2002. "The Challenge from Foreign-Invested Banks in China and WTO Accession." Paper presented at "Fourth International Conference on Sino-American Economic Relations under the WTO," Lingnan University, Hong Kong, May 6.

Li, David D., and Minsong Liang. 1998. "Causes of the Soft Budget Constraint: Evidence on Three Explanations." *Journal of Comparative Economics* 26 (1): 104–16.

Li, David D., and Changqi Wu. 2002. "The Ownership School vs. the Management School of State Enterprise Reform: Evidence from China." William Davidson Institute Working Paper 435, William Davidson Institute, Ann Arbor, MI.

Li, David D., Tao Li, Francis T Lui, and Hongling Wang. 2001. "Why Do Governments Dump State Enterprises? Evidence from China." Paper presented at Twelfth Annual East Asian Seminar on Economics, Hong Kong (China), October 15.

Li, Hongbin, and Scott Rozelle. 2004. "Insider Privatization with a Tail: The Screening Contract and Performance of Privatized Firms in Rural China." *Journal of Development Economics* 75 (1): 1–26.

Li, Jingwen, Dale Jorgenson, Youjing Zheng, and Masahiro Kuroda. 1993. *Productivity and Economic Growth in China, USA, and Japan (in Chinese)*. Beijing: China Social Sciences Press.

Li, Shaomin, Shuhe Li, and Weiying Zhang. 2000. "The Road to Capitalism: Competition and Institutional Change in China." *Journal of Comparative Economics* 28 (2): 269–92.

Li, Wei. 1997. "The Impact of Economic Reform on the Performance of Chinese State Enterprises, 1980–1989." *Journal of Political Economy* 105 (5): 1080–106.

Li Yining. 1992. "A Discussion of Two Types of Unbalanced Economies and the Main Line of Our Current Economic System Reform." In Yining Li, ed. *Zhongguo Jingji Gaige Yu Gufenzhi (Chinese Economic Reform and the Shareholding System)*. Beijing: Beijing University Press.

Li, Yuefen. 2002. "China's Accession to WTO: Exaggerated Fears?" UNCTAD Discussion Paper 165, United Nations Conference on Trade and Development, Geneva, Switzerland.

Lieberthal, Kenneth. 1995. *Governing China*. New York: W.W. Norton.

Lin, Justin Yifu. 1999. "Policy Burdens, Soft Budget Constraint, and State-Owned Enterprise Reform in China." Peking University Working Paper, Peking University, Beijing, China.

Lin, Justin Yifu, and Zhiqiang Liu. 2000. "Fiscal Decentralization and Economic Growth in China." *Economic Development and Cultural Change* 49 (1): 1–21.

Lin, Yi-min, and Tian Zhu. 2001. "Ownership Restructuring in Chinese State Industry: An Analysis of Evidence on Initial Organizational Changes." *The China Quarterly* (166): 305–41.

Linder, Jane C., Sirkka Jarvenpaa, and Thomas H. Davenport. 2003. "Toward an Innovation Sourcing Strategy." *MIT Sloan Management Review* 44 (4): 43–50.

Liu, Guy S., and Pei Sun. 2003. "Identifying Ultimate Controlling Shareholders in Chinese Public Corporations: An Empirical Survey." Asia Programme Working Paper 2, The Royal Institute of International Affairs, London.

———. 2005. "China's Public Firms: How Much Privatization?" In Stephen Green and Guy S. Liu, eds., *Exit the Dragon? Privatization and State Control in China*. Malden, MA: Blackwell Publishing.

Liu, Guy S., Pei Sun, and Wing Thye Woo. 2005. "Chinese Style Privatization: Motives and Constraints." In Stephen Green and Guy S. Liu, eds. *Exit the Dragon? Privatization and State Control in China*. Malden, MA: Blackwell Publishing.

Liu, Xiaoxuan. 2005. "The Effects of Privatization on China's Industrial Performance." In Stephen Green and Guy S. Liu, eds. *Exit the Dragon? Privatization and State Control in China*. Malden, MA: Blackwell Publishing.

Lloyd, Peter, Kerrin Vautier, and Paul Crampton. 2004. "Harmonizing Competition Policies." In Shahid Yusuf, M. Anjum Altaf, and Kaoru Nabeshima, eds. *Global Change and East Asian Policy Initiatives*. Washington, DC: World Bank and Oxford University Press.

Lo, Chi. 2004. "Bank Reform: How Much Does China Have?" *The China Business Review* 31 (2): 30–41.

Lubman, Stanley. 1999. *Bird in a Cage: Legal Reform in China after Mao*. Palo Alto, CA: Stanford University Press.

MacAvoy, Paul W., and Ira M. Millstein. 2003. *The Recurrent Crisis in Corporate Governance*. New York: Palgrave MacMillan.

Maddison, Angus. 1998. *Chinese Economic Performance in the Long Run*. Paris: Organisation for Economic Co-operation and Development.

Magretta, Joan. 2002. *What Management Is*. New York: The Free Press.

Majumdar, Sumit K. 1996. "Assessing Comparative Efficiency of the State-Owned, Mixed, and Private Sectors in Indian Industry." *Public Choice* 96 (1): 1–24.

Mallon, Glenda, and John Whalley. 2004. "China's Post Accession WTO Stance." NBER Working Paper 10649, National Bureau of Economic Research, Cambridge, MA.

Manion, Melanie. 2004. *Corruption by Design: Building Clean Government in Mainland China and Hong Kong*. Cambridge, MA: Harvard University Press.

Mathews, John A., and Dong Sung Cho. 2000. *Tiger Technology: The Creation of a Semiconductor Industry in East Asia*. Cambridge Asia-Pacific Studies. New York: Cambridge University Press.

McGoldrick, Peter, and Patrick Paul Walsh. 2004. "Reforms and Productivity Dynamics in Chinese State-Owned Enterprises." IZA Discussion Paper 1201, Institute for the Study of Labor, Bonn, Germany.

McKinsey Global Institute. 1999. *Russian Economy: Growth Is Possible*. New York: McKinsey Co.

McMillan, John. 1997. "Markets in Transition." In David Kreps and Kenneth Wallis, eds. *Advances in Economics and Econometrics: Theory and Applications*. Cambridge: Cambridge University Press, 210–39.

Megginson, William L., and Jeffery M. Netter. 2001. "From State to Market: A Survey of Empirical Studies on Privatization." *Journal of Economic Literature* 39 (2): 321–89.

Meyer, Marshall W., and Xiaohui Lu. 2005. "Managing Indefinite Boundaries: The Strategy and Structure of a Chinese Business Firm." *Management and Organization Review* 1 (1): 57–86.

Miwa, Yoshiro, and J. Mark Ramseyer. 2002. "Banks and Economic Growth: Implications from Japanese History." *Journal of Law and Economics* 45 (1): 127–64.

Moers, Luc. 2000. "Determinants of Enterprise Restructuring in Transition: Description of a Survey in Russian Industry." *Post-Communist Economies* 12 (3): 307–36.

Mohan, T. T. Ram. 2004. "Privatisation in China: Softly, Softy Does It." *Economic and Political Weekly* 39 (45): 4904–9.

Movshuk, Oleksandr. 2004. "Restructuring, Productivity, and Technical Efficiency in China's Iron and Steel Industry, 1988–2000." *Journal of Asian Economies* 15 (1): 135–51.

Mu, Jin. 2003. "SOE Bankruptcies Planned." *China Business Weekly* (129): 1–3.

Nabeshima, Kaoru. 2004. "Technology Transfer in East Asia: A Survey." In Shahid Yusuf, Anjum Altaf, and Kaoru Nabeshima, eds. *Global Production Networking and Technological Change in East Asia.* New York: Oxford University Press.

Nathan, Andrew J., and Perry Link, eds. 2001. *The Tiananmen Papers.* New York: Public Affairs.

National Bureau of Statistics. 1990. *Zhongguo Tongji Nianjian.* Beijing: China Statistics Press.

———. 1997. *China Statistical Yearbook.* Beijing: China Statistics Press.

———. 1999. *Comprehensive Statistical Data and Materials on 50 Years of New China.* Beijing: China Statistics Press.

———. 2002. *China Statistical Yearbook.* Beijing: China Statistics Press.

———. 2003. *China Monthly Economic Indicators.* Beijing: China Statistics Press.

National Statistical Office. 1989. *Zhongguo Gongye Jingji Tongji Culiao.* Beijing: China Statistics Press.

National Statistical Office Industry and Transport Bureau. 2000. Zhongguo gongye jiaotong nengyuan 50nian tonji culiao huibian, 1949–1999 [A compilation of 50 years of statistical materials on Chinese Industry, Transport and Energy]. Beijing: China Statistics Press, 2000.

Naughton, Barry. 1995. *Growing Out of the Plan.* New York: Cambridge University Press.

———. 1999. "How Much Can Regional Integration Do to Unify China's Markets?" Paper presented at Conference, "Policy Reform in China," Center for Research on Economic Development and Policy Research, Palo Alto, CA, November 18.

Nichols, Nancy A. 1994. "Scientific Management at Merck: An Interview with CFO Judy Lewent." *Harvard Business Review* 72 (1): 88–99.

"No Right to Work." 2004. *The Economist,* September 9.

Nohria, Nitin, William Joyce, and Bruce Roberson. 2003. "What Really Works." *Harvard Business Review* 81 (7): 42–52.

Nolan, Peter. 2001. *China and the Global Economy: National Champions, Industrial Policy, and the Big Business Revolution.* New York: Palgrave.

———. 2002. "China and the Global Business Revolution." *Cambridge Journal of Economics* 26 (1): 119–37.

Nolan, Peter, and Godfrey Yeung. 2001. "Large Firms and Catch-Up in a Transitional Economy: The Case of Shougang Group in China." *Economics of Planning* 34 (1/2): 159–78.

Norton, Patrick M., and Howard Chao. 2001. "Mergers and Acquisitions in China." *The China Business Review* 28 (5): 46–53.

"Nose to Nose." 2005. *The Economist*, June 23.

OECD (Organisation for Economic Co-operation and Development). 2002. *Science, Technology and Industry Outlook*. Paris: OECD.

———. 2004. *Understanding Economic Growth*. Paris: OECD.

Ohmae, Kenichi. 2002. "Profits and Perils in China, Inc." *Strategy+Business* 26 (First Quarter): 68–79.

Oi, Jean Chun. 1999. *Rural China Takes Off: Institutional Foundations of Economic Reform*. Berkeley, CA: University of California Press.

Oi, Jean, and Andrew G. Walder (eds.). 1999. *Property Rights and Economic Reform in China*. Palo Alto, CA: Stanford University Press.

Opper, Sonja. 2004. "The Political Economy of Privatization: Empirical Evidence from Transition Economies." *KYKLOS* 57 (4): 559–86.

Otsuka, Keijiro, Deqiang Liu, and Naoki Murakami. 1998. *Industrial Reform in China: Past Performance and Future Prospects*. New York: Oxford University Press.

"Out of Business." 1999. *Far Eastern Economic Review*, February 18.

Owen, Bruce M., Su Sun, and Wentong Zheng. 2004. "Antitrust in China: The Problem of Incentive Compatibility." SIEPR Discussion Paper 03–40, Stanford University, Palo Alto, CA.

Oxfam International. 2004. "Stitched Up: How Rich-Country Protectionism in Textiles and Clothing Trade Prevents Poverty Alleviation." Oxfam Briefing Paper No. 60, Oxfam International, Oxford, U.K.

Pagano, Patrizio, and Fabiano Schivardi. 2003. "Firm Size Distribution and Growth." *Scandinavian Journal of Economics* 105 (2): 255–74.

Park, Albert, and Minggao Shen. 2003. "Joint Liability Lending and the Rise and Fall of China's Township and Village Enterprises." *Journal of Development Economics* 71 (2): 497–531.

Pavlinek, Petr. 2002. "The Role of Foreign Direct Investment in the Privatization and Restructuring of the Czech Motor Industry." *Post-Communist Economies* 14 (3): 359–79.

Perevalov, Yurii, Ilya Gimadii, and Vladimir Dobrodei. 2000. "Does Privatisation Improve Performance of Industrial Enterprises? Empirical Evidence from Russia." *Post-Communist Economies* 12 (3): 337–63.

Perkins, Dwight H. 1966. *Market Control and Planning in Communist China*. Cambridge, MA: Harvard University Press.

———. 1968. "Industrial Planning and Management." In Alexander Eckstein, Walter Galenson, and Ta-Chung Liu, eds. *Economic Trends in Communist China*. Chicago: Aldine.

———. 1988. "Reforming China's Economic System." *Journal of Economic Literature* 26 (2): 601–45.

————. 2001. "Industrial and Financial Policy in China and Vietnam: A New Model or a Replay of the East Asian Experience." In Joseph E. Stiglitz and Shahid Yusuf, eds. *Rethinking the East Asian Miracle*. New York: Oxford University Press.

————. 2004. "Corporate Governance, Industrial Policy, and the Rule of Law." In Shahid Yusuf, M. Anjum Altaf, and Kaoru Nabeshima, eds. *Global Change and East Asian Policy Initiatives*. New York: Oxford University Press.

Perkins, Dwight H., and Shahid Yusuf. 1984. *Rural Development in China*. Baltimore, MD: Johns Hopkins University Press.

Perotti, Enrico C., Laixiang Sun, and Liang Zou. 1999. "State-Owned Versus Township and Village Enterprises in China." *Comparative Economic Studies* 41 (2–3): 151–79.

Perry, Tekla S. 2005. "Digital TV's 100-Meter Dash." *IEEE Spectrum* 42 (6): 46–51.

"Pivotal Privatisation." 2004. *Oxford Analytica*, February 10.

Pivovarsky, Alexander. 2001. "How Does Privatization Work? Ownership Concentration and Enterprise Performance in Ukraine." IMF Working Paper WP/01/42, International Monetary Fund, Washington, DC.

"Planning System To Be Reformed." 1984. *Beijing Review*, October 29.

Pomeranz, Kenneth. 2000. *The Great Divergence*. Princeton, NJ: Princeton University Press.

Poncet, Sandra. 2003. "Measuring Chinese Domestic and International Integration." *China Economic Review* 14 (1): 1–21.

Prasad, Eswar, and Shang-Jin Wei. 2005. "The Chinese Approach to Capital Inflows: Patterns and Possible Explanations." NBER Working Paper 11306, National Bureau of Economic Research, Cambridge, MA.

"Privatization Revived." 2003. *Oxford Analytica*, May 29.

"Prospects 2003: China." 2002. *Oxford Analytica*, December 6.

Prybyla, Jan S. 1978. *The Chinese Economy: Problems and Policies*. Columbia, SC: University of South Carolina Press.

Putterman, Louis, and Xiao-Yuan Dong. 2000. "China's State-Owned Enterprises: Their Role, Job Creation, and Efficiency in Long-Term Perspective." *Modern China* 26 (4): 403–47.

Qian, Yingyi. 1996. "Enterprise Reform in China: Agency Problems and Political Control." *Economics of Transition* 4 (2): 427–47.

————. 1999. "The Institutional Foundations of China's Market Transition." Paper presented at the Annual World Bank Conference on Development Economics, Washington, DC, April 29.

————. 2002. "How Reform Worked in China." CEPR Discussion Paper 3447, Centre for Economic Policy Research, London.

Qian, Yingyi, and Gerard Roland. 1998. "Federalism and the Soft Budget Constraint." *American Economic Review* 88 (5): 1143–62.

Qian, Yingyi, Gerard Roland, and Chenggang Xu. 1999. "Why Is China Different from Eastern Europe? Perspectives from Organization Theory." *European Economic Review* 43(4–6): 1085–94.

Radygin, A. D., and P. M. Entov. 2001. "Корпоративное управление и защита прав собственности: эмпирический анализ и актуальные направления реформ (Corporate Governance and Protection of Property Rights: an Empirical Analysis and Actual Avenues for Reform)." Institute for the Economy in Transition Working Paper No. 36, Institute for the Economy in Transition, Moscow.

Rajan, Raghuram G., and Julie Wulf. 2003. "The Flattening Firm: Evidence from Panel Data on the Changing Nature of Corporate Hierarchies." NBER Working Paper 9633, National Bureau of Economic Research, Cambridge, MA.

Ramirez, Carlos D., and Ling Hui Tan. 2003. "Singapore, Inc. versus the Private Sector: Are Government-Linked Companies Different?" IMF Working Paper WP/03/156, International Monetary Fund, Washington, DC.

Ravenscraft, David J., and F. M. Scherer. 1989. "The Profitability of Mergers." *International Journal of Industrial Organization* 7 (1): 101–16.

Ray, Subhash, and Ping Zhang. 2001. "Technical Efficiency of State Owned Enterprises in China (1980–1989)." Working Paper 2001–05, University of Connecticut, Storrs, CT.

"The Real Test of China's Appetite for Reform" 2003. *Financial Times,* January 28.

Reardon, Lawrence C. 1998. "Learning How to Open the Door: A Reassesment of China's 'Opening' Strategy." *The China Quarterly* (155): 479–511.

Reynolds, Bruce, ed. 1987. *Reform in China: Challenge and Choices.* Armonk, NY: M.E. Sharpe.

Richardson, Thomas, and Steven Barnett. 2000. "Fiscal and Macroeconomic Aspects of Privatization." IMF Occasional Paper 194, International Monetary Fund, Washington, DC.

Riskin, Carl. 1987. *China's Political Economy.* New York: Oxford University Press.

Roland, Gerard. 2000. *Transition and Economics: Politics, Firms, Markets.* Cambridge, MA: MIT Press.

Ross, Thomas W. 2004. "Viewpoint: Canadian Competition Policy: Progress and Prospects." *Canadian Journal of Economics* 37 (2): 243–68.

Rumbaugh, Thomas, and Nicolas Blancher. 2004. "China: International Trade and WTO Accession." IMF Working Paper WP/04/36, International Monetary Fund, Washington, DC.

"Russia: Government Aims to Cut State Property Holding." 2003. *Oxford Analytica,* March 18.

"Russia: Government Plans Next Wave of Privatization." 2003. *Oxford Analytica,* August 22.

"Russia: Small Businesses Confront Large Obstacles." 2003. *Oxford Analytica,* July 14.

Sachs, Jeffrey, Clifford Zinnes, and Yair Eilat. 2000. "The Gains From Privatization in Transition Economies: Is 'Change of Ownership' Enough?" CAER II Discussion Paper 63, Harvard Institute for International Development, Cambridge, MA.

Sachs, Jeffrey D., and Wing Thye Woo. 1997. "Understanding China's Economic Performance." Development Discussion Paper 575, Harvard Institute for International Development, Cambridge, MA.

Santos, Jose, Yves Doz, and Peter Williamson. 2004. "Is Your Innovation Process Global?" *MIT Sloan Management Review* 45 (4): 31–7.

Sappington, David E. M., and Joseph E. Stiglitz. 1987. "Privatization, Information, and Incentives." *Journal of Policy Analysis and Management* 6 (4): 567–82.

Schoar, Antoinette. 2002. "Effects of Corporate Diversification on Productivity." *The Journal of Finance* 57 (6): 2379–403.

Selden, Larry, and Geoffrey Colvin. 2003. "M&A Needn't Be a Loser's Game." *Harvard Business Review* 81 (6): 70–9.

Shanghai Statistics Bureau 2003. *Shanghai Statistical Yearbook*. Shanghai: Shanghai Statistics Bureau.

―――. 2004. *Shanghai Statistical Yearbook*. Shanghai: Shanghai Statistical Bureau.

Shenkar, Oded. 2005. *The Chinese Century*. Upper Saddle River, NJ: Wharton School Publishing.

Shih, Victor Chung-hon. 2003. "Not Quite a Miracle: Factional Conflict, Inflationary Cycles, and Non-Performing Loans in China." Unpublished Dissertation. Cambridge, MA: Harvard University.

Shirley, Mary M., and Lixin Colin Xu. 2001. "Empirical Effects of Performance Contracts: Evidence from China." *Journal of Law, Economics & Organization* 17 (1): 168–200.

Shleifer, Andrei, and Daniel Treisman. 2000. *Without a Map: Political Tactics and Economic Reform in Russia*. Cambridge, MA: MIT Press.

Slinko, Irina, Evgeny Yakovlev, and Ekaterina Zhuravskaya. 2003. "Institutional Subversion: Evidence from Russian Regions." CEFIR Academic Paper 32, Centre for Economic and Financial Research, Moscow.

Smil, Vaclav. 1993. *China's Environment: An Inquiry into the Limits of National Development*. Armonk, NY: M.E. Sharpe.

Smith, Abbie J. 1990. "Corporate Ownership Structure and Performance: the Case of Management Buyouts." *Journal of Financial Economics* 27 (1): 143–64.

Smith, Stephen C., Beon-Cheol Cin, and Milan Vodopivec. 1997. "Privatization Incidence, Ownership Forms, and Firm Performance: Evidence from Slovenia." *Journal of Comparative Economics* 25 (2): 158–79.

Smyth, Russell. 2000. "Should China Be Promoting Large-Scale Enterprises and Enterprise Groups?" *World Development* 28 (4): 721–37.

Smyth, Russell, and Zhai Qingguo. 2003. "Economic Restructuring in China's Large and Medium-Sized State-Owned Enterprises: Evidence from Liaoning." *Journal of Contemporary China* 12 (34): 173–205.

Smyth, Russell, Jianguo Wang, and Quek Lee Kiang. 2001. "Efficiency, Performance, and Changing Corporate Governance in China's Township-Village Enterprises Since the 1990s." *Asia-Pacific Economic Literature* 15 (1): 30–41.

"SOE Bankruptcies Planned." 2003. *China Business Weekly*, July 29.

Solinger, Dorothy J. 2002. "Labour Market Reform and the Plight of the Laid-Off Proletariat." *China Quarterly* (170): 304–26.

Sonin, Konstantin. 2003. "Provincial Protectionism." CEPR Discussion Paper 3973, Centre for Economic Policy Research, London.

Sonobe, Tetsushi, and Keijiro Otsuka. 2003. "Productivity Effects of TVE Privatization: The Case Study of Garment and Metal Casting Enterprises in the Greater Yangtze River Region." NBER Working Paper 9621, National Bureau of Economic Research, Cambridge, MA.

Steinfeld, Edward. 1998. *Forging Reform in China*. Cambridge: Cambridge University Press.

―――. 2004a. "China's Shallow Integration: Networked Production and the New Challenges for Late Industrialization." *World Development* 32 (11): 1971–87.

―――. 2004b. "Chinese Enterprise Development and the Challenge of Global Integration." In Shahid Yusuf, Anjum Altaf, and Kaoru Nabeshima, eds. *Global Production Networking and Technological Change in East Asia*. New York: Oxford University Press.

Stewart, Thomas A., and Louise O'Brien. 2005. "Transforming an Industrial Giant." *Harvard Business Review* 83 (2): 114–22.

Stiglitz, Joseph E. 1994. *Whither Socialism?* Cambridge, MA: MIT Press.

Sull, Donald N. 1999. "Why Good Companies Go Bad." *Harvard Business Review* 77 (4): 42–52.

Sull, Donald N., and Yong Wang. 2005. *Made in China: What Western Managers Can Learn from Trailblazing Chinese Entrepreneurs.* Boston, MA.: Harvard Business School Press.

Sun, Yifei. 2002. "China's National Innovation System in Transition." *Eurasian Geography and Economics* 43 (6): 476–92.

Sun, Yun-Wing. 1991. *The China Hong Kong Connection: The Key to China's Open-Door Policy.* Cambridge, U.K.: Cambridge University Press.

Tam, On Kit. 1999. *The Development of Corporate Governance in China.* Cheltenham, U.K.: Edward Elgar Publishing, Ltd.

Tan, Kong-Yam. 2004. "Market Fragmentation and Impact on Economic Growth." Beijing, China: World Bank. Processed.

Tanner, Murray Scot. 2004. "China Rethinks Unrest." *The Washington Quarterly* 27 (3): 137–56.

"TCL Spree Becomes a Cautionary Tale." 2005. *Financial Times,* May 24.

"Technically Speaking." 2003. *Business China,* May 26.

Teiwes, Frederick C. 2000. "The Chinese State during the Maoist Era." In David Shambaugh, ed. *The Modern Chinese State.* Cambridge, U.K.: Cambridge University Press.

Tenev, Stoyan, Chunlin Zhang, and Loup Brefort. 2002. *Corporate Governance and Enterprise Reform in China: Building the Institutions of Modern Markets.* Washington, DC: World Bank and International Finance Corporation.

Thompson, Emund R. 2002. "Competitiveness Concerns in Hong Kong: Business Fears and Government." *The Pacific Review* 15 (3): 443–67.

Thun, Eric. 2004. "Keeping Up with the Jones': Decentralization, Policy Imitation, and Industrial Development in China." *World Development* 32 (8): 1289–1308.

Tian, Lihui, and Saul Estrin. 2005. "Retained State Shareholding in Chinese PLCs: Does Government Ownership Reduce Corporate Value?" IZA Discussion Paper 1493, Institute for the Study of Labor, Bonn, Germany.

Tidrick, Gene, and Jiyuan Chen. 1987. *China's Industrial Reform.* Oxford: Oxford University Press.

"Time Bomb." 2004. *The Economist,* May 22.

Tornell, Aaron. 1999. "Privatizing the Privatized." NBER Working Paper 7206, National Bureau of Economic Research, Cambridge, MA.

"Unquotable." 2004. *The Economist,* December 28.

Urata, Shujiro, and Hiroki Kawai. 2002. "Technological Progress by Small and Medium Enterprises in Japan." *Small Business Economics* 18 (1–3): 53–67.

Vasiliev, Sergei. 1994. "Market Forces and Structural Change in the Russian Economy." *Economic Policy* 19 (supplement): 123–36.

Veugelers, Reinhilde, and Bruno Cassiman. 2003. "R&D Cooperation between Firms and Universities: Some Empirical Evidence from Belgian Manufacturing." CEPR Discussion Paper 3951, Centre for Economic Policy Research, London.

Wang, Hui. 2003. *China's New Order: Society, Politics, and Economy in Transition.* Cambridge, MA: Harvard University Press.

Wang, Jiann-Chyuan, and Kuen-Hung Tsai. 2003. "Productivity Growth and R&D Expenditure in Taiwan's Manufacturing Firms." NBER Working Paper 9724, National Bureau of Economic Research, Cambridge, MA.

Wang, Yan, Dianqing Xu, Zhi Wang, and Fan Zhai. 2004. "Options and Impact of China's Pension Reform: A Computable General Equilibrium Analysis." *Journal of Comparative Economics* 32 (1): 105–27.

Wang, Zixian, and Wenfeng Li. 2003. "Evaluation and Expectation: China's Accession to WTO." In *Theme Report Background Reports.* Beijing: Development Research of the State Council.

Warzynski, Frederic. 2003. "Managerial Change, Competition, and Privatization in Ukraine." *Journal of Comparative Economics* 31 (2): 297–314.

Wei, Zuobao, Oscar Varela, Juliet D'Souza, and M. Kabir Hassan. 2003. "The Financial and Operating Performance of China's Newly Privatized Firms." *Financial Management* 32 (Summer): 107–206.

Weiss, Andrew, and Georgiy Nikitin. 2002. "Effects of Ownership by Investment Funds on the Performance of Czech Firms." In Anna Meyendorff and Anjan V. Thakor, eds. *Designing Financial Systems in Transition Economies: Strategies for Reform in Central and Eastern Europe.* Cambridge, MA: MIT Press.

Wen, Mei, Dong Li, and Peter Lloyd. 2002. "Ownership and Technical Efficiency: A Cross-Section Study on the Third Industrial Census of China." *Economic Development and Cultural Change* 50 (3): 709–34.

Westney, D. Eleanor. 2001. "Japanese Enterprise Faces the Twenty-First Century." In Paul DiMaggio, ed., *The Twenty-First Century Firm.* Princeton, NJ: Princeton University Press.

Whalley, John. 2003. "Liberalization in China's Key Service Sectors Following WTO Accession: Some Scenarios and Issues of Measurement." NBER Working Paper 10143, National Bureau of Economic Research, Cambridge, MA.

"Why Are the Fads Fading?" 2003. *Financial Times,* July 12.

Wiemer, Calla, and Xiuhua Tian. 2001. "The Measurement of Small-Scale Industry for China's GDP Accounts." *China Economic Review* 12 (4): 317–22.

Williams, Mark. 2003. "Adopting a Competition Law in China." In Deborah Z. Cass, Brett G. Williams, and George Barker, eds. *China and the World Trading System.* Cambridge, U.K.: Cambridge University Press.

Williamson, Peter, and Ming Zeng. 2004. "Strategies for Competing in a Changed China." *MIT Sloan Management Review* 45 (4): 85–91.

Woetzel, Jonathan R. 2003. *Capitalist China: Strategies for a Revolutionized Economy.* Singapore: John Wiley & Sons (Asia) Pte. Ltd.

Woo, Wing Thye. 1999. "The Real Reasons for China's Growth." *China Journal* (41): 115–37.

Woo, Wing Thye, Fan Gang, Wen Hai, and Yibiao Jin. 1993. "The Efficiency and Macroeconomic Consequences of Chinese Enterprise Reform." *China Economic Review* 4 (2): 153–68.

World Bank. 1993. *China: The Achievement and Challenge of Price Reform.* Washington, DC: World Bank.

———. 1997. *China's Management of Enterprise Assets: The State as Shareholder*. Washington, DC: World Bank.

———. 2002. *Unified Survey*. Washington, DC: World Bank.

———. 2003. *China: Promoting Growth with Equity*. Report No. 24169-CHA. Washington, DC: World Bank.

———. 2004a. "Policies for the 11th Plan." Washington, DC: World Bank.

———. 2004b. "Russia: Country Economic Memorandum." Washington, DC: World Bank

Wu, Jinglian. 1988. "Zhongqi jingji tizhi gaige (The Way to Deal with the Several Stages of Mid-Term Reform)." *guanli shijie* 6 (21): 1–8.

Wu, Yongping 2005. *A Political Explanation of Economic Growth*. Cambridge, MA: Harvard University Press.

Wu, Zengxian. 1997. "How Successful Has State-Owned Enterprise Reform Been in China." *Europe-Asia Studies* 49 (7): 1237–62.

Wuhan City Statistics Bureau. 2004. *Wuhan City Statistical Yearbook*. Wuhan: Wuhan City Statistics Bureau.

Xiao, Geng, Joe Lu, Junling Xing, and Xiaoyun Yu. 2002. "Measuring Enterprise Performance in China: Do Better Enterprises Get More Resources?" Unpublished Paper. University of Hong Kong. Hong Kong (China).

Xiao, Jason Zezhong, Jay Dahya, and Zhijun Lin. 2004. "A Grounded Theory Exposition of the Role of the Supervisory Board in China." *British Journal of Management* 15 (1): 39–55.

Xie, Wei, and Guisheng Wu. 2003. "Differences between Learning Process in Small Tigers and Large Dragons: Learning Processes of Two Color TV (CTV) Firms within China." *Research Policy* 32 (8): 1463–79.

Xu, Lixin Colin, Tian Zhu, and Yi-min Lin. 2001. "Political Control, Agency Problems, and Firm Performance: Evidence from a National Survey of Ownership Restructuring in China." Washington, DC: World Bank. Processed.

Xu, Shanda, and Lin Ma. 1995. "Reform and the Market Economy and Tax in China." In Ahmad, Ehtisham, Gao Qiang, and Vito Tanzi, eds. *Reforming China's Public Finances*. Washington, DC: International Monetary Fund.

Yafeh, Yishay. 2002. "An International Perspective of Corporate Groups and Their Prospects." NBER Working Paper 9386, National Bureau of Economic Research, Cambridge, MA.

Yao, Yang. 2004. "Privatizing the Small SOEs." In Ross Garnaut and Ligang Song, eds. *China's Third Economic Transformation: The Rise of the Private Economy*. New York: Routledge Curzon.

Yarrow, George. 1986. "Privatization in Theory and Practice." *Economic Policy* 1 (2): 323–77.

Yeh, Tsung-ming, and Yashuo Hoshino. 2002. "Productivity and Operating Performance of Japanese Merging Firms: Keiretsu-Related and Independent Mergers." *Japan and the World Economy* 14 (3): 347–66.

Young, Alwyn. 2000. "The Razor's Edge: Distortions and Incremental Reform in the People's Republic of China." NBER Working Paper 7828, National Bureau of Economic Research, Cambridge, MA.

"Young, Bright, and Jobless." 2003. *Economist,* June 21.

Yudaeva, Ksenia, Konstantin Kozlov, Natalia Melentieva, and Natalia Ponomareva. 2003. "Does Foreign Ownership Matter: The Russian Experience." *Economics of Transition* 11 (3): 383–409.

Yusuf, Shahid, M. Anjum Altaf, Barry Eichengreen, Sudarshan Gooptu, Kaoru Nabeshima, Charles Kenny, Dwight H. Perkins, and Marc Shotten. 2003. *Innovative East Asia: The Future of Growth.* New York: Oxford University Press.

Yusuf, Shahid, M. Anjum Altaf, and Kaoru Nabeshima, eds. 2004. *Global Production Networking and Technological Change in East Asia.* New York: Oxford University Press.

Yusuf, Shahid, and Simon J. Evenett. 2002. *Can East Asia Compete? Innovation for Global Markets.* New York: Oxford University Press.

Zalduendo, Juan. 2003. "Enterprise Restructuring and Transition: Evidence from the Former Yugoslav Republic of Macedonia." IMF Working Paper WP/03/136, International Monetary Fund, Washington, DC.

Zhang, Anming, and Yimin Zhang. 2001. "Impact of Ownership and Competition on the Productivity of Chinese Enterprises." *Journal of Comparative Economics* 29 (2): 327–46.

Zhang, Anming, Yimin Zhang, and Ronald Zhao. 2002. "Profitability and Productivity of Chinese Industrial Firms Measurement and Ownership Implications." *China Economic Review* 13 (1): 65–88.

———. 2003. "A Study of the R&D Efficiency and Productivity of Chinese Firms." *Journal of Comparative Economics* 31 (3): 444–64.

Zhang, Chunlin. 2002. "Financing the SOE Sector: Institutional Evolution and Its Implications for SOE Reform." *China and World Economy* 10 (6): 3–11.

Zhang, Jun. 2000. "Market Size, Scale Economies and Loss-Making in China's Post-Reform State Manufacturing Industry." *East Asian Review* 4 (1): 3–25.

Zhang, Le-Yin. 1999. "Chinese Central-Provincial Fiscal Relationships, Budgetary Decline and the Impact of the 1994 Fiscal Reform: An Evaluation." *The China Quarterly* (157): 115–41.

———. 2004a. "The Impact of China's Post-1993 Financial Reform on State-Owned Enterprises: The Case of Shanghai." In Yasheng Huang, Anthony Saich, and Edward Steinfeld, eds. *Financial Sector Reform in China.* Cambridge, MA: Harvard East Asian Press.

———. 2004b. "The Role of Corporatization and Stock Market Listing in Reforming China's State Industry." *World Development* 32 (12): 2031–47.

Zweig, David. 2002. *Internationalizing China.* Ithaca, NY: Cornell University Press.

INDEX

ABOUT THE AUTHORS

Shahid Yusuf is economic adviser in the Development Economics Research Group at the World Bank. He holds a B.A. in economics from Cambridge University and a Ph.D. in economics from Harvard University in Cambridge, Massachusetts. He is team leader for the World Bank–Japan project on East Asia's Future Economy and was director of the *World Development Report 1999/2000: Entering the 21st Century*. Prior to that, he served the World Bank in several other capacities.

He has written extensively on development issues, with a special focus on East Asia. His publications include *China's Rural Development*, with Dwight H. Perkins (Johns Hopkins University Press 1984); *The Dynamics of Urban Growth in Three Chinese Cities*, with Weiping Wu (Oxford University Press 1997); *Rethinking the East Asian Miracle*, edited with Joseph Stiglitz (Oxford University Press 2001); *Can East Asia Compete? Innovation for Global Markets*, with Simon Evenett (Oxford University Press 2002); *Innovative East Asia: The Future of Growth*, with others (Oxford University Press 2003); and *Global Production Networking and Technological Change in East Asia* and *Global Change and East Asian Policy Initiatives*, both edited with M. Anjum Altaf and Kaoru Nabeshima (Oxford University Press 2004). He has also published widely in various academic journals.

Kaoru Nabeshima is an economist in the Development Economics Research Group at the World Bank. He holds a B.A. in economics from Ohio Wesleyan University and a Ph.D. in economics from the University of California, Davis. He is a team member for the World Bank–Japan project on East Asia's Future Economy and was a coauthor of *Innovative East Asia: The Future of Growth* (Oxford University Press 2003) and coeditor for *Global Production Networking and Technological Change in East Asia* and *Global Change and East Asian Policy Initiatives* (Oxford University Press 2004). His research interests lie in the economic development of East Asia, especially in the innovation capabilities of firms.

Dwight H. Perkins is the Harold Hitchings Burbank Professor of Political Economy at Harvard University in Cambridge, Massachusetts; he joined the Harvard University faculty in 1963. Most recently he was director of the Harvard Institute for International Development (HIID), from 1980 to 1995, and director of the Harvard University Asia Center, from 2002 to 2005.

He has authored or edited 12 books and more than 100 articles on economic history and economic development, many on the economies of China, the Republic of Korea, Vietnam, and the other nations of East and Southeast Asia. Topics include the transition from central planning to market economies, long-term agricultural development, industrial policy, and the underlying sources of rapid growth in East Asia.

He has served as an adviser or consultant on economic policy and reform to the governments of China, Indonesia, Korea, Malaysia, Papua New Guinea, and Vietnam. He has also been a long-term consultant to the World Bank, the Ford Foundation, various private corporations, and agencies of the U.S. government.

He served in the U.S. Navy (active duty 1956–58) and received a B.A. in Far Eastern Studies from Cornell University and an M.A. and Ph.D. in economics from Harvard University.